Prosodic Patterns in Conversation

Nigel G. Ward

University of Texas, El Paso

CAMBRIDGE
UNIVERSITY PRESS

CAMBRIDGE
UNIVERSITY PRESS

University Printing House, Cambridge CB2 8BS, United Kingdom

One Liberty Plaza, 20th Floor, New York, NY 10006, USA

477 Williamstown Road, Port Melbourne, VIC 3207, Australia

314–321, 3rd Floor, Plot 3, Splendor Forum, Jasola District Centre, New Delhi – 110025, India

79 Anson Road, #06-04/06, Singapore 079906

Cambridge University Press is part of the University of Cambridge.

It furthers the University's mission by disseminating knowledge in the pursuit of education, learning, and research at the highest international levels of excellence.

www.cambridge.org
Information on this title: www.cambridge.org/9781107181069
DOI: 10.1017/9781316848265

© Nigel G. Ward 2019

First published 2019

Printed in the United Kingdom by TJ International Ltd. Padstow Cornwall

A catalogue record for this publication is available from the British Library.

Library of Congress Cataloging-in-Publication Data

Names: Ward, Nigel (Nigel G.) author.
Title: Prosodic patterns in English conversation / Nigel G. Ward, University of Texas, El Paso.
Description: Cambridge; New York : Cambridge University Press, 2019. | Includes bibliographical references and indexes.
Identifiers: LCCN 2018048293 | ISBN 9781107181069 (hardback) | ISBN 9781316633618 (paperback)
Subjects: LCSH: English language–Prosodic analysis. | English language–Intonation. |
BISAC: LANGUAGE ARTS & DISCIPLINES / Linguistics / Phonetics & Phonology.
Classification: LCC PE1139.7 .W37 2019 | DDC 421/.6–dc23
LC record available at https://lccn.loc.gov/2018048293

ISBN 978-1-107-18106-9 Hardback
ISBN 978-1-316-63361-8 Paperback

Additional resources for this publication at www.cambridge.org/Ward

Prosodic Patterns in English Conversation

Language is more than words: it includes the prosodic features and patterns that we use, subconsciously, to frame meanings and achieve our goals in our interaction with others. Here, Nigel G. Ward explains how we do this, going beyond intonation to show how pitch, timing, intensity, and voicing properties combine to form meaningful temporal configurations: prosodic constructions. Bringing together new findings and hitherto-scattered observations from phonetic and pragmatic studies, this book describes over twenty common prosodic patterns in English conversation. Using examples from real conversations, it illustrates how prosodic constructions serve essential functions such as inviting, showing approval, taking turns, organizing ideas, reaching agreement, and evoking action. Prosody helps us establish rapport and nurture relationships, but subtle differences in prosody across languages and subcultures can be damagingly misunderstood. The findings presented here will enable both native speakers of English and learners to listen more sensitively and communicate more effectively.

NIGEL G. WARD is Professor of Computer Science at the University of Texas at El Paso, and Chair of the Prosody Special Interest Group of the International Speech Communication Association. He has published widely in human–computer interaction and speech technology as applied to spoken dialog systems, information retrieval, and second language learning.

Contents

Preface

This book presents the principal prosodic constructions of English dialog. I came to this topic in a roundabout way, after twenty-five years of research in spoken language processing (most recently with support from the National Science Foundation, Toyota Motor Corporation, and the Defense Advanced Research Projects Agency).

Building new applications requires new tools, and over the years I have accumulated a large collection. It started in 1993, at the University of Tokyo, with the gift of a pitch tracker (from Keikichi Hirose). Gradually I built a suite of tools for prosodic analysis (with help from Alejandro Vega, Paula Gallardo, Ricky Garcia, and others), complemented by freeware, especially Voicebox, Praat, and Elan (written by Mike Brookes, Paul Boersma, and others). A breakthrough came in 2011, with the addition of Principal Component Analysis to the workflow (suggested by Olac Fuentes).

This not only improved our application's performance, but revealed what looked like meaningful patterns. Departing from the norms of my research community – where the custom is to address the application at hand, maybe developing a new algorithm or two, but generally leaving knowledge discovery to the linguists – I decided to try to make sense of these patterns. I had the good fortune to find students willing to work with me for hours and hours, examining hundreds of dialog fragments to figure out the meanings of the prosodic constructions of English (Alejandro Vega, Paola Gallardo, Luis Ramirez, and James Jodoin). As we worked, I applied methods learned from my teachers at Berkeley in the late 1980s (George Lakoff, Charles Fillmore, and many others), especially about how to work out the connections between language forms and human intentions.

As data we used real conversations (mostly among students of the University of Texas at El Paso, and mostly recorded in my lab by Steven Werner, Esaul Campos, Saiful Abu, and Paola Gallardo). Additional data to support examination of specific phenomena was contributed by other scholars (Rachel Steindel Burdin, Jeremey Day-O'Connell, and Alejna Brugos).

With all this help I learned many things. Bursting to share them, I was able to devote a full year to writing (while working with Tatsuya Kawahara and his students and colleagues at Kyoto University, thanks to a Fulbright award and a leave from my home institution, the University of Texas at El Paso).

Aiming for a book that is both scholarly and readable, I have benefited greatly from discussions with colleagues (especially Oliver Niebuhr, Stefan Benus, Juergen Trouvain, Richard Ogden, Francisco Torreira, Gina Levow, David Novick, and Eric Freudenthal), and detailed comments on chapters (by Stefan Benus, Margaret Zellers, German Zarate-Sandez, Jeremey Day-O'Connell, Yoko Hasegawa, Timo Baumann, Keikichi Hirose, Anton Batliner, Yi Xu, Carlos Ishi, Keelan Evanini, Rasmus Persson, Colleen Myers, Isabel Ward, and Susan Ward). The cover art is based on a concept by Adan Contreras, and Helen Barton was my editor.

I sincerely thank them all.

1 Introduction

Beyond words, spoken language involves prosody: intonation, loudness, timing, and the like. In conversation prosody is vital: it enables people to mark things as important or incidental, show interest in something or change the topic, be sympathetic or business-like, and so on. Without prosody, conversations would be just alternating short speeches: the human element would be lost.

This book explains how speakers of American English use prosody to accomplish things in conversation. While native speakers do this without conscious awareness, that does not mean it is simple. Attempts to pin down the details have faced many challenges, but now, in a remarkable convergence, researchers in diverse traditions – experimental phonetics, formal phonology, conversation analysis, and signal processing – have independently begun using compatible styles of description. The shared core is the notion of prosodic construction. Prosodic constructions are recurring temporal patterns of prosodic features that express specific meanings and functions. These typically involve not only intonation but also energy, speaking rate, timing, and articulation properties, often with synchronized contributions by two participants.

For example, consider one that is common in active listening. A listener can show interest and engagement by periodically nodding or saying *uh-huh* or the like, but this is not done at random. Example 1 illustrates.

1) *A: well, it's someone's house.*
   B: yeah
   A: they're gonna, I mean, there's like, they're gonna be spinning.

The audio for this and other examples is available at www.cambridge.org/ward.

In this example, B has asked what kind of party A is talking about. A is not entirely sure, so she starts telling what she knows. Importantly, her pitch, shown with the wavy line in Figure 1.1, goes down on *someone's* and stays low for a moment, then B backchannels with *yeah*.

A: *well, it's someone's house,*   B: *yeah*

Figure 1.1 Pitch contour

	Speaker A	Speaker B
−600 ms	loudness increases	
−400 ms	pitch drops and stays low	
−300 ms	loudness decreases	
−100 ms	silence	
0 ms		backchannel, quiet, flat pitch
800 ms	resumes speaking, loud, fast, high pitch	

Figure 1.2 The Backchanneling Construction: A first approximation

This exemplifies a common pattern: a region of low pitch – typically below the speaker's 26th percentile for at least 110 milliseconds – is followed by a short response by the listener about a half second later. This is usually part of a larger construction, as follows: in the middle of an utterance the speaker goes louder and articulates more clearly a word or two, here *someone's*, then gently drops her pitch while reducing the energy, and then falls silent. The listener produces a backchannel, generally a quiet word in flat pitch, here *yeah*. The original speaker then says a few words with more energy, before resuming her normal speaking style. Figure 1.2 shows how these prosodic features are configured in time.

This pattern of interaction is not a meaningless ritual. It's used when a speaker has a multi-part package of information to convey. Winding up one part, A gives B the chance to display attention, interest, and readiness to process the next part. After B does this with a backchannel, A continues. Only then, in many cases, does the speaker deliver the truly important information. In the example, A reveals that *they're gonna be spinning*, implying that there will be dancing, only after the participants have jointly performed this prosodic pattern.

In casual conversation people typically use this pattern several times a minute, without awareness. In general, we use prosody without thinking about it. While we may struggle with the special rules for professional speaking – newsreading, political speaking, acting, and so on – like stressing the important words and pausing dramatically to underline important points, in fact, it is the prosody of conversation that is more complex. Rather than a few simple rules, there is a large set of resources to master. Effective speakers know these forms and meanings and deftly select among them and combine them on the fly to exactly fit the situation and their goals. This seems easy only because these skills are acquired in childhood; as adults, we are never aware of all this, except when learning a new language.

While not the first book on the prosody of English, this book goes beyond previous work in several ways.

First, this book focuses on the uses of prosody in conversation. Many previous books have focused on monologue or on simple exchanges, describing the proper ways to say things like *Excuse me, do you have the time?* and *Would you like tea or coffee?* However, the prosody of such sentences is trivial compared to what happens when people go beyond such basic routines to actually explain things, make plans, cooperate on a task, or get to know each other. Among other things, speakers in dialog generally pursue multiple goals simultaneously, and prosody is important in this.

Second, this book covers all of prosody, not just intonation. While pitch is especially salient, many other aspects of prosody – loudness variations, syllable durations, other timing properties, and so on – are also essential for conveying many meanings.

Third, this book reports some new discoveries, including a key element of politeness in offers and invitations (late pitch peaks), a way we convey positive regard (a simple pitch-intensity configuration), and an essential characteristic of urgent warnings (breathy voice).

Fourth, this book strives to catalog all the most important prosodic patterns in American English conversation. This would have been impossible even a few years ago, but the notion of prosodic construction enables previously scattered findings to be connected into a comprehensive model. As we will see, much of the richness of prosody in conversation boils down to the uses of such constructions, plus one simple combining process: superposition.

Fifth, this book focuses on the facts, not issues of theory. While prosodic phenomena are relevant to many central questions in linguistics, the book will discuss these only in passing: the focus is on accurately describing the facts of English prosody in conversation.

Sixth, this book relates dialog behaviors to the larger picture of human interaction. People are inherently social creatures, and for thousands of years philosophers and scientists have striven to work out what this implies about human nature. Yet some of the most interesting evidence has been hiding in plain sight, in the nuts and bolts of how people interact, moment-by-moment, in everyday conversations. Thus this book will occasionally digress to speculate about connections to cultural values and practices: not modern attributes like popular foods and entertainment, but the fundamental, deeply rooted ways in which Americans manage social obligations, reach decisions, and connect with other people.

Seventh, this book is intended for anyone with an interest in language. No previous knowledge of prosody or phonetics is assumed, and the International Phonetic Alphabet (/aɪ.piː.eɪ/) will not be used. The phenomena are described with a minimum of terminology and illustrated with many examples. These are crucial; to get maximum benefit from this book, please listen to the audio examples and then say each one out loud. If people are around, at least mouth them or speak them in your head. Prosody is processed using specific brain circuits (mostly in the right hemisphere, in contrast to words, which are processed on the left) and these are activated by auditory input. Just reading the examples may be interesting, but to fully experience the prosodic patterns you need to say them and hear them.

The book is in four parts. Chapters 2 through 4 lay the groundwork, each introducing a prosodic pattern and using it to explain fundamental concepts. Chapters 5 through 10 give historical perspective and explain how superposition-based modeling enables efficient discovery, interleaved with presentation of two more patterns. Then Chapters 11 through 13 catalog eighteen specific constructions involved in turn-taking, topic management, and expressing of stance, and finally, Chapters 14 and 15 give a wider perspective. We'll travel quickly, but I'll occasionally step off the path for anecdotes about research missteps and breakthroughs; for stories about the interesting prosody of children and foreigners; for speculations about culture, language learning, personality, social roles, emotion, politeness and rapport; and to debunk some myths.

Why should we care about the prosody of dialog? Most of the time we do just fine without thinking about it. But lack of awareness can cause problems. If we naively assume that prosody faithfully expresses intention and personality, someone who uses inappropriate prosody may seem impolite or insensitive, although the actual cause may be just a technical glitch in their pitch or timing, or a different idea about some pattern of English. If we instead see prosody as a system of its own, with its own logic and its own failure modes, we can reduce such misunderstandings.

I wrote this book out of frustration and hope. The frustration was from seeing valuable findings about conversational prosody go to waste, known and accessible only to scholars in a few isolated niches. At the same time non-native speakers of English, including many of my friends and co-workers, fail to communicate effectively because they never learned these constructions ... because they were never taught ... because their teachers lacked a resource on the facts of the prosody of dialog. My hope is that a clear account of prosodic constructions will help us all – scientists, teachers, co-workers, and friends – understand more deeply and communicate better.

2 Bookended Narrow Pitch Regions

The Bookended Narrow Pitch Construction is common and relatively simple: a good place to start. We'll take some time to examine both form and function, developing along the way the notion of prosodic construction. We'll then see how the disparate findings of previous work fit cleanly into a unified construction-based account, and finally speculate on what the prevalence of this construction says about American culture.

2.1 Marking Contrast

When people talk things over to reach a decision, they typically consider various factors. As they do, they generally indicate which support the previous point and which do not.

Suppose we're thinking about going on a hike tomorrow, and someone notes that the forecast says it will be warm. I might reply:

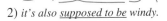

1) *yes, but it's also supposed to be windy*

with the pitch going up and down as suggested by the curves, with a region of narrow, nearly flat pitch in the middle, on the underlined words. This prosodic form indicates that there is a contrast, contradicting the implication that tomorrow's weather would be good for hiking.

The prosody is the key. Even without an explicit *but*, this prosody conveys contrast:

2) *it's also supposed to be windy.*

However, if this prosody is lacking, for example, if this sentence sounded like it were read from a book,

3) *it is also supposed to be windy*

without a region of narrow pitch, the meaning of contrast would be gone. Indeed, if I said it this way people might wonder whether I'd lost interest in the pros and cons of hiking tomorrow, and instead was just mentioning a random fact.

The same is true if I say

4) *it's supposed to be windy tomorrow.*

Again, without a narrow pitch region, it's not clear whether this is agreeing or disagreeing with the proposal. While locally coherent as a continuation of the weather topic, it lacks a clear relation to the question of whether to go hiking. You might wonder whether I consider windy days to be invigorating and see this as another reason to go, or whether I'm attempting to change the subject.

In fact, this prosodic pattern is so strongly associated with contrast that it can force otherwise implausible interpretations. If my response to your hiking suggestion were instead

5) *it's also <u>supposed to be</u> beautiful*

there would still be a contrast implied. While figuring out the nature of the contrast may require some work – perhaps to infer that I think that the day is too beautiful to waste on a hike – the prosody clearly marks this as contrasting in some way with the proposal.

A real example I overheard the other day was

6) *If you <u>were doing that</u> during working hours,*

For this I didn't have to speculate about the meaning – the contrast was explicit in what the speaker said next: *that would be a different story.* In form, this example differs from the others so far in that the region of narrow pitch is not low but high. While less common, this is not rare.

Here's an example from one of my corpora. S and G are discussing program development environments, and S mentions the iPhone. He suggests using it for programming and wonders why people don't:

7) S: *you could program easier on that, per se, so I don't know why*
   G: *well, the, I mean <u>the problem with</u> that is, to do like, to compile*
      …

G prefaces his response with a narrow pitch region, signaling his intent to present information that is incompatible with S's assumption.

The type of contrast conveyed by this form varies: it may contrast with something the other person said, as in the examples above, or with the speaker's own previous statement. An example of the latter happens right after the example used in Chapter 1:

8) H: *is it going to be a rave-type party? or like,*
   C: *well, it's someone's house.*
   H: *yeah*
   C: *there's gonna, I mean, there's like, they're gonna be spinning
        so, in that sense . . . maybe, but it's just at someone's house*
   H: *yeah, yeah*
   C: *and it's like <u>in the middle of the night, that too,</u> but. . .*

Here C is giving H the pieces of information she has, as evidence for or against H's supposition that it might be a *rave-type* party, with dancing. With the repeated mentions of "just at someone's house," C is implying that it won't be a rave, but then she provides some information suggesting the contrary, that it might be a rave after all, and she naturally marks this as contrasting.

Incidentally, this construction is sometimes co-constructed, performed by two speakers together. For example, in a discussion about whether the recording set-up was correct, the two speakers said

9) J: *I can't hear <u>you</u>*
   S: *without the <u>micro</u>[phone, right?*
   J: [*<u>without that microphone,</u> at all*

in overlap, where "[" marks the same timepoint in both utterances. Getting the timing right for this is not easy; success is a feat of linguistic synchronization that demonstrates a high degree of mutual understanding and being mentally "in sync."

2.2   Stronger and Weaker Forms

The connection between this prosodic pattern and a meaning of contrast has been verified experimentally. Kurumada and colleagues[1] set out to investigate how prosody affects interpretations of sentences of the form *it looks like a zebra*. She started with two stimuli: a "neutral" prosodic form, intended to mean that *it looks like a zebra (and it probably is)*, and a contrastive one, intended to imply that *it looks like a zebra (but don't be fooled; it isn't really)*. As seen in Figure 2.1, the contrastive form, below, has the pattern discussed above, with a region of narrow pitch bookended by regions of wider pitch.

Kurumada presented subjects with these stimuli and a pair of pictures. They had to choose whether each utterance was referring to the picture of an actual

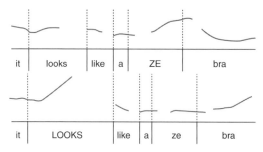

Figure 2.1 Neutral and contrastive variants of the same sentence, showing the pitch line and the time regions spanned by each syllable[2]

zebra or to the picture that only resembled a zebra. As expected, they tended to select the "real zebra" interpretation more for the neutral prosody than for the contrastive prosody, confirming that this prosodic pattern really does convey contrast.

Kurumada next investigated the nature of the form–function connection, in three ways. First, she observed that the prosodic form did not entirely determine the interpretation. The neutral form was interpreted as meaning "really is a zebra" not 100 percent but only 60–90 percent of the time, and the contrastive form was interpreted that way not 0 percent but 20–40 percent of the time. Second, she demonstrated that subjects' interpretations could shift when they had other sources of evidence. In one experiment, she gave subjects lots of exposure to stimuli with unambiguous wordings, such as *it is a zebra*. As expected, this increased their tendency to interpret sentences with *looks like* as indicating "not really," for both prosodic forms. In a third follow-up experiment, she exposed subjects to lots of stimuli where contrastive prosody was used but there was actually no contrast: where the animal really was a zebra. As expected, this weakened their tendency to interpret such stimuli as contrastive, presumably since they had learned that prosody was not a reliable cue in the experiment. Overall, these experiments show that the contribution of prosody to the overall interpretation is probabilistic, not absolute.

Kurumada also considered the question of whether prosodic marking of contrast was categorical or not: all-or-nothing or a matter of degree. To investigate, she created a family of twelve stimuli by warping the prosody in stages from the neutral form to the contrastive form. As Figure 2.2 shows, subjects were less likely to choose the "really-is" meaning as the contrastive prosody became stronger. That is, the strength of contrast correlated with the strength of this prosodic pattern. Thus this pattern is not all or nothing, but rather it can be present to a greater or lesser degree. This differs starkly from the more

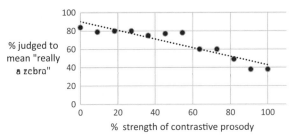

Figure 2.2 Percentage of times that the subjects thought the sentence referred to an actual zebra, as a function of the prosodic form. On the x axis are the variant forms, with the neutral prosody at the left, the contrastive prosody at the right, and in the middle intermediate points for variants warped progressively between the two[3]

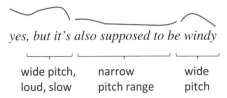

yes, but it's also supposed to be windy

| wide pitch, | narrow | wide |
| loud, slow | pitch range | pitch |

Figure 2.3 The three main components of the Bookended Narrow Pitch Construction

familiar property of language elements to be either present or not, with no middle ground. For example, there's nothing between the words *cupcake* and *cupcakes*; no way to pronounce the last /s/ weakly and thereby convey that I ate more than one cupcake but less than two. But prosody works differently: its perception here is not categorical, but a gradient phenomenon.[4]

2.3　The Narrow Pitch Region and the Bookends

Now that we've seen a function of this pattern, let's consider its form more carefully. There are three components, as suggested in Figure 2.3.

The first is the region of narrow pitch. Every speaker has his or her own typical pitch range, but this pattern involves a region where the pitch range is much narrower. It is seldom completely flat, typically having slight pitch bumps at lexically stressed syllables, but is clearly compressed in range. The narrow pitch region is typically around 400 to 900 milliseconds, which is commonly three or four words, depending on word length and speaking rate.

The location of the narrow pitch region can vary; it is not tied to any specific words. This can be seen in alternate forms of a response to the hiking suggestion

10) *well, yeah, I saw <u>that it will hit 80, but it's</u> also supposed to be windy*

11) *well, yeah, I saw that it will hit 80, but it's also supposed to be windy.*

Both convey a clear contrast.

This pattern has two more components: the leading and trailing "bookends."[4] These enhance the salience of the narrow pitch region and are necessary to the pattern. If the first bookend is missing, a narrow pitch region can sound like a vague musing:

12) *<u>it's also supposed to be</u> windy*

and without a tailing bookend, a narrow pitch region can sound incomplete:

13) *it's also <u>supposed to be windy</u>*

as if the speaker hasn't finished deciding what he wants to say.

The bookends can take different forms. Most commonly they exhibit high pitch with wide pitch range, increased loudness, and slowing, but other patterns are also possible, as long as they clearly end the region of narrow pitch, as in

14) *I'd feel wrong graduating <u>in May, and still having a class left</u> over*

where the last two words, *left over* are very low in pitch, indeed creaky. This example conveys a contrast between this option and the alternative, namely graduating in December.

These examples illustrate that all three components are part of the pattern. This configuration of prosodic components therefore deserves a name: I call it the "Bookended Narrow Pitch Construction."

While this characterization is new, many aspects of this construction have been noted before. Let's consider two classic perspectives, each of which reveals something interesting.

One perspective highlights the ways in which this construction resembles some kinds of focusing. In particular, the bookends often resemble the pattern used to focus a word, and the region of narrow pitch resembles "post-focus compression," in which a focus-related pitch peak is generally followed by a region of reduced pitch range.[5] Semantically also, the bookends can relate to focus. Despite the similarities, this construction cannot be reduced to mere focus, for three reasons. First, this construction includes a right bookend, whereas focus generally needs only one pitch peak.[6] Second, the meaning of this construction involves more than focus, as illustrated above. Third, the left bookend does not necessarily align with a semantically contrastive word. For example, the left bookend comes on *I mean* in Example 7, and in Example 14,

---

Bookended Narrow Pitch Construction (Preliminary)

Function: express contrast with something that has just
been said or implied

Form:

timespan	prosodic properties
0 – 200 ms	high or wide pitch, loud, slow
200 – 600 ms	narrow pitch range
600 – 700 ms	high or wide pitch

Figure 2.4 The Bookended Narrow Pitch Construction: a first approximation.

it comes on *graduating*, rather than the word *May*, which is actually being contrasted.

A second perspective treats this pattern as an intonation contour, ignoring all aspects of prosody other than pitch height. Historically this was represented in one of two ways, either as an overall contour or as a symbolic description, as a sequence of levels, such as [L*+HL-H%], specifying the sequence of highs and lows using ToBI notation.[7] Notational questions aside, the intonation-contour perspective highlights the importance of the narrow pitch region, rather than treating it as just an uninteresting default way to fill in the gap between two peaks. Drawing this pattern as a contour also has a visual immediacy, and emphasizes that it is a configuration in time. The disadvantages of the contours approach are an over-emphasis on pitch height, at the expense of other prosodic features, and in particular an inability to indicate pitch-range properties. Although the narrow pitch region may be high or low relative to the bookends, when we diagram it as a contour, the middle part needs to be drawn at some specific height. A similar problem arises for approaches to prosody which limit the descriptive vocabulary to two symbols, L and H, for low and high (L and H) targets. Since the middle region is low more often than it is high, descriptions in this style typically denote it with some variant of "L," but this fails to describe the allowable variability in height, let alone the importance of the narrowness of pitch.

Avoiding these various pitfalls, Figure 2.4 summarizes the construction as seen so far. This is truly a construction: it exhibits four properties. It is: (1) a specific temporal configuration of prosodic features, (2) with a specific meaning, (3) with no rigid alignment to specific words or phrasings, and (4) with the ability to be present to different degrees. These are the first four key properties of prosodic constructions.

2.4   Uses in Contradictions

Historically this construction has received a fair amount of attention in linguistics, starting with Liberman and Sag.[8] At the 1974 Chicago Linguistics Society meeting they famously presented the question-response sequence seen in Figure 2.5.

The response was performed on a kazoo, to convey the pitch pattern without using words. Nevertheless, the meaning was clearly some kind of contradiction: one could imagine it accompanying phrases like *you don't have a pet whale*. Thus Liberman and Sag demonstrated that an intonation contour can have meaning, independent of the words it is performed on, if any. Another example from their paper was, in response to someone bemoaning that *my fate is sealed: I've been diagnosed with elephantiasis*, the response:

15) *Elephantiasis isn't incurable!*

again clearly showing a bookended narrow pitch. Based on such examples they claimed that this was a meaningful intonation contour: the Contradiction Contour.

While the examples are compelling, the general claim, that this contour itself means contradiction, was not universally accepted. The mapping between the meaning of contradiction and this contour is clearly not one-to-one – there are uses of this contour that don't involve contradiction, and contradictions that are expressed with other prosodic forms – and such exceptions made many unwilling to accept the idea of intonation contours as meaning-bearing units.[10] For many years the field of prosody research was split, divided between those for whom such examples were too convincing to ignore and those for whom the exceptions were too salient to overlook.[11]

Fast forward twenty-five years. By the new millennium the field of linguistics had come to accept that language behavior seldom follows exceptionless rules, but rather should be described in terms of statistical tendencies. (Of course, this is really just common sense: insisting on exceptionless rules would

M: *Hey Ivan, how about on your way to school this morning you drop off my pet whale at the aquarium?*

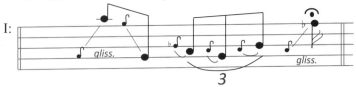

Figure 2.5 A snappy response to a ridiculous request[9]

imply, for example, that the word *cat* has no meaning, because sometimes *cat* refers to things other than housecats, and sometimes people refer to cats using other words.)

In 2003 Hedberg and colleagues decided to revisit the issue of whether there really was a contradiction contour.[13] Their question was not whether contradiction and this contour always co-occur, but whether the connection is more common than one would expect by chance. Whereas the debate in the 1970s relied on made-up examples, Hedberg set out to see what people actually do. By this time, linguists had developed large corpora, and methods and tools to support their analysis, but Hedberg's work was still Herculean: she and her colleagues painstakingly identified all contradictions in over twenty-three hours of dialog data and prosodically categorized each. Their results showed that, first, well, things are complicated, with several variant forms used in different contexts, but second, contours like those seen in Figure 2.6 were frequent enough with this meaning to justify the name "Contradiction Contour" after all.

In 2012 Lai followed up experimentally.[14] She had subjects act out scripted dialogs that included a sentence contradicting something said by the other. Figure 2.7 shows the intonation of several contradictions produced in different contexts by one speaker. Overall, Lai too found a strong correlation between contradictions and this form.

Recent evidence thus supports Liberman and Sag's claim: this form does have this meaning. But the exceptions are not something to dismiss. Rather,

Figure 2.6 Hedberg's illustration of the "classic" Contradiction Contour, spanning about 800 milliseconds[12]

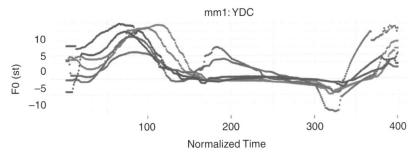

Figure 2.7 The pitch (log F_0) of contradictions produced by Lai's subject mm1, stretched linearly to align the endpoints[15]

they are a source of insight, which we will exploit in the next section to pin down this construction's meaning.

2.5   Other Meanings

The Bookended Narrow Pitch Construction↑ is associated not only with contrast and contradictions, as seen above, but also with complaining and expressing grudging admiration. After some examples of these uses, we'll consider what all these functions have in common.

2.5.1   Uses in Complaints

The Bookended Narrow Pitch Construction is common when complaining, as in

16) *it's annoying, how much, um homework is given.*

17) J: *can you hear me?*
       S: *yeah, but I hear a lot of static.*

Like contrasting, in complaining the narrow pitch region is not limited to appear in specific places; it can span various word sequences. For example, it might be positioned like this:

18) *well, I don't like to complain, but . . .*

or a little earlier

19) *well really, now I don't like to complain, but . . .*

with no significant change in meaning.

The connection between narrow pitch and complaining was first observed by Ogden, looking at British English.[16] In one of his examples the speaker was describing an unsatisfactory resort experience. After noting that only a few rooms had functioning air conditioners, she reiterated her point with

20) *the   rest   of 'em   were   broken.*

In another example, the speaker talked about dogsitting an animal who gets active too early:

21) |well it /seems her time for getting {↑ \up}_f is six o'{↑ \clock}_f|

(In Ogden's notation the vertical bars indicate boundaries (pauses), the arrows and slanted lines indicate peaks, and the subscript f indicates relative loudness (forte). Here there are two regions of narrow pitch, on *her time for getting* and on *is six o'*.) Ogden concludes that, in complaints, "the pitch span is often narrow" and set off by "accented syllables" that "are often loud . . . and their pitch peaks . . . high in the speaker's range." Despite the differences in dialect and in notation, this is almost certainly the Bookended Narrow Pitch Construction.

Another property that complaints may exhibit is "a high degree of rhythmicity,"[17] as in the previous example and in

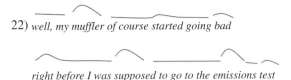

22) *well, my muffler of course started going bad*

right before I was supposed to go to the emissions test

as a result of the repeated bookended narrow pitch regions. This seems to be common when telling stories.

While the examples so far have been complaints about third parties, people also of course also complain directly to someone. Examples of this are lacking in most recorded conversations, but it's not hard to imagine how they might sound.

23) *we've been waiting twenty minutes and we still haven't seen a waitress.*

Consider also the set-up line in the classic joke: *A man in a restaurant finds a fly in his soup, so he calls over the waiter, and says,*

24) *Waiter, what's this fly doing in my soup.*

If said with the Bookended Narrow Pitch Construction, this is clearly a complaint, but if this prosody is absent or weak, it can be a question, which enables the second part of the joke: *so the waiter peers at the soup, and says "I believe he's doing the backstroke, sir."*[18]

Incidentally, if you speak some of these examples as complaints, with full feeling, you may naturally add certain facial expressions or gestures. In general, complaining can involve much more than just prosody. There are, for example, tendencies to use certain lexical items, such as expletives, to reference certain semantic categories, such as quantities of time or money, and to include certain sounds, such as tongue clicks.[19] Complaining also tends to fit into conversations in certain ways, with implicit conventions for when they are appropriate and for how the conversation can proceed after a complaint is voiced: the listener may empathize, apologize, mention an analogous personal experience, minimize the issue, joke about it, and so on.[20] A truly comprehensive treatment of complaining would cover all of this, but in this book we'll focus on only the prosodic aspects of each construction.

2.5.2   *Grudging Admiration*

The Bookended Narrow Pitch Construction can also express grudging admiration, as in an assessment of a software package:

25) *there's a graphical interface builder, called Xcode, it's a huge development environment. I mean, it, it does like, <u>it does</u> <u>everything</u>. As far as I've seen.*

Grudging admiration conveys not only that something is good, but that this praise is not given lightly: it implies that this is an informed opinion by a speaker who is knowledgeable and has high standards.

Uses of grudging admiration often include nuances of the other functions. This example includes also contrast: a contrast between the quality of this software and the normal property of software to do less than you expect. Consider also

26) *Professor, you really <u>kicked my butt with that</u> last assignment*

as a student once told me. I heard this as expressing not only grudging admiration for the sophistication of the assignment, but also a mild complaint, plus a claim that there was a contrast with his normal level of performance.

This is a good point for a digression on a pervasive difficulty for attempts to relate meaning to prosody: the possibility of different interpretations for any example. Occasionally I present an audio clip to the research group and ask the dozen members for thoughts on the meaning conveyed by the prosody. Going around the table we usually find more than one interpretation. For example, the prosody on the statement about the party *in the middle of the night* (in Example 8) may not only convey contrast, as mentioned above, but also simultaneously downplay the information and perhaps humorously call attention to that downplaying. Some readers may have already noticed other meanings for the examples in this chapter, in addition to the functions I am using them to illustrate. In general, for the examples in this book, please try to see at least the meanings I describe; listening to the audio clips will help with this. If the claimed meaning is still not apparent to you, try listening to another example: even if one example doesn't work for you, hopefully the others will.

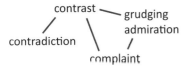

Figure 2.8 Functions of the Bookended Narrow Pitch Construction, with some connections

2.5.3 Connections among the Meanings

We have seen that this one construction serves at least four functions: contrast, contradiction, complaining, and grudging admiration. This may seem untidy, but things like this are not uncommon in language. For example, many words have multiple meanings, with the interpretation of any specific instance usually clear from the context.

In fact, this construction is polysemous, in that the possible meanings are closely related, rather than being discretely ambiguous. The polysemy may be present in a single example. For example, the complaint in Example 20 also includes a contrast: the contrast between functioning air conditioners and broken ones. Contradictions also necessarily involve contrast: a contrast with something explicitly stated by the other speaker.

Thus we can describe these four functions of the Bookended Narrow Pitch Construction as a "family" of meanings, as summarized in Figure 2.8.

2.6 The Core Meaning: Consider This

We have now arrived at a rather untidy idea of the meaning of this construction, involving four related functions. To more precisely characterize the meaning, let's consider some alternative prosodic ways to express these functions, to see how they differ in nuances.

Considering first the function of contrast, speakers have a choice of which prosodic form to use.[21] For example, in the hike-planning scenario, I could have chosen to express concern about the wind with a strong downward slope:

27) *it's supposed to be windy tomorrow.*

With this sharp fall, the utterance seems to disclaim any interest in persuading you to see things my way; it would be suitable if my intention were to end the discussion and walk away. In contrast, the same sentence with a Bookended Narrow Pitch pattern could serve as part of an agreement-seeking process, inviting you to consider the contrasting information and perhaps change your opinion.

Complaints also can be expressed in other ways. One alternative is to use a high nasal voice – to whine:

28) *nobody ever listens to anything I say.*

As Ogden notes, in some complaints the pitch is "sustained above the speaker's average."[22] Another way to complain is with a grumble, consistently using low creaky voice

29) *those stupid politicians will never understand.*

This form may, incidentally, be more common for complaints about distant third parties.

Interestingly, both whining and grumbling may involve regions of narrow pitch, but these are ongoing and open-ended, rather than bookend-delimited. The difference is that those without bookends seem more self-directed, less concerned about putting out information for consideration by the listener, and less intended to be productive in the sense of identifying a problem that can be solved by further discussion.

Another way to complain is with a long pitch fall,

30)   *I really don't like it when you do that*

as a bald declaration of displeasure. After this the speaker could walk away, or a parent could use this to scold a child without allowing a response. In contrast, the bookended-narrow version,

31)   *I really don't like it when you do that*

invites the listener to consider this information and leaves it open for discussion, maybe leading to a compromise.

Contradiction also may be expressed without using narrow pitch regions. Strongly falling pitch is yet again a possibility, as might occur on

32) *you're wrong.*

Sharp pitch movements, wide pitch range, and occasional falsetto is another way to contradict, as seen in children's squabbles, typically sequences of accusations and denials:

The Consider This Construction

Function: offer some information which the speaker knows, but which the listener may not; to offer it up for consideration by the listener, and for the sake of advancing the discussion, which is expected to continue; as when expressing contrast, contradiction, complaint, and grudging admiration

---

Form:

timespan	prosodic properties
0 – 200 ms	high or wide pitch, loud, slow
200 – 600 ms	narrow pitch range
600 – 700 ms	high or wide pitch

mnemonic: Bookended Narrow Pitch

Figure 2.9 The Bookended Narrow Pitch Construction: Summary Diagram. The times are typical values, but may be much longer[23]

33) Y: *why'd you take two of them?*
   N: *I didn't take two of them*
   Y: *yeah you did*
   N: *I did not*
   Y: *yeah, yeah you did*
   N: *uh-unh*
   Y: *yeah.*

In contrast to these two forms, contradictions expressed with bookended narrow pitch regions seem to invite the listener to consider something and to continue the conversation in light of that new information.

Thus, across these functions, there seems to be a core meaning that is consistently present when this construction is used, and lacking when it is not: the speaker is offering some information which the listener may not know, and is offering it up for consideration and for the sake of advancing the discussion, which is expected to continue.

This seems to be the specific, core meaning of the Bookended Narrow Pitch pattern. Accordingly, we also refer to it as the Consider This Construction, as summarized in Figure 2.9.[24]

To those familiar with traditional philosophical accounts, this may seem surprising as the meaning for a linguistic element. Early theories of semantics assumed that meanings are mostly objective, relating language elements to things that are independently visible in the world – rocks and trees, buildings and food, throwing and eating – and to propositions about them. For this construction, however, the meaning is of a different kind:[25] it involves the relations between the dialog participants and their ongoing exchange. From an interactional perspective this is not a surprise: language exists for human purposes, so we can expect many meanings to relate to human needs. Here the specific need is that, in dialog, speakers often need to help listeners understand the spirit in which something is being said, to help them interpret and respond to it appropriately. So it is not unreasonable that the English language has a prosodic construction to serve this purpose.

2.7   A Family of Constructions

So, we have found for the Bookended Narrow Pitch Construction a single core meaning, across the various uses. But is the meaning truly at this level? Let's consider two alternative levels of description.

First, meaning may inhere at a more specific level. Indeed, most previous descriptions of this construction have discussed how it can convey one of the more specific meanings: contrast or contradiction. While this may be partly due to the small numbers of examples treated by early researchers, the more specific meanings may have more specific prosody. For example, complaints may involve nasal voice and wider pitch range on the bookends, whereas grudging admiration may involve creaky voice and more modest bookends.

Second, some of the meaning may inhere at a more abstract level. Each individual component of this construction seems to have its own meaning, albeit a very abstract one. For example, narrow pitch regions often express some kind of negative stance, and pitch peaks often focus or mark things for special attention by the listener, or flag intent rather than just self-directed mumbling. These component meanings are present in the overall meaning of the Bookended Narrow Pitch Construction, although they do not fully account for its specific meaning. That is, this construction as a whole means more than the sum of the meanings of the parts.

The abstract component meanings are suggested in the top half of Figure 2.10, and the more specific "daughter" constructions in the bottom. Overall, meaning and form are inherited down from one level to another, as suggested by the arrows. Since each of these levels is a useful level of description, we cannot say that prosodic meaning is exclusively at one level. While in this book the focus will be at the middle level, we will occasionally also examine more abstract and more specific mappings.

Incidentally, in this figure, the meaning of the mother construction is given as the conjunction of three clauses. This is purely to be concise, and is not intended to imply that the meaning of this construction is properly captured by a logical conjunction of independent clauses. While traditional theories of meaning favor such descriptions,[26] the meaning here, as for all constructions, seems to be more "holistic," a sort of unified gestalt,[27] such that this construction is appropriate to the extent that the speaker's intention matches this gestalt.

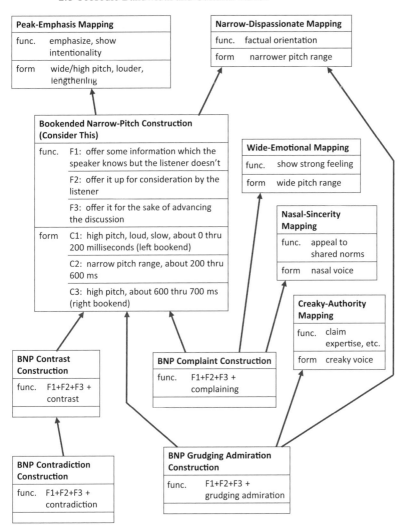

Figure 2.10 The Bookended Narrow Pitch Construction as part of a hierarchy. For the daughter constructions the forms are not shown, since they are simply the combinations of the forms of the parents

2.8   Prosodic Bandwidth and Cultural Values

Prosody is a limited resource. Everything that we do with prosody is done with just a few basic elements: pitch, energy, speaking rate, and so on. Although these can appear in many combinations, the number of possible configurations is not unlimited.[28] One limiting factor is the length: most constructions seem to span at most a few seconds. Another limiting factor is the potential for confusability: if two constructions were to differ by only a semitone over only a fraction of a second, listeners would find it hard to distinguish the two. Humans' limited ability to learn and to reproduce different forms may also limit the number of patterns a language can have.[29] Thus the bandwidth of prosody is limited, and the number of roles it can serve may number only in the dozens.

At the same time, there are many demands on prosody. Beyond pragmatic and dialog functions, it also is used to convey emotion and attitude, indicate clause boundaries and syntactic dependencies, and much else besides.[30]

Across languages, the limited bandwidth of prosody is allocated differently. In Mandarin, for example, prosody is pervasively used to convey lexical identity: tones differentiate words with the same phoneme sequences. As a result, less of the bandwidth is available for other uses.[31] And indeed, functions that in many languages are expressed by prosody, such as indicating questionhood or indicating newness, are in Mandarin mostly expressed with grammatical particles.

From this perspective, it is interesting to ask why the community of English speakers chooses to dedicate a chunk of precious prosodic bandwidth to contrast-related meanings, especially when other language communities make different choices.

Perhaps we can find an answer in the culture. The ties between language and culture are deep, and the lexical and grammatical resources available in a language can make it easier for speakers to focus their attention on certain aspects of the world, communicate about certain aspects of things, and even reason in certain ways.[32] So, what it is about the common thought patterns of English speakers that makes the Bookended Narrow Pitch Construction so necessary? There are several possibilities.

Regarding the function of indicating contrast, while in some cultures it's a bit rude to explicitly mark contrasts, Americans often welcome differences of opinion and healthy debate. On a team, having aired the issues, all members can feel better about whatever final outcome results: explicitly considering multiple factors can make the final conclusion feel solid and shared. This activity is often part of problem solving, an activity that Americans are generally fond of. In doing so, Americans like to feel that they're making progress, to feel that each statement in a discussion is contributing, in some way, to the ultimate conclusion. Statements that don't clearly contribute, that don't line up either for or against the proposal at hand, are felt to be a waste of time. These habits and preferences are culture-dependent, not universal. Mexicans, for example, can be put off by American business people's focus on lining up the pros and cons and quickly deciding on a plan, rather than taking the time to explore also how the stakeholders feel personally about the options.[33]

Regarding the function of contradicting, this also is something that Americans are comparatively comfortable with. We are willing to, as the idioms say, "tell it like it is," and "let the chips fall where they may." Other cultures have different preferences. In Seoul I once almost missed a flight because the gate attendant was too polite to tell me directly that I was mistaken. Korean culture, it is said, prefers to avoid things that could cause someone to lose face.[34] Still, Americans too have limits. Imagine the boss wants to do something that's not right. If you contradict her directly,

34) *that's not possible, because we <u>can't skip the quality checks</u>*

you're putting your job on the line, so you might choose to make the point in a different way, with different prosody.

Regarding complaining, Americans generally like to be upbeat; people who complain too much, or in the wrong contexts, can be labeled whiners. At the same time, Americans also like to identify and solve problems, and often this starts by noticing something wrong and mentioning it. The *a lot of static* example above was such a case: immediately afterwards, S went to adjust the audio equipment, which solved the problem.

When I'm advising students, after 10 to 15 minutes of discussion, I expect to hear them complain about something. If I don't hear that, I wonder why: whether the student is not consciously aware of what's good or bad in his academic life, whether he is unwilling to identify problems and share responsibility for solving them, or whether I've failed to establish enough rapport for him to be open with me.

Other cultures view complaining differently. In Japan there is a greater value on accepting whatever fate brings, with correspondingly less complaining. In Mexican culture, students from Mexico tell me, complaining is more common. Rather than a general negativity, this may reflect a cultural practice of sharing difficulties to lighten individual burdens. In any case, I've been told that Mexicans learn to dial back the complaining when interacting with Americans.

Regarding the phenomenon of grudging admiration, Americans are known for being judgmental, for liking to measure and evaluate, and for being competitive, always comparing themselves to others. Sometimes grudging admiration includes a nuance of reluctance to accept that other people are doing well, or even annoyance at others' success. Perhaps not coincidentally, all examples of grudging admiration in my data are from male speakers.

So the existence of this construction in English may have deep-seated cultural reasons.

2.9   Summary

This chapter has identified a prosodic construction, the Bookended Narrow Pitch Construction, and described its form and its functions, as summarized back in Figure 2.10.

This took a lot of pages, not because the construction is particularly complicated, but because I needed to bring together the previously unconnected insights of forty years of research. I also needed to explain the notion of prosodic construction. To recap, the key idea is that dialog prosody can be described in terms of prosodic constructions, and that each of these:

1. is a temporal configuration of prosodic features,
2. has a meaning,
3. is not necessarily closely aligned with words,
4. can be present to a greater or lesser degree,
5. can share aspects of meaning and form with related (sister and daughter) constructions.

Although the specific term "prosodic construction" is not yet in common use, much recent work in prosody is centered on temporal patterns of prosodic activity that express specific meanings and functions in this way.[35]

This chapter also introduced some of the methods this book will rely on. In particular, to arrive at a full understanding of this construction, I used a bottom-up, form-based investigation. That is, I started with an observed form and looked to see which functions and activities it is associated with. This was a productive strategy here, leading not only to the discovery of grudging admiration as a relevant activity, but also to the discovery that contrasting and complaining are prosodically similar, something that previous work had not noted.

The Bookended Narrow Pitch Construction is a relatively simple example, usually appearing in the middle of a conversation. The next chapter will introduce a construction involving more features, and which can pop up out of the blue.

3   Downstep Constructions

English has a specific prosodic construction for getting immediate action, though it is applicable only when certain conditions hold. This chapter explains the form and function of the Minor Third Construction in great detail. It also considers some issues in mental representation, language learning and socialization, and cross-cultural communication.

3.1   Two Long, Flat, Downstepped Syllables

Imagine you're in conversation with someone and her phone vibrates. She stops stop talking, says

1) ^{hang} $_{on}$

and answers it. (This chapter will use letter height to indicate pitch height.) The step down in pitch makes the meaning unambiguous: she wants you to wait a moment. In contrast, the same words without a pitch downstep

2) *hang on*

would lack that clear implication, and may sound like she's talking to herself, not you. Thus the impact comes from the prosody; indeed, it would mean the same even if used with other words, such as *just a sec*, *uh-oh* or *oh dear*.

In addition to the pitch downstep, this prosodic construction requires a level pitch on both the pre-downstep and post-downstep parts, and it requires both parts to be long.

This prosodic construction is also used for calling people. Indeed, it is so typical of this function that it has been called the "Calling Contour."[1] Thus if I need to get the attention of my two-syllable daughter, I can call her:

3) $^{Su\text{-}}$ $_{san.}$

When calling people whose names have more syllables,

4) ^{Juli} $_{an}$

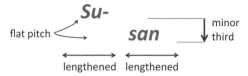

Figure 3.1 Some salient properties of the downstep construction

5) *Alex* $^{an\text{-}}$ *der*

the stressed syllable aligns with the higher syllable of the construction. Here, as usual, dialog prosody and lexical accent work nicely together: stressed syllables like to be long and high, which suits the needs of this construction. This last example also illustrates another common property of the construction: extra syllables before the stressed one tend to be lower in pitch, resulting in an upstep before the downstep.

The construction is less well suited to one-syllable names, but it can still be applied, by splitting up the syllable to make "docking sites" for both parts of the construction:[2]

6) $^{Joo\text{-}}$ *ohn.*

The same happens with

7) $^{over\ hee\text{-}}$ *ere.*

Dictionaries say that the word *here* has one syllable, but that's just the default; communicative needs can override that. Since the first word has no stress to contribute, the Minor Third Construction aligns twice with the stressed word, breaking it apart to do so.

But such alignments are not optimal. Their awkwardness may be one reason why people with one-syllable names have two-syllable nicknames, such as *Johnny* for *John*, and why people whose names have non-initial stress have stress-initial nicknames, such as *Alex* or *Sandy* for *Alexander*.

Figure 3.1 illustrates the most salient components of this construction. More detail will come after we examine its meaning.

3.2   The Core Meaning: Cueing Action

Consider the knock-knock joke, as in

8) *Knock* $_{knock!}$
   Who's $_{there?}$
   Carmen.

Figure 3.2 The rhythm of knock-knock jokes

Carmen who?
Carmen let me in already! ("Carmen" pronounced like "come and").

The opening line, *knock knock*, always exhibits the same prosodic form. If you use different prosody your joke will be off to a poor start, but an enthusiastic downstep obliges your hearer to respond; if they don't, they'll appear antisocial or uncultured. The hearer is also obliged to respond quickly: too slow and they'll seem dim-witted. In effect, the *knock knock* initiates a rhythmic call-response sequence, as illustrated in Figure 3.2, with the response coming in on the beat.

This pattern is important in various types of play, where it generally cues an immediate response. In Marco Polo, the pool game, the person who is "it" produces the downstepped call, *Marco*, and then all the other players respond by calling out *Polo*, in rhythm and in unison. On the playground, *nyah-nyah*, as in *nyah-nyah, you can't catch me* (9), cues the hearer to chase the taunter. In hide-and-seek, *ready or not, here I come* (10) cues the others to remain still, and *ollie-ollie-all-come-free-oh* (11) cues them to reveal themselves and return to base. Similarly,

12) *tag:* ^{*you're*} *it*

is a cue to try to tag back.

This construction can also cue action in less structured games. For example, in a cooperative videogame, player O was unsure whether to move ahead, but was spurred to action by a response with a downstep:

13) *O: do I wait for you?*
    G: no, it's okay, I got _{*it.*}

Sometimes the function is not to cue an action but to cue stopping an action or refraining from an action. In a videogame, as one player was approaching a hazard, the other said

14) *come on ...* ^{*oh*} *kay*

to cue the other to stop moving and take stock of the situation. We already saw how a downstepped *hang on* or *just a sec* can require the hearer to stop talking, not do anything, and not go anywhere. More harshly, a downstepped *stop that* (15) cues cessation of action.

Indeed, this pattern does this even without words. If a toddler is reaching for the cookies before it's snack time, you can say

16) $^{unh\text{-}}$ $_{uh}$

to make him desist.

While this pattern is conventionally associated with specific words and specific situations, it can also be used in new ways and in novel situations. For example, at a wrestling match where the people in front were taking too long to get settled, someone called out

17) *down in*^{front} $_{please}$

to cue them to sit down quickly.

Interestingly, many doorbells also embody this pattern. First, they have two chimes, with the second one downstepped. Second, each chime is constant in pitch, like the flat pitch of the prosodic pattern. Third, the timing is the same: doorbells have fairly long reverberation, like the lengthened syllables, and an appropriately timed interval between the chimes. While doorbells use no words, their rings still demand swift responses:

18) ^{ding} $_{dong}$ ...*come in*
    ^{ding} $_{dong}$ ...*just a second*
    ^{ding} $_{dong}$ ...*who's there?*

Thus this prosodic pattern is not only part of our language; it is designed into our environment. The exact downstep is usually three semitones: a minor third. (Some doorbells have instead a major-third downstep, which has a slightly different nuance, feeling to me more like an announcement than a summons.[3])

To be clear, the Minor Third Construction involves more than just a pitch downstep; that is, it is more than just an intonation contour. More discussion will follow, but for now let's just consider the differences between doorbells and foghorns. Foghorns also have a pitch drop and two long flat syllables. But their timbre is muddier, the duration longer, and the pitch drop greater. They do not have the same psychological effect: we do not feel obliged to respond.

Let's get back to business: pinning down the meaning of this construction. Across the uses seen above – calling someone, starting a joke, asking for attention, cueing the cessation of action, cueing action – the shared meaning is invoking a response that is required by some social norm. To see that this meaning actually comes from this construction, let's consider what difference this prosody makes. With it present,

---

Minor Third Construction (First Approximation)

Function: cue the hearer to do something

Form:

two syllables with flat pitch
each syllable lengthened
downstep in pitch between the syllables

Figure 3.3 The Minor Third Construction: a first approximation

19) ^{thank} $_{you}$

is quite likely to elicit a response. This form would be appropriate if the wait-ress had run out to you with your forgotten coat, and you wanted to express that you really appreciated it. She'd surely reply with *you're welcome* or *no problem*. In contrast,

20) *thank you*

with a flat or gently downsloped pitch is much less likely to get a response. This form is what you'd use when the ticket-taker hands you back the ticket stubs; you wouldn't expect him to respond.

Similarly, if the counter man closes the interaction with a downstep:

21) *you have a* ^{good} $_{one}$

you're likely to give a polite response, such as *you too*, to complete the ritual. But with a weaker rendition, with less lengthening and a smaller downstep,

22) *you have a good one*

you probably won't feel that a reply is needed or wanted.

Figure 3.3 summarizes the construction as discussed so far.

3.3   Conditions and Contexts of Use

Thus the Minor Third Construction is a powerful way to get people to do things. However, you can't use it just anytime. It's appropriate only if four specific conditions hold.

The first condition is that there is an obvious action for the hearer to perform. This condition is clearly true in games and ritualized play at times when there is only one relevant next action, and the only question is when to perform it. In less constrained contexts, the Minor Third is still appropriate only when there is just one possibly relevant action.[4] For example, in a two-player videogame,[5] at one point the experienced player prompted the novice to

23) $^{go\,for}$ it.

While this would have been odd if there were many possible actions, in the context there was only one, and the novice player immediately started moving in the obvious direction.

The second condition is that there is a social norm that compels the hearer to perform the desired action. For example, if it is my daughter's chore to clean up after dinner, I can cue that action with a pitch downstep or two:

24) $Isa\text{-}_{bel,}$ ^{dinner} $_{clean}$

but if this week that's not her chore, this prosody would be inappropriate; I'd have to use a different approach to get her to help.

Conversely, if there is a relevant social norm, it's proper to use the Minor Third Construction even in situations where one would not normally be permitted to speak, let alone demand someone to do something. For example, if the professor has forgotten to turn on the microphone, then any student has the right to say *excuse me* and tell her. Even though it's usually rude to interrupt someone, especially someone of high status, turning on the microphone is something that any student can rightfully ask for.

The third condition is that the invoked action be easy to do. This can be seen from the fact that this construction is not appropriate as a way to request something complex or open-ended. For example, a cry of distress of the form

25) $^{he\text{-}}$ -elp

would be strange or even humorous.[6]

The fourth condition is that the cued action needs to be performed right away. It's appropriate to say *down in front please* if the match is about to start; since an obstructed view for even a second could cause you to miss seeing a throw. Conversely, if there is still a minute before the match starts, this prosody would be rude.

An apparent counterexample to this is the pervasive *have a good one* (26). While syntactically this is an imperative, instructing you how to spend the rest of your day,[7] this invariably functions as a cue. For example, at the check-out counter this cues you to take your purchases and move on, since other customers are waiting.

In general, getting people to do things for you is tricky. Books have been written on the many ways to make requests, including the complex interpersonal strategies and linguistic resources involved in doing so politely.[8] But if the four conditions above hold, you can get someone to do something with just a couple of words and the right prosody. To summarize: (1) there has to be a single expected action that is obviously appropriate in the situation, (2) this action must be something that the speaker can rightfully expect of the hearer,

(3) it can't be a big deal, and (4) it should be done immediately. (While it is convenient to list these in this way, again I do not mean to imply that these are independent conditions, nor that speakers check whether all are precisely true before using this construction. Rather this construction's meaning is a gestalt, and speakers use it when there is an acceptably good match between this gestalt and the current situation, including their intention.)

The rest of this section will explore the implications of these conditions.

One implication is that there is seldom a need to use the Minor Third Construction during a conversation: it's seldom necessary to demand an immediate response when you're sitting down talking to someone. It is accordingly rare in my main corpus. Nevertheless, it does occur, for example in formulaic closings

27) *you're* welcome

28) R: *bye* e
    J: *bye*

and sometimes between close friends

29) S: *we were talking for seven* min utes
    J: *really*

30) S: *what did you* get on *that one?*
    G: ninety nine
    S: (throws up his hands, lurches back in his chair, and raises his eyebrows in a display of astonishment).

While, in general, to use the Minor Third Construction in conversation can seem controlling and rude, between friends there may be enough trust for the speaker to know that the listener will be happy following his lead, especially when the speaker also happens to be the dominant person in the dialog.

Another implication is that this construction can be used even when the speaker and hearer were not previously interacting. This is unusual. In general, people seldom communicate much until after some sort of greeting, a *hello* or whatnot. However, many uses of the Minor Third Construction come with no warning whatsoever. For example, some kid may just walk up to you on the playground and unleash a *knock knock*. Why is the Minor Third Construction exempt from the general requirement for interactions to be prefaced by greetings? The answer may lie in the fact that greetings are not a mere social ritual; they also serve to provide voice samples so the interactants can estimate each other's current standard pitch height, pitch range, and so on. This helps them properly interpret future utterances. This may be, incidentally, why greetings are common when meeting new people, and why we usually greet each other each day when we meet in the morning: people's voices change slightly from day to day, so it's helpful each morning to provide a fresh voice sample, to enable the listener to recalibrate.[9] The Minor Third Construction, however, is identifiable even without such calibration, since its key components – flatness, duration, and downstep – do not depend on the speaker's typical pitch height or range, and can thus be detected without having information on them. Thus it is well suited for use when one needs to immediately initiate an interaction, even with a stranger.

While on the topic of this construction's components, it's worth noting that several are motivated, not arbitrary. First, since the Minor Third Construction is often about getting someone's attention, flatness is appropriate by virtue of "its salience alone, its difference from 'normal'" speech, which is seldom flat.[10] This connection is seen also in other uses of flat pitch, as part of "stepped intonation" or "stylized intonation," that make things stand out.[11] The loudness, duration, flatness, and harmonicity also add salience, again serving the function of getting the hearer's attention. Second, the Minor Third Construction indicates that the speaker is done for the moment and that the social-activity ball is now in the interlocutor's court. This function is quite generally expressed, in many contexts, by some kind of downward movement of pitch,[12] and by lengthening and a drop in intensity. Thus, even though the downstep has the starring role, the supporting players also contribute to the meaning and identifiability of this construction.

3.4   Stronger, Weaker, and Mangled Forms

Like all constructions, the Minor Third Construction can be performed strongly or weakly. This can be done by accentuating or attenuating the various components. For example, if a teacher's *good morning* doesn't evoke a response, she may say it again with more energy, longer syllable durations, and a larger pitch downstep. She may also move the downstep later in the phrase, going from

31) ^{good} *morning*

to

32) *good* ^{morn} *ing*

where the preliminary upstep makes the remaining syllables more clearly high, and thus a more salient match to the construction's form. (And if the students miss such an obvious cue to demonstrate that they are paying attention, the next follow-up may be a scolding.)

Conversely, to make the cue less insistent, you can reduce the energy, syllable durations, and downstep. A less insistent form might be appropriate, for example, if you'd like to give someone an opportunity to say *hi*, but without requiring it.

33) *good morning*

The strength of the construction may also correlate with the magnitude of the action being invoked. If you're trying to get through a crowd, and just want someone to move over a bit to let you by, your *excuse me* (34) may have just a modest downstep. Or if you want to pose a question to a counter man who is already looking in your general direction, a modest downstep is enough. But if you need to get someone's full attention, in a situation when they haven't even noticed that you're there, your *excuse me* (35) will need stronger prosody.

Such fine-tuning is common but not universal. Some companies script their employee–customer interactions, specifying what words to use, without thinking about the prosody. When I walk through the door at a local drugstore, I always hear

36) *welcome to* $^{Wal\text{-}}$ *greens*

with a clear downstep, even when the employee is not looking at me. This is odd, since there's no appropriate response, despite the prosodic implication that there is one.

Other companies do better. For example, when you leave an airplane, the flight attendants often are positioned to give you a parting smile and a phrase, but it's never a

37) $^{good\text{-}}$ *bye*

or a

38) ^{thank} *you*

since that would oblige the customers to say something in return, which could be tiresome after a long flight. Instead, the flight attendants produce mangled forms of the downstep construction, lacking some essential component. You may hear

39) $^{bu\text{-}}$ *bye*

with the first syllable shortened rather than lengthened. Sometimes the pitch fall is buried in the middle of a syllable, making it more gradual and less salient. At other times the second syllable is higher in pitch, or has a wavy contour rather than a flat one. Any of these alternations mangles the construction enough to nullify the cueing effect.

Table 3.1 *Average parameter values for a phrase with minor-third intonation and the same phrase spoken in a declarative style. * marks parameters where the difference is significant.*

Property	Minor Third	Declarative	Units
pitch variability	0.68	0.86	standard deviation in semitones
total duration*	579	290	milliseconds, both syllables
pitch fall*	2.3	4.4	semitones
pitch height*	96.2	86.1	semitones above 1 Hertz
intensity fall*	4.1	6.2	decibels
harmonicity*	13.3	8.6	decibels

3.5   A Configuration of Fifteen Prosodic Properties

So far I've been a little vague about this construction's form, but this section will remedy this. While interesting in their own right, the details will also help us better understand the nature of constructions.

3.5.1   Measured Properties

In the 1970s there was a wave of interest in prosody, mostly about intonation contours, but accurate phonetic description was elusive. For this construction in particular this was true because it usually lives out in the wild, in situations where recording is inconvenient or impossible. It wasn't until 2010 that someone figured out a way to gather data that was both controlled and realistic: Day-O'Connell realized that, among the various uses of this construction, knock-knock jokes are something that people can naturally perform in the lab. He later devoted much of his Fulbright year to recording these and other instances of this construction, and, for comparison, people saying the same words in simple declarative sentences.[13] He then measured various aspects of both. In addition to pitch features, he measured intensity, which correlates closely with perceptions of loudness, and harmonicity, which correlates with perceptions of a singing-style voice, as opposed to a rougher voice and muddier timbre. Tables 3.1 and 3.2 summarize his key findings.

His first three measurements confirmed three already-noted properties of this construction: the syllables of this construction: (1) are flat in pitch (have low variability), (2) are long, (3) have a pitch fall. But the pitch fall in this construction is not just any pitch fall: it is special in two ways. First, it is not as large as falls in many other contexts. Second, it is relatively consistent in magnitude: 50 percent of the time its span is between 2 and 4 semitones, that is, within one semitone of the minor third interval. This suggests that this

Table 3.2 *Average parameter values for the pre-downstep and post-downstep syllables of the Minor Third Construction. Units as above.*

Property	First syllable	Second syllable
pitch variability	0.65	0.72
duration	210	364
harmonicity	11.8	17.1

downstep is not a mere side-effect of other prosodic processes, but something that speakers explicitly control. No Pythagorean exactitude is involved, but this magnitude is distinctive, which is why we can refer to this as the Minor Third Construction.

Day-O'Connell's measurements also showed that (4) this construction is overall relatively high in the pitch range of the speaker, and that the syllables of this construction are (5) fairly even in intensity, in that the second syllable is only slightly quieter than the first, and (6) high in harmonicity. Further measurement revealed differences between the two syllables: as seen in Table 3.2, the second syllable is (7) less flat, (8) longer, and (9) more harmonic than the first. If you listen again to an example or two, all these properties should be readily apparent.

From the literature we know two more things about this construction: (10) the downstep occurs during an intensity dip, during silence or at a syllable boundary, and (11) there is often a preceding upstep. Further, Niebuhr's measurements of the analogous German construction[14] suggest that (12) the Minor Third Construction is typically louder than other constructions, and (13) the pitch flattening is not limited to the primary two syllables, but also affects the lead-in syllable, when present. Both of these properties are readily observed to be true also of the English construction.

So, the Minor Third Construction is much richer than it first appeared. It is not just a phenomenon of intonation, but a multistream configuration of diverse prosodic features. Figure 3.4 presents an improved summary, showing the four conditions of use and somewhat more phonetic detail.

3.5.2 Distinguishing Properties

Thanks to these studies, we have a good understanding of the average form of this construction. However, that is only half the battle: a complete description must also specify how this construction differs from all others. Day-O'Connell's studies did not address this question, since the data collection

Minor Third Construction (Second Approximation)

Function: cue the hearer to do something
    1) when there is a single obviously appropriate action
    2) when doing this action is required by a social norm
    3) when this action is easy to do, and
    4) when this action should be done immediately

Form:

timespan	prosodic properties
0–200 ms	region of high, flat pitch
200–300 ms	syllable boundary
300–600 ms	region of mid-range, flat pitch, about 3 semitones below the first

mnemonic: Action Cueing

Figure 3.4 The Action Cueing Construction (The Minor Third Construction): second approximation

was designed so that every recording was obviously a Minor Third example or obviously not. To investigate the boundaries required a different method: iterative refinement of a formal description.

Thus Ricky Garcia and I set out to develop a description that would fit all and *only* the instances of this construction. Being minimalists, we started with a very simple description, and then incrementally refined it as necessary. For this process we first created seed collections of positive and negative examples of this construction. For the negative examples, we used almost everything in 100 minutes in a collection of telephone conversations.[15] In telephone conversations people are usually just talking, with no need to cue immediate actions. The exceptions were when dealing with an incoming call-waiting signal, with something like *hang on*, and when ending the call, with something like *bye-bye*. For our initial set of positive examples, we augmented such cases with some recordings by Day-O'Connell and some productions in our own voices.

Our first-pass formal description was a subroutine that tested for three basic properties in two adjacent syllables: flatness, lengthening, and drop. If these were found, it would flag that region as a possible instance of the Minor Third Construction. Applying this subroutine to an hour of recorded dialogs, it found most of the positive examples, but it also matched many cases that were not instances of this construction. While similar to the Minor Third Construction in some ways, each clearly differed in form, to our ears, and differed in function, as judged by its role in the dialog where it occurred.

We then examined these false positives to determine where our description needed improvement. One issue was disfluencies. In these cases, a word or phrase was followed by a drop to a floor-holding *uh* that was long and lengthened, as in

40) ^{I} *uh...*

Although these cases matched our simple description, having the three basic properties, there was a difference: invariably the *uh* was low in the speaker's pitch range. This told us that prosodic forms that deviated from the canonical form in this way were on the other side of the perceptual boundary: no longer perceived as instances of the Minor Third Construction. In terms of our model, this told us how to improve it, and so we added an additional clause to specify that a Minor Third Construction could not end low. This was not a surprise; as noted earlier, the whole construction is high in the pitch range, and high-in-range entails not-ending-low-in-range.

After adding a clause to take care of this, the next major kind of false positive was the backchannel cueing pattern, as discussed in Chapter 1. To exclude such cases we added another clause to our model, to specify that the drop in pitch could not be gradual, but had to happen over a short interval (14). Another type of false positive was in some productions of list intonation. To rule these out required yet another clause, to specify the existence of a period of silence after the second syllable (15).[16] After adding these new clauses, our description was fairly solid, matching almost all of the true instances of this construction, and only rarely matching examples of other things.

The point of all this detail is to show that the construction involves more than three simple components: it has at least fifteen specific properties. To be sure, not all fifteen need be present in any particular case; many can be omitted, especially in weak forms. That is, producing the downstep and a few of the other properties may suffice to cue the appropriate action, since listeners don't require perfect productions in order to recognize your intention. Nevertheless, these fifteen properties are commonly present, and we can think of them as components of the ideal form.

3.5.3   A Gestural Score

Now we finally have a comprehensive description of the Minor Third Construction, so let's try a visualization to see how all the properties relate. Figure 3.5 lays them out along a timeline,[17] illustrating how they might underlie the realization of a typical production of *class, good morning*.

In this figure the width of each bar indicates the strength of effects over time. For example, the strength of the lengthening feature increases over the construction, slightly stretching the lead-in syllable, strongly stretching the highest syllable, and most strongly stretching the post-downstep syllable. Harmonicity has the same shape. For height, the effects are strongest pre-downstep, but

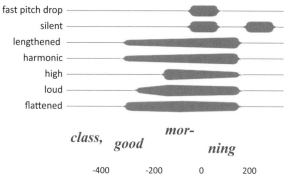

Figure 3.5 Approximate temporal domains of influence of the prosodic features of an instance of the Minor Third Construction. Times in milliseconds

also extend over the post-downstep syllable: it is still not low in the speaker's range. The loudness feature is similar, although it starts earlier and the drop-off is more gentle, meaning that the second syllable is only slightly quieter than the first.

This representation may remind you of an orchestral score, describing at each moment what each instrument needs to be doing. It's also like a control program. For example, the high-pitch bar indicates roughly the time over which the glottal muscles need to pull, and the bar width indicates how strongly. Such coordination among muscles is not rare. Consider hitting a baseball: the muscles of the torso, shoulders, elbows, and wrists must all contribute, each pulling at the appropriate times with suitable force, and synergistic muscles must simultaneously work to stiffen and constrain the motions.

In this representation the components are not concatenated pieces, as in my earlier descriptions, but overlapping gestures. This has several advantages, especially when compared to the earlier motley list of fifteen clauses. Some of these are technical, so if representation issues are not your thing, you may wish to skip ahead to the next section.

One advantage of this representation is conciseness. In particular, it avoids the need to explicitly specify that there may be a preceding upstep. Since the temporal extent of the flattened feature is longer than that of the high pitch feature, a lead-in syllable will necessarily be flat and less high than the following syllable. Thus the occasional occurrence of an upstep can be seen as the natural result of the temporal spans of the various component properties, rather than an arbitrary, unexplained fact.

A second advantage is that it helps us see how children might learn this construction. It's daunting to think of learning the conjunction of fifteen specific properties, but a temporal score over seven features seems like something that children could easily learn, given enough examples. A child might form a prototype, with all these properties, and save it in her mental inventory of constructions. Later, with exposure to more examples, this might be generalized in order to form a general construction.[18]

A third advantage is that this representation reminds us that the components are gestures and not instantaneous. For the human voice, setting the control parameters for harmonicity, say, or flat pitch, is not something that can be done instantaneously: shaping the glottis to produce sound with the desired properties needs a little start-up time. So, for example, for flatness to be at full power during the pre-downstep syllable, it may have to start early, during the previous, pre-upstep syllable. I think of it as like a pizza-factory conveyor belt, with the workers trying to customize each pizza to order. But as the pizzas go by, trying to "add extra cheese" or "add double meat" to just one may be difficult, and occasionally a little extra topping may end up on a pizza next to the intended one. This would be especially true if they were zipping past at four or more per second, with no gaps between them, like syllables in speech. Prosodic control is neither fast enough nor accurate enough to get the toppings exactly aligned up with the pizzas: features like harmonicity and flatness may spill over.

A fourth advantage is that this representation suggests how this construction may be superimposed with other constructions. In particular, the bars in Figure 3.5 indicate effects, not absolute settings, so the lack of a bar extending over some time does not mean the value is low, rather that it is unspecified there. For example, this construction says nothing about the height of the lead-in syllable. Its height, or lack thereof, may be determined or influenced by the pitch profile of other constructions present, either adjacent or superimposed.

A fifth advantage of this representation is that it leverages a general fact about the nature of articulatory targets: that some parameters take precedence over others. In particular, when there is no sound, as indicated by the regions where the silence bar is wide, other effects, such as loudness and high pitch, are suspended. This is a special case of a general tendency in speech production: articulatory targets can be abandoned when other nearby targets demand behaviors that make them unreachable.[19]

Parenthetically, while Figure 3.5 is an adequate description of the known facts of this construction as it might apply to one specific rendition of *good morning*, it lacks generality in one important respect: it doesn't describe its association properties, that is, the rules about how it can align with different word sequences and how its timeline can stretch, spread, shrink, or warp nonlinearly to enable alignment with the stressed syllables of the words used. The rules governing such alignment can be very complex.[20] Furthermore, it is not a one-way process: not only do a syllable's intrinsic durations affect the timing of a construction's components, the construction in turn influences the timing and durations of the syllables. Such alignment tendencies and processes have been seen as a central issue in prosody, and some aspects of it have been well studied.[21] For this particular construction, we know that the pitch drop tends to align with a syllable boundary (a break in voicing being necessary because the human voice cannot instantaneously jump in pitch.[22]) Modeling how this works in detail remains as a challenge.

So, those are the detailed facts of this construction. In future I won't go into so much detail, in part because only for this one construction is there is a solid understanding of the details.

3.6   Another Downstep Construction

Thus we see that the Minor Third Construction, simple as it seems, involves many component properties. While some of these may be just fine points of style, others are critical. In particular, their values distinguish this construction from the use of downstep in a very different construction: the Giving-In Construction.

This construction is a recent discovery. In 2013, Oliver Niebuhr gave his class as homework the task of labeling the intonation patterns in a segment of a reality TV show.[23] One of the students came back reporting a difficulty: one of the utterances did not fit any known pattern. This occurred in an acted court trial, when the defendant, after being judged guilty, produced a grudging apology with a clear but small pitch downstep. She observed this in German, but the same can happen in English, as in

41) *I'm* *sorry.*

There are many ways to apologize, but this form is prototypically appropriate when an admission of guilt is required. The same pattern occurred when a player in a videogame slipped up, and acknowledged his fault with

42) *my* *bad.*

This instance is slightly mangled and slightly jokey, but the downstep is there and this is clearly an acceptance of responsibility.

The same form can also be used in conceding a point, as when a speaker admits that he had overstated the extent of coding in his current class:

43) J: *but, don't you do most of the coding in Software 2?*
       S: *yeah, but it...* *It's* *true.*

It can also occur in expressions of resignation, where the speaker is accepting fate.

44) *oh* *well.*

Across these uses there is a common meaning: the speaker is in an awkward, negative situation, he accepts that the situation is not something he can change,

---

The Giving-In Construction

Context: speaker is in a negative situation
Function:
    speaker accepts the situation
    speaker signals the desire and intent to move on

Form:
prosodic properties

a small pitch downstep
very long post-downstep syllable
moderately high pitch
fairly flat pitch
slightly creaky voice

Figure 3.6 The Giving-In Construction

he acknowledges this fact, and he does so to close out the topic and to allow the interaction to move on.

Figure 3.6 summarizes this, the Giving-In Construction.

Charles Fillmore described two types of linguists: "splitters," who like to find fine distinctions among different forms and uses, and "lumpers," who like to find generalizations across different forms and uses. In earlier sections we successfully lumped many diverse uses of downsteps into one construction, the Minor Third Construction. Should we also unify the Giving-In and Minor Third Constructions?

Historically, back in the days when intonation was the sole focus of attention and before careful measurements were possible, theorists were unable to distinguish these two: after all, both exhibit downstep.[24] However, on other prosodic features there are many differences: the Giving-In Construction exhibits less flatness of pitch, voicing that is modal or creaky rather than harmonic, a longer post-downstep syllable, lower pitch overall, and a smaller pitch drop.

Beyond the differences in form, the two constructions differ greatly in their implications. Consider two ways a child may answer a call to dinner. She may say

45) $I'm$ coming

with a small downstep etc., indicating reluctance, resignation, and protest,[25] or use a larger downstep, along with the other properties of the Minor Third Construction, to convey an altogether different attitude:

46) $I'm$ $com\text{-}$ $ing.$

In the first case you'd probably want to go fetch her; in the other she's cheerfully cueing you to wait a moment: she'll be right there, so don't start without her.

Thus these two constructions are not relatives but neighbors, bumping shoulders with each other in a narrow perceptual space.[26] That is, they inhabit close but distinct ecological niches.[27]

3.7   Language Learning and Socialization

A happy moment for parents is baby's first social laugh. This often comes during a game of peek-a-boo. My family does it like this: first get baby's attention, then cover your eyes and say *peek-a*, then downstep to *boo*,

47) $^{peek\ a}\ _{boo}$

while dramatically opening your hands to reveal a big smile. Then the baby laughs. Other families do it differently, but generally include most of the features of the Minor Third Construction, and always aim for the same response.

Most Americans have experienced peek-a-boo as babies, and indeed it is listed as a developmental milestone by the National Institutes of Health, at 9 months, as an early indicator of the normal development of social interaction.[28] This is really very early: at 9 months babies are just starting to recognize a few words. We can describe peek-a-boo as a tool that English-speaking parents use to train their babies to respond to language patterns and to meet socially imposed obligations.[29]

As evidence, consider the fact, readily verifiable on YouTube, that some parents will repeat the game dozens of times in a single play session, never twice exactly the same, giving baby enough stimuli to learn to identify the essential components of this form, those that are constant in the midst of unimportant variation. Sometimes the variation is small; other times large, as illustrated in Figure 3.7.

(Parenthetically, babies' enjoyment of peek-a-boo may also relate to another critical skill they need to learn. Younger babies notice objects but don't keep track of them: if something is not visible, it doesn't exist. If you were designing a first lesson in object permanence, you'd probably want to use something very familiar (Daddy's face), hide it just briefly (two seconds), cue baby to notice it and respond (the Minor Third Construction), and add some reward for doing so (the smile). Peek-a-boo includes all these elements: it is perfect for this purpose. Then, once your baby has acquired the concept of object permanence, they are ready for the next challenge, learning to remember the locations of hidden objects, the focus of other fun games.)

Another important milestone in child development comes much later: learning to admit it when you have behaved badly. The Giving-In Construction is part of this. I remember it vividly from kindergarten. When required to

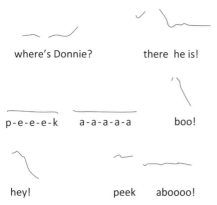

where's Donnie?   there he is!

p-e-e-e-k   a-a-a-a-a   boo!

hey!   peek   aboooo!

Figure 3.7 F$_0$ traces for three renditions of peek-a-boo in one play session[30]

apologize, you had to say *I'm sorry* and to say it "sincerely," that is, with the right prosody, including the small downstep. This ritual also had gestural and postural components: you also had to look at the person you were apologizing to, chin down. As we learned this construction, we learned that even if you think you are in the right, you sometimes have to accept the judgment of the person with authority. Mastering this pattern had a concrete reward: after performing it, you'd be released from the hot seat and allowed to go off and play, or to sulk. As adults, we know that there is much more to apologizing,[31] but this is still an essential social skill.

Knock-knock jokes also have a role in development. In second grade or so they spread like the flu, infecting all the kids in the class, and sometimes their families too; then in two weeks the epidemic is over. Knock-knock jokes are significant in at least two ways. They may be children's first experience with puns and thus of phonetic awareness, as they come to realize that the sound components of words are malleable and manipulable. They also provide a way to practice social norms, as children learn when and how to cue appropriate actions and tune up their reflexes for responding swiftly and appropriately.

There is yet another downstep-based construction: that involved in cursing. This is also acquired at a certain stage, perhaps towards the end of elementary school. Cursing is a very special form of language, with its own syntactic patterns and rules,[32] so it's not surprising that it also has distinctive prosody. An example is

48)   *screw you* *green thing*

said by a videogame player approaching the green-mud obstacle that had killed her on the previous round. But with this being the only example in my data, figuring out the general pattern, and how it relates to the other downstep constructions, must be left for future research.

3.8   Cueing and Apologizing across Cultures

The Minor Third Construction is not universal. On the train from Kansai airport the person in the seat in front said something. After a moment I realized he was talking to me, and a moment later understood his words. After answering his question, I thought about why I'd been so slow on the uptake. His pitch contour was probably a factor. He'd said

49) $excu^{se}$ ^{me} $_{e_e}$

with a fade-out in loudness, as indicated by the letters getting smaller. Although the phonemes were all correct, the prosody was wrong for his intended effect. He was using instead the prosody of his native language, Japanese, namely a rise-fall pattern commonly used for social cueing functions.[33]

Japanese are stereotyped as timid and non-demanding, but I suspect this may arise in part from this language difference: the pattern that they use to get action is something that sounds, to English speakers, like nothing at all. But why, you may wonder, don't they just learn how to do it right in English? I suspect that it's not that simple. The Japanese rise-fade construction may be as deeply fundamental as the English Minor Third, rooted similarly in the Japanese equivalent of peek-a-boo.[34]

Other languages also have peek-a-boo equivalents. In Fernald's survey,[35] the language prosodically most similar to English is German, and there is evidence for similar prosody in at least two other Germanic languages: Dutch and Swedish.[36] This is not just for babies: German, like English, uses the Minor Third Construction for many social cueing functions, and rather more widely.[37] For example, you hear it on *bitte* when airport security cues you to walk through the metal detector, and when the bakery server calls you up for your turn at the counter. Germans are stereotyped as obsessed with control, order, and social obligations; perhaps this is due in part to the more pervasive use of this prosodic construction.

German is similar to English also in its Giving-In Construction.[38] Managing guilt and forgiveness is essential to how a society upholds standards of right and wrong. Different cultures handle guilt and submission in different ways,[39] but German and English handle it similarly, at least in the ritual prosody of apology. Considering all the ways the two languages have changed over two millennia, evolving to mutual unintelligibility, it's remarkable that the prosody of this socio-cultural pattern has stayed constant. Given that this construction is also learned very early, we may wonder whether children's acquisition of prosody might be recapitulating the evolutionary development of their language.

We might also wonder whether some downstep-related constructions are intelligible across species. Dog owners frequently use the Minor Third Construction, for example when calling

50) Γ_i- *do*

Even if dogs don't actually understand this construction, the fact that owners use it attests to how basic and essential it seems.

3.9   Summary

This chapter has presented a prosodic construction with a limited but powerful social control function. While so basic and simple that even a child can use it, this construction has an exquisitely specific form, involving many prosodic features beyond just intonation. There is also a great amount of detailed knowledge involved in the proper use of this construction in terms of the social conditions of use.

In what follows the descriptions will be snappier: having now established how constructions work, subsequent chapters will present only the most salient aspects of each. But before looking at more constructions, let's devote a chapter to examining other ways that prosody can convey meaning.

4   Creaky Voice and Its Functions

Arnold Schwarzenegger's famous line as the Terminator,

1) *hasta la vista, baby*

is remembered not for the words, but for how he said them. One aspect was the use of creaky voice. Not limited to heroic performances, this voice quality also plays important roles in daily conversation.

While creaky voice is not among the traditional features addressed by models of prosody, it plays related roles in dialog[1] so it is appropriate to examine it here. Being less familiar, it may need some explanation, so this chapter will start with a quick review of the fundamentals of human pitch.

4.1   Pitch and the Glottis

The production of pitch is one of the marvels of the human body.[2] Way down in your throat, down past the uvula, used for gargling, and below the false vocal cords, used for growling,[3] is your voicebox (larynx). This contains two folds of tissue, the vocal folds. These are the gatekeepers of the glottis, a narrowing in the passage connecting the lungs and trachea to the pharynx, nose, and mouth. As you inhale and exhale, the vocal folds stay out of the way, but they can swing in to meet up and seal the glottis, as suggested by Figure 4.1. They do this, for example, when you strain to lift a heavy weight; this holds the air in your lungs and thereby helps stiffen your upper body.

Sometimes a closure opens briefly to let out a puff or two of air, as in

2) *u-u-aah.*

This occurred at a tense spot in a videogame. While there was no physical exertion, there was intense mental effort, marked by a glottal release, spelled here as -*u*-, as the player tried to jump on a swaying beam, before falling into the green mud with a frustrated *aah*.

Closures can also occur in the middle of speech. For example, in the middle of

3) *uh-oh*

there is a glottal closure of about 70 milliseconds.

 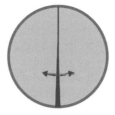

Figure 4.1 The vocal folds, from above, looking down the throat. On the left, closing; on the right, about to open

Figure 4.2 Waveform for /a/ in rising pitch: sound pressure level as a function of time

As always, I recommend listening to the audio examples, especially here, since glottal closures are not part of the standard phonetic inventory of English, and the orthography is ambiguous. While a dash often indicates a glottal closure, at least in comic books, it may also mean other things.[4] Incidentally, an apostrophe can also mark a glottal stop, as in *Hawai'i*, which is a borrowing from Hawaiian, where the glottal stop is phonemic, comprising one of the eight consonants of the language.

Isolated closures and openings like these are, however, unusual in English. More commonly, the vocal folds open and close repeatedly. In each cycle, they swing in to meet up and block the airstream, but hold together only a moment, until the outgoing air forces them apart, letting out a tiny puff of air. Then, if the tension is right, they close again. This open-close cycle usually repeats dozens or hundreds of times per second.

Figure 4.2 illustrates this. Here the y axis shows the sound pressure level, thus, where the curve is above the dotted line, the air pressure is momentarily greater than average. At the very left, the air pressure is low, corresponding to a momentary interruption of the airflow by a glottal closure. The glottis opens, a moment later, with a puff of air, as seen in the figure by the first upspike. This pattern is repeated across the figure: each closure being followed by a tiny puff.

This basic pattern is partly obscured by the additional wiggles in the waveform. For current purposes these are just a nuisance; they result from the fact that people have heads on their necks, rather than emitting sound directly from their throats. These specific wiggles are the result of the puff bouncing around inside my mouth, combining with the remnants of previous puffs as they resonate with my palate and tongue, which was shaped to produce an /a/, specifically one in the last syllable of *Marianna*. In addition to adding wiggles, the supraglottal articulators (the tongue, lips, and so on) affect the relation between the waveform and the perceived pitch, but for now we will ignore such complications.[5]

For the listener, these little puffs follow each other too quickly to be individually heard. Rather they are perceived together as pitch, that is, as a tone of a specific frequency. In Figure 4.2 we see 32 puffs over a duration of about 0.24 seconds. Thus there are, on average, around 133 (= 32/0.24) cycles per second: so the pitch is about 133 Hertz. But this rate is not constant over time: Towards the left of the figure the pitch is about 110 Hertz, but over time the puffs get closer together and the pitch rises, to about 150 Hz at the right edge.

The frequency of the glottal pulses, and thus the pitch, depends on several factors, including two that speakers cannot control.[6] One is their anatomy, including the length of their vocal folds. Just as longer strings vibrate more slowly, longer vocal folds tend to take longer to open and close. Different people have vocal folds of different lengths. For example, males usually have larger larynxes, visible as their Adam's apples, and thus deeper voices. Another factor is the dynamics of the airflow. In particular, when less air passes through, less energy is imparted to the vocal folds and their vibration generally slows. This is why frequency correlates with loudness, and why the pitch unavoidably drops when the speaker runs out of air at the end of a long utterance.[7]

But some things are directly under the speaker's control: notably the muscles of the larynx. These can pull the vocal folds to change their length, shape, and stiffness, and this affects how the vocal folds interact with the airflow and thus the pitch. For example, tighter and shorter vocal folds cause higher pitch, and longer and looser vocal folds lower pitch.

4.2   The Production and Perception of Creaky Voice

In speech, the waveform is usually periodic, that is, the glottal pulses come at a steady pace, as the glottis smoothly cycles between closed and open states. But sometimes the intervals between glottal pulses vary. Consider the sound

4) *baaa*

as in a first grader's rendition of the sound that sheep make. Here there is a lot of variation in the intervals between pulses, as seen in Figure 4.3. While the signal looks periodic in places, we can't really find a nice repeating sequence: some puffs you'd expect to see are missing, others are strangely small or large, and others appear in odd places. We perceive this as creaky voice.[8]

Figure 4.3 Waveform for the creaky /a/ in *baaa*

Figure 4.4 Pitch values detected across an instance of *the marmalade* that ends in creaky voice

Creaky voice is well named. Think of a door with a creaky hinge. Adding oil silences it, because the lubricating film enables the two pieces of metal to slide over each other smoothly. Without oil they may stick. Typically they stick just a little, then the friction breaks and they advance a little, and the cycle repeats. Each time the friction breaks, there is a little burst of sound. If you open a creaky door very slowly you may hear the individual sound bursts, but usually they come too quickly for that; instead you hear a continuous sound. The metal's imperfections have no particular pattern, so the sound bursts are not periodic. Thus what you hear is not a tone, but a creak. The same is true for the human voice: an aperiodic sequence of puffs can be perceived as creaky.

Such departures from periodicity can also be seen in pitch diagrams. Figure 4.4 shows what a pitch tracker finds for a pronunciation of *the marmalade* (5). In the middle, the smooth pitch contour falls apart, turning into a jittery scattering of points. These are places where the pitch tracker momentarily found some small region of periodicity. While visually these look high in pitch, what we hear is not high pitch but creaky voice.

Some of the factors involved in producing creaky voice are anatomical: as people age, the vocal folds get stiffer and don't vibrate as smoothly, and smokers may have chronically creaky voice, due to damaged vocal folds. Other factors are dynamic. Creaky voice is often a side effect of low pitch and quieter voice. Shower singers know that you can expand your range and hit lower notes if you sing louder. But even so, we all have our limits, as suggested by Ladefoged's recipe for creaky voice: "singing the lowest note that you can, and then trying to go even lower."[9] When you do, the airflow is not adequate to keep the lengthened vocal folds opening and closing at a regular rhythm. Creaky voice and low pitch thus often occur naturally together.

But speakers also have some degree of control over the degree of creakiness in their voice, and they use this in meaningful ways, to serve specific communicative purposes.

4.3   General Uses of Creaky Voice

To isolate the meaning contribution of creaky voice, let's consider how the same words can sound with and without it. Imagine a top executive, after an underling has briefed him on a plan to buy a smaller company, declaring

6) *I like it*

with the meaning "I approve." This will probably have creaky voice, as indicated by the asterisks. If you say this like a boss, you'll probably feel the creaky voice. Say it a few more times, and you may also start to feel powerful and important, quite naturally so, since creaky voice is associated with authority and control.

Now imagine the same exec at home, praising his aunt's casserole. Though the words may be the same,

7) *I like it*   (non-creaky)

they certainly won't sound the same. With no special authority over casseroles, his voice will probably not be creaky.

Creaky voice is not rare, but to find examples faster in real data I wrote some code. This exploits the fact that in modal, non-creaky voice, changes to the frequency of glottal pulses are necessarily gradual, since the muscles of the larynx can only act so quickly.[10] Apparently faster pitch changes are therefore a good indicator of creaky voice.[11] The more such sudden changes in any small time window, the stronger the perception of creakiness there. I applied this creakiness detector to 40 minutes of dialog[12] and listened to a few dozen places where the creakiness was strongest, in order to infer the typical functions. The rest of this section illustrates what I found.

Consider a statement made after some discussion of interesting topics in computer science, when the speaker said

8) *applications of AI [that] I'm a little *familiar with*: machine learning . . .*

In this example, the creaky detector identified the most creaky region as being on *familiar with*, but that's just the extreme; this utterance is fairly creaky throughout. This is typical: creakiness usually builds up gradually and fades out gradually, rather than being tightly localized to a word or two. In this example, the creaky voice serves to convey that, despite the modesty of the phrasing, the speaker really is knowledgeable about AI applications.

The knowledgeability expressed by creaky voice can be of many kinds. In

9) *I told him, here's the maze, and here's everything I did,*
   *and *that's it*. Like what else am I going to do?*
   It's like really straightforward, like,
   *there's nothing special about *how my maze looks**

the speaker is reporting how he explained his program to the teaching assistant. He was there, so he knows what he said, and it's his program, so he knows what's in it. For both reasons, he has authoritative knowledge of what he's talking about, and the creaky voice indicates this.

Consider also

10) S: *it went to sleep while we're recording? [no] it's still recording, apparently*
    J: **yeah*, the light's green*

where S is unsure whether the computer is still recording the conversation. J, however, was in a position where she could see the recording indicator, and her creaky voice reflects her superior knowledge, based on direct perception. Incidentally, this example illustrates that creaky voice is not always associated with low pitch: the word *yeah*, especially at the start, is very creaky, even though it sounds higher in pitch than the non-creaky *green*.

People may also be confident about their own feelings, and when they are, they may show this with creaky voice, as in

11) **I just love* playing online, how competitive it is.*

In contrast, a speaker who was less sure, perhaps feeling only that *I kind of like playing online* (12), would probably not use creaky voice,

Another use of creaky voice is in distancing oneself from something. In the next example, two students are talking about who should run the club next year, and one says that he doesn't need to have a prestigious position like president or vice president. He then restates his point, again disclaiming any desire for prestige, and his voice becomes creakier and creakier:

13) *It could be ... me as secretary, or, I dunno, whatever.*
    I mean, I could care less.
    I mean, if it's, if it's a position there, I mean, *whatever*.

Distancing is also present when creaky voice is used in grudging admiration. This can be heard in an example used earlier as an illustration of the Bookended Narrow Pitch Construction, which also has superimposed creaky voice

14) *I mean, it, it does like, *it does everything. As far as I've seen.**

Grudging admiration invariably involves some emotional distance, since people don't express grudging admiration for someone or something close to them. The use of creaky voice for grudging admiration also connects with other functions, in that it is generally said by someone with expert or authoritative knowledge of the topic. Figure 4.5 summarizes the uses of creaky voice seen so far. Although there doesn't seem to be a single core meaning, all of the uses are related, forming a family of meanings.

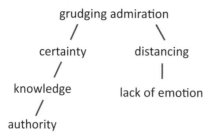

Figure 4.5 Some functions of creaky voice, and some connections among them

---

Creaky Voice Mapping

Function: express authority, knowledge, certainty, distancing, lack of emotion, and/or grudging admiration

---

Form:

timespan	prosodic properties
any region	creaky voice

Figure 4.6 The general prosody–pragmatics mapping of creaky voice

At this point we can truly appreciate the appropriateness of the Terminator's tone of voice. Having overcome all obstacles and about to destroy the evil, in this scene he is in a position of power and control. He is also completely sure about what he needs to do, and entirely distant from any emotional involvement. All of these are associated with creaky voice: adding them up gives the opportunity for a memorably creaky performance.

Since creaky voice is a single feature, with indeterminate temporal extent, we can't call it a construction; but there is nonetheless a mapping between form and function. Figure 4.6 summarizes.

4.4   Conflicting Judgments

My phonetics teacher, Geoff Pullum, once illustrated creaky voice by imitating an airline pilot saying *we'll be flying at an altitude of 31,000 feet* with a Southern accent and in a very creaky voice. He joked about the pilot seeming low-energy or even lazy, which surprised me, since I'd always admired pilots' voices, liking the way that they showed confidence despite the responsibility for getting a planeload of passengers safely to the destination. Since creaky voice can do so many things, it's not surprising that sometimes people can have different ideas about what it's expressing.

In recent years, language mavens have criticized the new generation of young women for frequent use of creaky voice (often called "vocal fry"): to them it sounds unprofessional or unladylike.[13] It is true that people may use creaky voice to claim knowledge or authority that they don't really have (in which case they may be tagged as "bitchy" or "full of it"). It is also true that, in experiments with people listening to short audio clips without context, voices that are more creaky can be judged less hireable;[14] perhaps they seem distant, indifferent or disengaged.

But in real life, listeners don't judge people based on isolated voice samples, and speakers don't produce speech without reasons. Rather, they use creaky voice for specific purposes at specific times. A woman may speak with creaky voice, as may a man, on topics about which she has authority or certain knowledge. If you don't believe that women can know anything, or you don't understand the creaky/knowledgeability connection, then it's natural to think that creaky voice is indicating something else, such as a bad attitude. But more often people use creaky voice appropriately, helpfully conveying their knowledge level. For example, I know one young woman who in her first class with me lacked confidence and showed that clearly in her voice, but now, as a Ph.D. student, she uses creaky voice frequently, especially when talking about things within her area of expertise.

Another source of misperceptions may be the role of creaky voice in marking identity and affiliation with a social class, gang, or subcultures.[15] Many subcultures have their own styles of speech. Some also have their own music, often with a distinctive singing style. For example, country music favors nasal voice and J-pop favors falsetto (which makes sense given the typical sincerity of the one and the cuteness of the other). Classic hip-hop is rich in ejectives. Creaky voice also has a genre where it is pervasive: hard rock. Think of any AC/DC song. This is fitting: the common themes of rock music – individualism, detachment, and fantasies of power – relate nicely to the functions noted above. Such associations with rebellious subcultures may be another reason why language mavens dislike creaky voice.

4.5   Paralinguistic versus Linguistic Communication

In Chapters 2 and 3 we saw how specific configurations of prosodic features could form constructions that bear meanings. However, creaky voice does not need to be part of a larger construction to convey meaning: it can do it alone.

In this, it functions more as a "paralinguistic" form of communication than a linguistic one.[16] Basic linguistic elements have, according to Saussure, no meanings in themselves; they are able to express meanings only when combined with other elements.[17] For example, a /k/ in isolation means nothing, but as part of the word *cat* it enables us to talk about small felines. Further, proper linguistic combinations, like *cat*, are supposed to map to meaning in arbitrary ways. There is nothing inherent in the sounds of this word that makes it suitable for referring to cats rather than dolphins or houseflies: the mapping is purely arbitrary. Creaky voice, however, does not work like this, at least not in English:[18] it is thus generally not linguistic but, rather, paralinguistic.

Paralinguistic communication is non-arbitrary and involves direct mappings from properties of the speech signal to other things. These include physiological effects: for example, people who are sleepy tend to speak quietly and slowly. Recent research has established that the voice conveys all sorts of non-linguistic things: intoxication, depression, autism, stress, anger, fatigue, social role, fertility, age, gender, various medical conditions, and many more. In particular, prosodic features are important in all of these discriminations.[19] Emotion in particular is often conveyed by prosody,[20] with some prosody–emotion correlations having direct connections to physiology, although others are arbitrary and language-dependent.[21] There is even evidence the brain has specific neural systems for the paralinguistic aspects of prosody, separate from those for linguistic prosody.[22]

Now, it would be convenient for research if we could draw a sharp line between paralinguistics and linguistics. For phonemes we almost can: most phonemes are purely linguistic, with only a limited number of non-arbitrary, sound-symbolic mappings.[23] However, for prosody the linguistic and paralinguistic roles are tightly linked.[24] Let's look at pitch height as an example.

4.5.1   Paralinguistic Aspects of Pitch Height

Larger animals tend to have longer vocal tracts and larger larynxes, and thus, like larger organ pipes and longer strings, tend to have lower frequencies, that is to say, deeper voices.[25] The laws of physics also apply to human voices, so larger people also tend to have lower pitch.

In wolf packs social dominance correlates well with physical size, but human social hierarchies are more complex. For us, low pitch relates not only to size but also to status, as Ohala observed.[26] At work you probably use lower pitch when talking to the new guy than when talking to the boss. That is, pitch height can paralinguistically indicate dominance or submissiveness.[27] While rooted in the physical correlation between large size and low pitch, pitch height has thus been adapted to a new function.

The use of pitch height has also been adapted a step further, to indicate knowledge and authority. Even when I'm talking to my boss, if the topic is something I know more about, I'll tend to speak in a deeper voice. In a sense, the status disparity varies with the situation, If I ask my daughter which color shirt to wear, I'm deferring to her superior fashion sense, and if in the next moment she asks me about calculus, the roles will switch. This ability to adapt roles to the immediate context and needs is fundamental to human society. Incidentally, I'm not sure that all cultures exercise this fluidity equally. In traditional Japanese culture, for example, the boss was assumed to know more

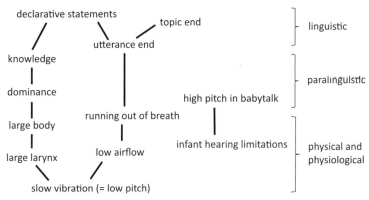

Figure 4.7 Some linguistic and paralinguistic functions of pitch height, their connections, and their roots

than his underlings about every topic, to be always right, and to be always in control.

In English, the connection between knowledge and pitch height has also been adapted yet one step further: at the sentence level, statements usually end low, but questions can end high. This is in line with the mapping between the more knowledgeable person using lower pitch.

Another factor affecting pitch height is seen in babytalk ("motherese"): people speaking to babies or young children tend to use higher pitch, probably in part because infants' hearing is more acute for higher frequencies, and in part because there is obviously no need to flaunt dominance over infants. Interestingly, people also tend to use higher pitch with puppies and other small dogs.[28]

Yet another factor affecting pitch is airflow: speakers naturally tend to drop in pitch as they run out of air. This connection also has been adapted as a linguistic signal: speakers use pitch height to indicate how far they are into an utterance, and how much longer they intend to speak.[29] Further, we may refrain from dropping the pitch at the end of an utterance to signal that there is more to come. Thus, other things being equal, non-final clauses end higher in pitch than the last clause in a sentence.

Thus pitch height is determined not only by basic anatomy and physiology, but also by paralinguistic mappings and by more-or-less linguistic structures built on them. Figure 4.7 summarizes.

Having now explained and illustrated the notion of paralinguistic prosody, we're ready for a deeper look at the meanings of creaky voice.

4.5.2   Paralinguistic Aspects of Creaky Voice

After that long digression, let's return to creaky voice. Since it is more paralinguistic than linguistic, we may expect its meanings to be motivated, rather than

Figure 4.8 Some correlates and functions of creaky voice, roughly grouped by type

arbitrary. Indeed, two links to fundamental properties of human speech are easy to see. First, as noted above, older speakers tend to have more creaky voices. In a society where those with more knowledge and more authority are generally older, there are thus correlations between creaky voice and these traits. People are surely sensitive to these correlations, both now and during the evolution of English, so these may underlie some general meanings of creaky voice. The second link comes from the correlations between low airflow, low loudness, and creaky voice.[30] People who are disengaged or dispassionate may put little effort into their speech, resulting in quieter and creakier voices. This motivates associations between creaky voice and attitudes like detachment, distancing, or lack of emotional involvement. Figure 4.8 illustrates these connections.

Given that the meanings of creaky voice have two fundamental roots, namely age and airflow, which don't relate in any tidy way, it is easy to see how hearers may interpret it differently in some situations, as marking responsibility versus laziness, for example, or knowledgeability versus lack of interest.

Down near the roots, prosody–meaning mappings are closely linked to human physiology, so we can expect them to be common across languages. The creaky–authority mapping, for example, is seen not only in English, but also in Japanese, where even three-year-olds will use it when explaining things to two-year-olds. However, as we get further from the roots, there can be more variety: languages differ in how they extend the fundamental mappings to new meanings.[31] For example, Japanese has a construction with creaky voice that can draw attention to a possible breach of group norms.[32] While related to authority and distancing, this mapping extends it in a more specific way. In Tzeltal, a Mayan language, creaky voice can be used for commiseration. This also is not arbitrary, since "creaky voice, having as a natural source low speech energy, can implicate calmness and assurance, and thence comfort and commiseration."[33] In general, as we get further from the fundamental roots, prosodic meanings are less paralinguistic, less primordial, more arbitrary, and more language-specific.

4.6   The Primordial Roots of Prosodic Meanings

In addition to paralinguistic and linguistic uses of prosody, there are also iconic uses.[34] Earlier we saw *baaaa* for imitating sheep sounds. The timing of *knock knock* can imitate the rhythm of knocking on a door. The sound of something small and metallic dropping on a hard floor can be imitated with a short sound, like *plink* (15), and something larger with a longer sound, like *clatter*. Sometimes iconicity is used in extended ways. For example, the correspondence between sound duration and object size extends even to things that produce no sound, as in *it was a bi-i-ig fish!* (16).[35]

To refer to all non-arbitrary uses of prosody, both paralinguistic and iconic, I will use the term "primordial mappings." Such mappings have been noted by numerous researchers and studied under many names, including sound symbolism, non-arbitrary prosody, language-independent prosody, honest signals, and biological codes.[36]

Table 4.1 lists some likely primordial mappings. Many are quite speculative. Let's consider just one here: the connection between sharp final intensity drop and taking charge. This is present in a drill sergeant's *hup two three four* while leading a parade-ground march: each syllable ends sharply, that is, in a clipped end. (The exact consonant used for this may vary: it might be a glottal stop, a /p/, or a /t/.) Here the strong initial consonants mark the moments when the soldiers' heels should hit the ground, and the clipped ends reinforce the message of control, as befits the need to precisely synchronize every movement of twenty men. Similarly, the glottal stop in *uh-oh* helps convey that, whatever just fell or broke, the situation is now under control. Clipped ends also feature in *yep*, *nope*, and similar forms.[37]

Looking at Table 4.1 again, the list of functions seems quite untidy: no rational person designing a communication system would pick these functions. But of course there is no rational design to language. Rather, these diverse functions arise from the diverse things involved in the production of sound, which connect, directly or metaphorically, to diverse aspects of meaning and human interaction.

Language has been described as a human invention, but for many aspects of prosody, the roots are much deeper.

4.7   Minor Constructions

Creaky voice, although largely primordial, is also part of at least one specific construction. This is the one used, for example, by a woman to admire a picture of someone's baby, as in *awww, how cute!*[52]

17) *awww.*

This form has a very specific prosody: high pitch, creaky, nasal, loud, and lengthened, with two pitch peaks, one very early in the syllable and one at the

Table 4.1 *Some likely primordial prosody–meaning mappings*

Feature	Representative meaning or function
low pitch	dominance
high pitch	submissiveness, babytalk, engagement, insistence, unpredictability[38]
pitch fall	completion, certainty[39]
high beginning	new topic
low beginning	continuation of topic[40]
high ending	continuation, incompleteness[41]
low ending	finality, end of turn, certainty[42]
sharp pitch movements	excitement, anger
narrow pitch range	negativity, disengagement, lack of interest[43]
flat pitch	attention-getting
wide pitch range, pitch peaks	attention-getting, emphasis, enthusiasm, effort[44]
creaky voice	authority, distancing, etc.
harmonicity	social ritual
falsetto	cuteness, strong feeling[45]
breathy voice	seductiveness,[46] off-topic-ness
vibrato	warmth, encouragement
nasal voice	appeal to shared knowledge,[47] sincerity
late peaks	non-action-orientation
glottal stop	effort, warning[48]
loudness	importance
quietness	lack of engagement
sharp final intensity drop	taking charge
gradual final intensity drop	bid for empathy
longer duration	larger referent[49]
consonant lengthening	negative sentiment[50]
phonological reduction	semantic bleaching[51]

Figure 4.9 The pitch of *awww* in *awww, how cute*

end, as seen in Figure 4.9. Incidentally, these peaks may be due in part to the glottal stops which usually precede and follow *awww*. The creakiness is an essential part, and is reflected in the spelling: the repeated letters indicate not only lengthening but also creaky voice. (This is a common comic-book way to represent creaky voice, as in Charlie Brown's *arrgh* (18) and the pirates' *arrr* (19).) Figure 4.10 summarizes this; I'll call it the Awww of Cute Construction.

Although Awww of Cute includes creaky voice, its meaning is distinct from any of the uses of creaky voice seen above, and its contexts of use are very far from those in any Terminator movie. At the same time, Awww of Cute does

Awww of Cute Construction

Function: admire a cute baby, kitten, etc.

Form:
    generally fairly flat in pitch
    small initial pitch peak
    small final pitch peak
    high pitch throughout
    creaky voice throughout
    nasal throughout
    loud throughout
    long duration

Figure 4.10 The Awww of Cute Construction

relate to a more general meaning of creaky voice: that of distancing. One cannot appropriately say *awww* in reference to your own baby, or a baby you're holding, or a baby that you are responsible for. It may also be more common when the baby is asleep or otherwise not to be touched, and may reassure the mother that, although her baby is irresistibly cute, you'll keep a respectful distance.

While *awww* has many other uses, including the *awww* of spectators reacting to a missed goal, this particular construction is very limited in the contexts where it can appear, in the sounds it can appear with, and in the meanings it can convey. It also tends to come with a restricted set of gestures, such as a sappy smile and a cocked head. Constructions like this can be called "minor constructions," to distinguish them from the general constructions seen so far, which, to recap, can commonly occur superimposed with other constructions, can contribute to multifaceted, composite meanings, and can be used with all sorts of words. We can think of the general constructions as the prosodic analogs of general grammatical forms, and the minor constructions as the prosodic analogs of idioms.[53]

English has many other minor constructions. Many of these are associated with specific words or non-lexical expressions. The word *wow*, lengthened and with a steadily falling contour, from extreme high to extreme low, is common way to show appreciation, for example of a gift.[54] Another example is *meh* (20). Fashionable a few years ago, this always seemed to appear with its own specific prosody, including high pitch and breathy voice. Another minor construction, briefly in vogue a decade ago, involved the word *bad*, more commonly written *baaad* to mark its special prosody, usually including creaky voice, and used as a term of praise. (This form is said to be traceable back three centuries to the Creole language Gullah in the time of slavery.[55]) Another minor construction was observed half a century ago: Bolinger noted that the word *see?* could be used as an "exultant exclamation with the meaning 'I told you so' " when said with a "very slow upgliding drawl."[56] I don't think I've heard this usage for decades, but similar prosody has recently reappeared on backchannels, most commonly on the word *right* as an expression of strong agreement, as in

21) M: *there's this game out there … it's called like Deux Ex*
    J: *oh my god, right?*
    M: *have you played it?*
    J: *yes, I love that game.*

Interesting as they are, this book won't say much more about minor constructions: we'll focus on the general constructions, plus a few primordial mappings.

4.8   Summary

By considering some meanings of creaky voice, this chapter has illustrated the continuum of ways in which prosody can convey meaning. As Figure 4.11 suggests, these range from the physiological and paralinguistic, up through the general constructions, including mothers and daughters, to the very specific minor constructions.

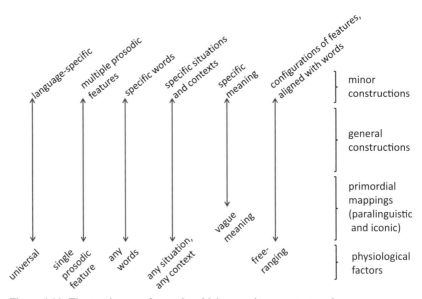

Figure 4.11 The continuum of ways in which prosody conveys meaning

Because prosody has both paralinguistic and linguistic aspects, Bolinger described it as a "half-tamed savage."[57] It would be convenient if these two aspects could be cleanly separated, but most prosodic features have both paralinguistic and linguistic functions, often closely related,[58] as we saw earlier, with the primordial mappings that surface in the meanings of the components of the Bookended Narrow Pitch Construction and the Downstep Construction. Thus one prosody–meaning mapping can relate to mappings at other levels. Further, a single mapping may span different ranges on the different scales of Figure 4.11.

This is all bad news for elegance-minded theorists, as it suggests that no single simple model can handle all of prosody, and it sits ill with traditional views, which are the topic of the next chapter. But this complexity is not a problem for us in this book, since our aim is merely to describe the facts as accurately as possible, using any appropriate vocabulary, however eclectic.

5   Perspectives on Prosody

This chapter steps back from the facts of English to consider different perspectives on prosody. After a look at the traditional view, with its limitations and biases, it overviews advances over the centuries. These explain why the descriptions in this book may differ from others you may know.

5.1   The Historical Roots of Prosodic Descriptions

The study of English prosody can be traced back to 1569,[1] in an era when modern English was emerging as a standard, and when London was becoming rich. Members of the merchant classes were starting to have leisure time, including time to think about writing and speaking well. They also had motivation to do so: in a hierarchical society with the court at the top, they could "better themselves" by acquiring the social graces, that is to say, by learning to act more like the nobility. An important part of this was proper language use, including standard pronunciation and polite intonation. This path for social advancement is seen in the movie *My Fair Lady*, in which Eliza Doolittle leaps from the bottom of the social hierarchy to the top, just by changing her way of speaking. Interestingly, while the Professor's teaching addresses only her phoneme-level pronunciation, by the time of her appearance at the embassy ball, transformed from street seller to lady, she has somehow also acquired upper-class prosody.

Fiction aside, in the late 1500s, grammarians were trying to establish how English should be written and spoken. Trying to pin down both form and function, they faced challenges with both.

Regarding form, since they lacked the ability to record and replay, early grammarians were limited to describing what they could notice with an attentive ear. This had several implications. First, among the various locations where prosody appears, the most salient are utterance ends. Speech is ephemeral and memory is fleeting, so if you have no recording device, what you'll remember best of an utterance is its last second or two, so that is what they focused on. Second, among the various prosodic features, the most salient is often pitch, and so the early grammarians focused on intonation. Third, among the many genres of language use, only a few were really accessible. Recitations of poetry, for example, were convenient to study since one can hear the exact same sequence many times, the pace is slow, and the prosody is well aligned with the words. None of these things is true for conversation, so it was quite out of reach for early scholars. Thus early scholars focused on pitch rises and falls at the end of utterances in monologue.

Regarding function, early grammarians had little conception of the diverse ways people use language to accomplish things – linguistics had yet to be invented. There was only a nascent understanding of grammar, including the ways sentences can differ in their basic grammatical form. For example, aux-inversions (as in *have you eaten?*) are a solid syntactic indication of questionhood. Could grammar also explain prosody? It certainly seemed promising. They noted, for example, that questions have rising final intonation more often than do statements. (Today we might describe this as a statistical tendency, but statistics was also yet to be invented.) Conveniently for those seeking guidance on how to speak elegantly, this tendency was stronger in the prestige dialect, Southern English, so by reserving final rises for questions, one could avoid sounding provincial or rustic. (Then, as now, in many regions of the British Isles, statements do not reliably go down at the end.[2]) So the early grammarians naturally came to the opinion that polite questions should end with a final rise and that statements should fall. Things seemed to be coming together nicely; in fact, so well that some of these observations got baked into our orthography. For example, the custom of marking questions with a special symbol at the end dates back to this same time period.[3]

The result of these early investigations was sets of rules which do things like tie utterance-final prosodic forms to grammatical structures. This is the historic core of what has been called the "British tradition" in prosody, and such rules have been influential ever since.

However, sad to say, such accounts are not only incomplete but also often wrong. For example, even in the prestige dialects of English, the claim that "questions go up," is not accurate in general, even for yes/no questions: it's not true today,[4] and there's no reason to think it was true in the past: many studies have failed to find reliable connections between pitch rises and questions,[5] regardless of whether questions are defined syntactically or pragmatically. The prosody of questions is in fact highly variable, as we have already seen.[6]

It's also not true that the prosody of sentence ends matters most. While final prosody can be important, speakers usually don't wait until the very end to flag their intention. This is shown, for example, by experiments in which subjects hear only the first part of a sentence and are asked to judge whether it will turn out to be a question or statement; in general, they do very well.[7] For questions in particular, there are usually additional prosodic indications of the communicative function earlier in the utterance.[8] Spanish punctuation, perhaps recognizing this, marks questionhood both at the start and the end of sentences.

But for an arbitrary decision made centuries ago, English might do the same. *¿Quién sabe?* [9].

Yet such inaccuracies have been generally overlooked, then and now. There are several likely reasons for this.

One reason was that people were quite happy to acquire a stylized version of English. Indeed, using prosodic patterns that were obviously the product of education and effort was a way to show off: to distinguish oneself from the common folk who spoke in whatever style they had just picked up naturally.

A second reason was that most learners had little interest in the everyday uses of English. The ambitious middle classes were concerned less with improving communication with friends and co-workers than with being more dignified and impressive at social functions. I imagine great formal banquets, where proper speaking was essential for performing introductions, engaging in polite small talk, honoring guests, and making toasts. Such ritual behavior is quite unlike the real-time give-and-take of normal conversation, and lacks most of the complexities of dialog prosody.

A third reason was that the truth or falsity of such rules matters little. In conversation, end-of-utterance prosody is seldom uniquely critical to communicating meaning and intention: that is, it has low functional load. Consequently, this part of the prosodic bandwidth is largely available for marking social identity, such as region, gender, age, marital status, and, of course, social class. In terms of a continuum between pure function and pure fashion, utterance-final prosody may be nearer the latter: it can be vital to making a good first impression, but is seldom decisive in effective communication.

Thus, even though the early grammarians were limited in what they could discover, their insights still found an eager market: the many people who wanted guidance on how to speak with "proper" intonation.

This section has provided a very selective overview of early prosody research. Readers interested in accurate and comprehensive descriptions – including coverage of the various schools and theories, representations and models, claims and controversies – may wish to consult the excellent general overviews by Pike, Crystal, Fox, or Laver,[10] or a more specialized survey.[11]

The rest of this chapter will consider a few ways in which these old ideas persist, together with new approaches that are leading to a more accurate understanding.

5.2   From Prescriptive to Descriptive

Early work in prosody was largely prescriptive: concerned more with what people should do than with what they actually do. Much popular writing on language still follows this tradition, serving the low end of market with simple rules.[12] For example, the converse of "questions go up" is "statements go down," and students going for job interviews are regularly advised to complement steady eye contact and a firm handshake with appropriate prosody: "use falling-pitch to show confidence," "avoid uptalk," and so on. Maxims like these are firmly rooted in the traditional view of prosody.

Such statements are meant to be good advice, and may have some basis in reality. But a little bit of knowledge can be a dangerous thing. For example, a language maven[13] can easily hear a prosodic feature like uptalk or creaky voice and see it as an expression of attitude ("today's young women are lacking in confidence," or "uppity" or "lackadaisical"), without understanding that speakers actually use such features in specific contexts to convey certain meanings.

Such advice is not entirely without value: it encourages us to pay more attention to how we speak and how other people perceive us. But modifying our behavior based on such simplistic views can make us seem phony or even impede communication.[14] It has been suggested, for example, that the voice coaching received by Margaret Thatcher, early in her political career, not only gave her a lower voice and a more commanding presence, but also interfered with her uses of prosody for turn-taking, creating unnecessary awkwardness in interviews.[15] However, more recent work has shown that simply speaking in a deeper voice will not reliably make people perceive you as stronger or more dominant.[16] So simple prescriptive statements about how to speak must be viewed with caution.

While there will always be people who like simple rules for how to behave, we now have better ways to describe language: linguistics is now recognized as the science of accurately describing how people really use languages, including their prosody.

5.3 From Grammar to Functions

While early descriptions of intonation related it to grammatical forms, advances over the centuries have revealed many more things that prosody relates to. An early expansion considered the prosody of semantically different types of questions: yes/no questions, choice questions, and so on.[17] Another focus of interest has been the prosody relating to propositional meanings, especially those phenomena that are easy to study in the laboratory, such as the prosody of contrastive focus in sentences like *I see a red circle, not a red square*. Other work has expanded our knowledge of how prosody relates to speech acts and dialog acts,[18] such as statements, greetings, backchannels, and so on. This work has culminated in broad categorizations of prosody as it relates to various inventories of diverse functions, including clause linkages, lists, greetings, new information, and contrastive focus.[19] However, these favorite classic research topics do not include all the things that are important in dialog.

Another stream of research has positioned itself as a reaction to meaning-based approaches. Reviving a classic dichotomy, this addresses not the "rational" but the "emotional" functions of prosody. There have been numerous studies in this vein,[20] exploring how to discriminate between joy, fear, sadness, and so on, generally in acted utterances. Such efforts are, however, rather marginal to the goal of understanding the prosody of dialog. Full-blown emotions are rare in most conversations, are seldom purely paralinguistic, and are usually enacted in orderly ways in coordination with other dialog activities.[21]

Thus, for the purposes of this book, simple semantic functions and pure visceral emotions are both only marginally relevant. Prosody in dialog generally seems to connect more often with pragmatic functions involving interpersonal relationships, speakers' goals, and communicative contexts.[22] Fortunately, recent years have seen a growing interest in the actual human uses of language, rather than what disembodied intelligent agents might do in philosophers' abstract worlds.[23] Of particular note is work in interactional linguistics, which has indeed focused on dialog.

5.4   From Monologue to Dialog

As noted above, early studies of prosody focused on monologue, such as public speaking. Even today, most research on prosody focuses on monologue or "near-monologue" situations, such as experimental subjects reporting on colors and shapes, or tourists asking the way to the breakfast room. Such "one-shot" utterances lack most of the richness of ongoing interactions: the complexities that arise when participants get down to the business of really communicating. Such near-monologue behaviors may also have an element of performance: they are spoken in public places, may be overheard by others in the room, and help display the social role and status of the speaker. Despite the atypical properties of monologue genres, such data are still popular as an object of study. There are many reasons for this.

One reason is that such data enable the generation of aesthetically pleasing pitch tracks. For dialog data, pitch tracks often come out spotty and jumpy. To get graceful, smooth pitch curves requires talented speakers or postprocessing with smoothing filters, or both. The result can be elegant curves that beautifully illustrate rise, rise-fall, and the other cute creatures in the traditional little menagerie. Obtaining such nice curves also requires careful selection of phoneme sequences, to get constant voicing and avoid strong microprosodic effects.[24] In this book, I use this trick once below, borrowing the phonetics-lab favorite, *Marianna made the marmalade*, for exactly these reasons.

Monologue and near-monologue scenarios are also convenient for controlled experiments. For detailed phonetic studies it can be helpful to have subjects produce intonation contours (tunes) on demand, one sentence at a time, using words chosen by the experimenter. Such speech, being produced in an idealized situation, can avoid all the "corruptions" arising in everyday interactions, where speakers are affected by time pressure, memory lapses, uncertainty in what to say and how to say it, sneezes, and other complications, especially the unpredictable behavior of conversation partners.

Thus most prosody research still uses monologue data. This is sometimes cast as a strategic move, part of a strategy to first solve monologue, and only then tackle dialog. But a monologue-first strategy risks leading us to theories and frameworks that work for monologue only, precluding the accurate modeling of dialog phenomena. In contrast, if the most basic form of language use is unscripted social interaction, it makes sense to start with it. This point has been made by Clark and many others,[25] and a reaction against monologue-centered research is at the heart of the research tradition known as conversation analysis and its descendant, interactional linguistics. Originating outside linguistics and inspired more by anthropology and sociology, these approaches examined true dialog phenomena from the start. Historically, this work grew with the availability of portable tape recorders:[26] in the 1960s and 1970s; these enabled scholars to capture real language, "in the wild," and bring it back to the lab for intensive study. Within these traditions, the importance of prosody has long been recognized.[27] While early work in this tradition tended to be impressionistic rather than precise and to shy away from quantitative methods or general claims,[28] more recent work is combining detailed analyses of dialog behavior with accurate prosodic descriptions:[29] a powerful combination.

5.5 From Intonation to Prosody

Intonation has always been top dog in descriptions of prosody.[30] Originally due to the perceptual salience of pitch and to the convenient availability of music notation for recording it, a disproportionate focus on intonation is still common today.

One reason for this is the sheer visual appeal of pitch tracks. Automatic pitch trackers became generally available in the 1970s, and researchers were happy to see that the intonation contours we perceive can often be seen directly in automatically generated graphs; this fact still makes intonation easier to study than other aspects of prosody.

Another reason is that pitch is relatively robust. Loudness, in contrast, is vulnerable not only to variation in the distance from the speaker's mouth to the microphone, but also to all kinds of noise.[31] Lengthening and timing properties are sensitive to the lexical content and the vagaries of the speaker's thought processes. Pitch, despite microprosodic complications, is less affected by such factors.

Another reason for the common focus on intonation may be the types of data that researchers preferred. While we no longer aspire to speak like the nobility, we still admire speakers with noble voices. Politicians, actors, and newscasters are common role models, not necessarily for you and me, but certainly for engineers trying to develop synthetic voices. Studies of newscasters were especially influential in early formal models. In the 1980s, when speech synthesis researchers started to realize the importance of prosody, their primary challenge was achieving intelligibility. Newscasters are paragons of intelligibility, so it was natural to study them. (Incidentally, we often admire not only their clarity, but also their authoritative and yet human style. While showing little emotion, in accordance with news conventions, newsreaders do humanize the news. Currently we know only a little about how this is done, but good prosody is certainly an important part of a good "radio voice").[32] Newsreading is, however, prosodically atypical in many ways. Newsreaders consistently distinguish stressed and unstressed syllables, to help with intelligibility. Since news copy may involve long and syntactically complex sentences, newsreaders devote a lot of the prosodic bandwidth to marking structure and boundaries, including sentence and topic boundaries. Due to transmission issues, broadcast speech could not vary much in loudness, to avoid listeners wondering whether the signal was fading and reaching for the volume knob.[33] Newscasters also avoid creaky and breathy voice, as they reduce intelligibility. Thus, the prosody of news is atypically centered on intonation.

Whatever the reasons, intonation has always been the primary focus in studies of prosody, and intonation-only models were the primary interest of many influential scholars. At times very aggressive claims have been made. For example, in the middle of the last century, the "4-3-4" pattern (where smaller numbers represent higher pitch) was proposed to represent "repudiation."[34] However, few such claims have stood the test of time. Half a century ago it seemed enough to present an (invented) sentence or two that exhibited both some claimed meaning and some specific intonation contour. But today the standards of evidence are higher, and the field has seen repeated failures to confirm claims that some specific meaning truly inheres in the intonation alone.

While intonation is even today the top dog, examination of the other aspects of prosody also has a long history. Many studies consider at least the "big three" aspects of prosody: pitch, loudness, and timing. These are a familiar set, partly for historical reasons. The word *prosody* itself comes from a Latin word describing word accent,[35] which in turn comes from a Greek word describing poems set to music. Indeed, for centuries, the word "prosody" in English was used primarily to refer to the study of the rhythm of poetry.[36] For both song and poetry, the relevant prosodic properties are indeed the big three.

But even the big three are only part of the story: as illustrated above, there are other properties of speech which pattern with them and have dialog significance.[37] These include creaky voice, breathy voice, precision of articulation, and nasalization. While these are not usually thought of as prosodic features, they are often similarly suprasegmental, that is, they often span speech regions much wider than one segment or phoneme. They also frequently have dialog significance, and are thus increasingly often studied together with the big three prosodic features.

Until recently, these various types of prosodic feature were mostly studied one at a time. That is, researchers would focus on one or another "stream" of information: pitch-related, timing-related, reduction-related, and so on. However these streams are seldom independent. Even things that seem simple and unitary may involve multiple types of features. Stress and prominence, for example, are signaled by high pitch, lengthening, and loudness.[38] (Incidentally, in English, pitch is the most heavily weighted feature in stress, but this varies across languages.) While stress is usually a single percept – we don't perceive the components separately, rather we just perceive "is stressed" – measurements show that all three features are involved. It is not the case, for example, that instances of the Minor Third Construction occur as fortuitous conjunctions of an independent pitch pattern, an independent lengthening tendency, and so on.

In general, many phenomena involve configurations of prosodic features of different types. Effectively identifying and describing such "multistream" phenomena is a great challenge,[39] but one that is increasingly being addressed.

5.6   From Symbolic to Quantitative

In this book I have freely used ad hoc symbols for various acoustic properties, such as the asterisk for creaky voice. These symbols are merely mnemonic devices for audible properties; that is, they are intended as phonetic symbols. Many other approaches, however, ascribe real significance to symbols: making them the building blocks of a phonological theory of intonation or prosody. This section discusses why this approach was popular and why more recent models tend to be more quantitative.

In the last century, many prosody researchers were inspired by symbolic analyses of other language phenomena. For example, the usual way to get started in phonology is to look for contrasting items. If we can determine that in English /b/ and /p/ can stand in contrast, since *pin* and *bin* mean different things, then we know that those two phonemes need to be included in the inventory of English sounds. Some scholars have approached prosody in the same way. For example, Brazil starts his book on English intonation by declaring his intention to examine only phenomena that he can see as involving "a set of oppositions."[40] This approach is, however, very limiting: it ignores the fact that prosodic forms may be not merely present or absent, but present to varying degrees. While prosodic forms can be perceived categorically in some circumstances,[41] such results are only found with certain experimental methods and for certain types of data.[42]

Using contrastive methods naturally leads to a set of symbols, one for each member of the set of identified sound components. In phonology these are symbols from the International Phonetic Alphabet; in prosody various symbol sets have been proposed. For example, Bolinger used A, B, and C, for downslope, upslope, and downstep contours, respectively, and ToBI uses H and L for high and low, with additional markings like *, %, and – for alignment and other properties.[43] Having a set of symbols, one can then conveniently state formal rules, such as rules for stress prominence in sentences, and rules for where stress falls in derived words, like *discontinúity* from *discontínuous* and *phénom* from *phenómenon*.[44] However, rules and symbols work much less well for prosody as it occurs in actual dialog. For example, even to define what H and L mean in real language data is surprisingly challenging.[45] In addition, descriptions of intonation contours in terms of symbol sequences – such as CAC in questions, or H*H*L-L% versus L+H*L-H% for neutral versus contrastive prosody,[46] quickly get unwieldy.

Part of the appeal of symbol-based accounts is their seductive elegance. Theoreticians love claims like "despite the apparent complexity, prosody is really all just X," where X may be prominences and pauses, tones and boundaries, highs and lows, rises and falls, and so on. An appropriate symbology can then be invented for X, and a school of research founded. However, there are several problems with this. First, such abstract theories can lose touch with the realities of language: saying little substantive about either how the symbolic level maps to meanings or how it maps to acoustic realizations.[47] Second, although simplicity is a virtue, extreme reductionism is ill-suited to the description of prosody, where, as we have seen, a lot of meaning is bound up in specific, richly complex patterns. Third, the use of theory-specific terminology and symbols has impeded communication between different schools of research. (This is, incidentally, one reason why this book strives to describe everything directly and concretely, without specialized terminology.) The fourth problem is that symbolic models are ill-suited for superposition, the topic of a future chapter.

Despite these well-known problems, symbol-based approaches have enduring appeal, in part because of their familiarity. We all spent much of first grade learning to work with symbolic descriptions of sound, so as adults this seems natural, even unavoidable. But let's take a minute to consider how surprising it is that symbolic descriptions of language *ever* work.

Ultimately every sound we make is the result of muscle motions and their effects on the tongue, lips, and other articulators. Since no movement is instantaneous, every property of every sound we make has some temporal extent. These include steady-state properties, such as the tongue forming a vowel shape, and dynamic properties, such as the lips coming together for a consonant closure. The various muscle motions required, that is to say, the articulatory gestures, often overlap. This is as true of phonemes as it is of prosody: coarticulation is pervasive. For example, some of what characterizes the vowel sound in *spin* is actually found in the time segments devoted to the surrounding consonants.[48] Thus, the physical reality underlying every sound we make, phonemic or prosodic, is due to gestures.

For phonemes we can usually forget this, and instead describe things at an abstract level. This is because the temporal extents are relatively small and generally well aligned, often to within tens of milliseconds. This is because the movements of the tongue and lips are fast and precise, so the synchronization of oral gestures can be very accurate.[49] We can therefore conveniently treat these aspects of speech as composed of discrete little sound packages, or "segments," standing in sequence like books on a shelf. And so alphabets work fine for these sounds, and the science of sounds-as-symbols, namely phonology, has been a great success.

Prosody, however, is different. Human larynxes are not as fast or as precise as tongues and lips,[50] as suggested earlier with the pizza conveyor belt metaphor. Thus, symbolic representations are much less useful for prosody: we need more detail on the timing of gestures than any symbolic account can give.

These problems are well known. In reaction to the limitations of symbolic modeling, there is increasing interest in quantitative modeling. This encompasses a wide range of approaches, from modestly just gathering statistics on some aspect of a symbol-based model, to fully automatic modeling. By relying on automatically extracted prosodic features, the latter steers clear entirely of specialized notations and terminology, in favor of descriptions that directly relate functions to low-level features that can be directly heard and directly computed.[51] These approaches have been especially successful for applications, thanks not only to robust automatic feature detectors and large data collections, but to the availability of sufficient computational power.[52]

Purely quantitative modeling, however, has its own weaknesses. Recently, most applied work in prosody has used "black-box" models, typically generic neural-network architectures. Applied to huge corpora, these learn thousands of parameters that together enable the performance of some task or other. For practical purposes this may be enough, as has been found for several specific tasks, including generation of prosody for highly intelligible speech synthesis,[53] recognizing emotion from prosody, predicting turn ends, and diagnosing medical conditions. However, such models have two weaknesses. First, they are not reusable: having built one model, to then build a new model for a different task or demographic group requires one to start from scratch, with a new data collection and annotation effort. Second, such models lack any recognizable representation of knowledge about prosody: they are truly black boxes, in the sense of being opaque to analysis and understanding.

Thus the challenge is to develop models of prosody that are quantitative but also understandable to human researchers and human readers.

5.7   Teaching Prosody: Techniques and Trends

Many people want to improve their speaking skills, and teachers at all levels are there to help, from speech therapists to debate coaches to communication professors. But perhaps the greatest need is among non-native speakers. Prosody is a great challenge for them: even when their other language skills are good, non-native speakers often have saliently non-native prosody.[54] Unfortunately, prosody is seldom much discussed in courses on English as a second language,[55] and if taught at all, it is mostly presented along traditional lines.

Traditional teaching of prosody certainly has some value. For example, if you're aspiring to work in tourism, it's important to know a proper way to say *would you like some more tea?* This is not a trivial matter, since appropriate prosody here can make or break your career.[56] Teachers usually recommend the use of the classic final rise of "International English" for this purpose. This is universally safe, although it must be noted that native speakers have dozens of dialectal, subculture-specific or casual ways to make offers – such as *you look like you might be ready for another beer* – that may seem more sincere or be more engaging.

Traditional rule-based instruction is convenient for some learners and even more so for teachers. Rules like "questions go up" are easily taught – just like times tables, state capitals, and spelling – with worksheets, rote memorization, and written tests. This is great if you're a busy teacher with many students. In contrast, truly teaching the prosody of language is labor-intensive. Today learners mostly acquire effective prosody outside the classroom, via expensive private tutoring or expensive semester-abroad programs. Further, while many learners are able to pick up the patterns organically, in the course of interacting with native speakers, some never do.

While we're on the topic of teaching English, it's worth saying a few words about rhythm.[57] Rhythm is a salient part of English prosody; at least when we hear someone speaking English with the rhythm of a different language, perhaps one with different rules for placing stresses, or one without a stressed/unstressed distinction at all. Rhythm is important for intelligibility, and for giving a good first impression. Quite a lot is known about the stress and rhythm of English, especially how words are accented, and this can be taught. This is, however, not necessarily of the first importance for communicative effectiveness:[58] people with excellent stress patterns are certainly more pleasant to listen to, but not necessarily easier to interact with.

In any case, most teaching of the prosody of English as a second language follows ancient traditions. This is, however, demonstrably inadequate: if prosody were truly based on simple rules, nations where it is taught that way would be superpowers in English proficiency, but we all know cultures where both teachers and students are dedicated and diligent, but the outcome, in terms of English communication ability, is disappointing. It is not hard to infer why: among the various functions of prosody, the dialog-related aspects can be the most important – since incomplete command of these forms can impact interactional competence and interfere with the achievement of communicative goals[59] – yet these aspects are poorly handled by traditional descriptions and teaching methods.

But things are rapidly changing. There are increasing efforts to improve the teaching of second-language prosody: to base it on real language behaviors and to make it more effective.[60] One thing that may help is teaching prosodic constructions explicitly. When I've borrowed an ESL class and taught a construction or two, the students could readily understand, appreciate their significance, and learn to produce them.[61] Be that as it may, teaching prosody effectively is today more an art than a science, and will likely stay that way for the foreseeable future. Helping students acquire conversational prosody is likely always to require teachers with sensitive ears, good voice control, creativity, and patience.

5.8   Implications

This chapter has explored the lasting influence of the limitations of traditional approaches to prosody. These underlie what you learned about intonation in grade school and what you hear from commentators in the media. Although hallowed by generations of repetition, such maxims have little relevance to the prosody of dialog.

This chapter has also noted that, as linguistics has become a science, there have been numerous advances in tools, methods, and topics of study, moving in the direction of more comprehensive, function-oriented, qualitative, and dialog-focused studies. While different advances have been embraced by different schools, recently we are seeing work that exploits these advances in combination. In particular, the notion of prosodic construction is useful for this.

But challenges remain. Beyond the historical and methodological issues, the prosody of dialog is intrinsically hard to study. Prosody mostly operates at or beyond the limits of human perception: phenomena happen very fast, many of the meaningful patterns involve multiple streams of prosody, the signals are often subtle, and multiple patterns are generally superimposed. Moreover, many of these patterns are acquired early in life and are thus processed without conscious awareness and not available to introspection.

Thus new methods are needed. In this chapter we've examined and rejected many old and comfortable, yet constraining, ideas about prosody. We're now free to move on to build a new view, albeit one that includes what is valuable from other perspectives. After two more empirical chapters and some discussion of superposition, I will present a big-data method that combines many of the strengths of the diverse schools and methods. After that, we'll be fully prepared to move quickly through a dozen constructions.

6   Late Pitch Peak and Its Functions

We remember Martin Luther King's

1) *I have a dream*

not just for the words, but also for how he said them. His prosody makes it clear that he's engaging in a feat of deliberate imagination, and that he's inviting us to share in this dream and help make it real. This all comes from the prosody. Without it, the same four words could mean something mundane, as in, *I have a dream cruise planned for next year* (2). The key property of the prosody is something special on the words *I* and *dream*.

This chapter will explain this "something special." After dissecting some syllables to explain the form, we will examine its many functions and its core meaning.

6.1   Pitch and Intensity Alignment and Disalignment

English, like every language, is made up of syllables. Most syllables have a vowel in the center and consonants at the edges. Since vowels are usually louder than consonants, the intensity profile of the archetypal syllable looks something like this:

$$\cap$$

That is to say, over time the loudness increases, stays high for a bit, and then decreases. Loudness is, acoustically, achieved by greater airflow. Now, greater airflow past the vocal folds generally causes faster vibration, by the laws of physics. So the pitch also typically goes up and then comes down over the course of a syllable, and thus tends to have the same shape as the intensity profile, and the two tend to be aligned, as illustrated in Figure 6.1.

In this particular syllable – a kendo battle cry *yaa* (3), yelled at full volume – the physics governed: the speaker wasn't much controlling her vocal folds, and the pitch closely tracks the intensity. The same is typical of *yay* (4) as a response to sudden good news: in free, uncontrolled expressions of joy, the pitch contour tracks the intensity contour.

Figure 6.1 A archetypal syllable: pitch above, in black, and intensity below, in gray

| okay | so | now | yeah | | so | now | learn | drone | five |

Figure 6.2 Pitch (black) and intensity (gray) over two phrases

In Figure 6.2, in contrast, the pitch line tracks the intensity only for the first part of the utterance

5) *okay, so now, yeah, so now, learn Drone*⁹ *Five*⁹.

At the end the pitch contour saliently departs from the intensity contour, and in particular, there are two pitch peaks which come late relative to an intensity peak, on the words *drone* and *five*.

I'll refer to this phenomenon as "late peak." This figure also illustrates my motivation for using the balloon, ⁹, to mark this: it suggests the pitch floating up, not tethered to the intensity.

To better appreciate the sound of late peaks, consider two renditions of the same word:

6) *what Marianna made was the marmalade*

presents *the marmalade* as a pure fact, without suggesting any further implication. But

7) *Marianna made the mar*⁹*malade*

is suggestive, indicating that there is some implied message beyond what the words literally say: perhaps we should try some of her marmalade, or perhaps we should re-evaluate her culinary skills.

Figures 6.3 and 6.4 show the pitch and intensity contours of these two examples. In both of them the lexically stressed syllable, *mar*, is lengthened, but only in the factual rendition does the pitch peak come within that syllable. In the suggestive rendition it comes later. (In addition, the pitch goes higher and the syllable containing the pitch peak is longer. While not coincidental, these differences are not our focus here.) This phenomenon, of a pitch peak occurring *after* the syllable that is longest and loudest, occurs in many other contexts

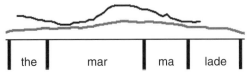

| the | mar | ma | lade |

Figure 6.3 Pitch and intensity of *the marmalade* in a purely factual utterance

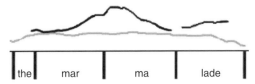

| the | mar | ma | lade |

Figure 6.4 Pitch and intensity of *the marmalade* in a suggestive utterance

in English, with many meanings. But before we consider the uses of late peak, it's worth a note on its discovery.

Although some aspects of prosody have been known for millennia, late peak is a recent discovery. It was first described in 1977, as distinguishing in some Swedish dialects between words that would otherwise be homonyms,[1] and it was pinned down experimentally only in the late 1980s.[2] Its existence can be demonstrated in production studies. In English, for example, Barnes et al.,[3] asked people to produce short phrases in two ways, once spoken so as to convey uncertainty and once spoken to convey incredulity. Considering first the uncertain utterances, they observed that these had the usual close alignment of pitch and intensity peaks, with the offset between the two averaging a mere 16 milliseconds. However, in the incredulous recordings: the pitch peaks generally occurred significantly after the intensity peaks. Compared to their position in the uncertain utterances, they were on average 77 milliseconds later. This was a consistent pattern, suggesting that this is not just sloppy behavior.

In general, humans are very good at precisely aligning actions, and not only in speech.[4] For example, gestures while speaking frequently align with stressed syllables, and the apex of the gesture even tends to align with the exact pitch peak.[5] Indeed, humans strongly tend to produce actions in alignment,[6] for example when finger tapping rapidly with both hands, even in experiments where subjects are asked not to align. So it seems likely that late peaks are the result of speakers doing something special to overcome the general tendency: effortfully making the pitch peak *not* align with the intensity peak.

Knowledge of the existence of late peak has been pretty much limited to a few tight communities of phoneticians and phonologists, some using different terms for similar phenomena, including "delayed peak," "rising pitch accent," and "scooped contour."[7] The few thorough studies of this phenomenon have mentioned its pragmatic functions only in passing, instead focusing on its phonetic details, correlations with speaking style and social roles, and implications for phonological theory.[8] This chapter will instead aim to identify what late peak is actually used for.

6.2   Making Suggestions

Chapter 3 discussed one way in which prosody can be used to get people to do things, with the Minor Third Construction. That tactic only works where there is a social norm you can invoke, but English also has other ways, as in

8) *I suggest⌐ you lis⌐ten to the audio⌐ for the exam⌐ples.*

(This suggestion is actually a real one: do please listen to the examples and if possible say them yourself, with feeling; this is the best way to appreciate how late peaks contribute to the meaning.)

A real-life example of late peak in a suggestion was already seen above, in Figure 6.2, where the speaker was giving advice on how to get better at a videogame,

9) *so now⌐, learn Drone⌐ Five⌐.*

In this example late peak is slightly present on the word *now*, and strongly present on the words *Drone* and *Five*.

Late peak is also seen in

10) *why⌐ would you do five⌐, if you still have one left?*

said so as to imply that just four classes this semester would be a better choice, and on our old friend,

11) *it looks like a ze⌐bra.*

While earlier we saw this as an example of a "neutral," non-contrastive utterance, it also may include a nuance of suggestion. With the late peak, as seen in Figure 2.1, it sounds like the speaker is suggesting that the listener interpret the ambiguous picture as being really a zebra. With an aligned peak, it's purely a statement,

12) *it looks like a zebra*

with no suggestion implied.

Parenthetically, the diversity of grammatical forms in suggestions is noteworthy:[9] in just these few examples we see declaratives, imperatives, and a question. Thus it is not the syntax that determines the function; rather, in each case it is the prosody that makes it clear that a suggestion is being made.

Be that as it may, the magnitude of late peak seems to correlate with the magnitude of a suggestion. If I'm inviting my daughter to shoot some baskets after dinner, it can be quite mild,

13) *Isabel, read⌐y for some basketball?*

but if I'm inviting another family to join us for a three-day rafting trip, there will be multiple strong late peaks:

14) *we were ʔthinking it would be great ʔif you could come.*

6.3   Offering, Inviting, Requesting, and Threatening

Late peaks are also common when making offers, whether conditional or unconditional:

15) *okay Hen ʔry, I'll trade you two sheep for one wheat ʔ*

16) *you ʔlook ʔlike you might be ready for another beer ʔ*

17) *would ʔyou care for something to drink?*

Many offers exhibit question syntax.[10] Following standard practice, I'll mark these with question marks, although this does not indicate any consistent prosodic property. In particular, the traditionally prescribed final rise is optional in offers. Without a final rise you can still make a nice offer, provided one or more late peaks are present, as in the beer offer. But the opposite is not true: without a late peak near the beginning, the same sentence will sound cold, businesslike, tired, or impolite:

18) *would you like something to drink?* (no late peak)

The other day at the fast food counter I was asked:

19) *would you like two apple pies for a dollar?*

with no late peaks. This first struck me as rude, but perhaps the counter person was being helpful: her prosody usefully conveyed that she was not making a sincere offer – she didn't really think I'd like two pies – but rather she was just mouthing some words her manager had told her to say.

In any case, the final rises that are present on some offers differ from commonplace up-and-fade-out rises; rather they can resemble other late peaks. This can be seen by comparing a non-offer question, a question-type offer, and a non-question offer.

20) *was the word baked pota ʔto?*

21) *(would you like a) baked pota ʔto?*

Figure 6.5 shows the pitch and intensity of these examples. In shape, the final syllable of the *potato* offer (middle) looks more like the final syllable of the *beer* offer (right) than like the final syllable of the confirmation question (left). Perceptually also, the two offers sound rather similar.

Figure 6.5 Pitch and intensity. Left: query (question syntax), center: offer (question syntax), right: offer (declarative syntax). Audio examples 20, 21, and 16, respectively

Thus I speculate that the final-syllable high pitch in offers, when it occurs, may result from a general process that adds late peaks to all stressed sylla-bles across some timespan, including the last one. While some theorists like to sharply distinguish between accent-related pitch shapes and boundary-related pitch shapes,[11] here they do seem to be related.

Be that as it may, late pitch is also common in invitations,

22) *we͏ͨcould go out to see a mo͏ͨvie or something tonight͏ͨ*

and pre-invitations,

23) *so do you have any͏ͨthing planned͏ͨfor͏ͨtonight͏ͨ?*

In the same way,

24) *what͏ͨare you doing?*

is likely to be a preface to something, like an offer of help or suggestion to take a break. However, without a late peak

25) *what are you doing?*

is likely just a request for information.

Similarly, you might ask

26) *do you͏ͨlike tea?*

if you're hoping your guest will say yes so you can bring out your tea pearls and make a friendly pot, but if you're just taking a survey on beverage preferences, there would probably be no late pitch peak:

27) *do you like tea?*

In sentences without lexical marking of invitation, late peaks can make the intention clear. Conversely, without them, even a promising line like

28) *I found this great little place for lunch*

can fall flat.

Late peaks are also common in requests,[12] as in

29) *[can you] hit record͏ͨfor me͏ͨ?*

This can be seen in the difference between

30) *it's cold in here*

meant as an observation, and

31) *it's cold in here*$^\wp$

as an implicit request for the window to be closed.

To digress for a moment, back in the 1970s the field of Artificial Intelligence was starting to develop dialog systems able to address users' needs conversationally. Fascinated by examples like these,[13] researchers developed sophisticated methods for inferring whether ambiguous sentences were conveying only the literal meaning or in addition an "indirect speech act" such as a request. While such sophisticated inference may be unavoidable for text-based dialog systems, for spoken dialog systems that are able to pay proper attention to what the user is saying, including the prosody they use, clever inference may in fact not be needed.

Requesting is in any case a common dialog act. An interesting special case is requesting agreement. The following utterance occurred after the other player had proposed going on to the next game level:

32) *but I*$^\wp$ *need to get, I still need to get three, the three gems.*

Late peaks also occur in aggrieved requests.

33) *hey, could you*$^\wp$ *guys keep it down?*

The same utterance without a late peak would be more of a demand and much less polite:

34) *hey, could you guys keep it down?*

Flight attendants similarly say

35) *could you please put your seat back up?*

with a final rise to make it polite, but no late peak, making it unambiguously a command, not a request.

While many requests ask for action, others ask only for information.

36) *oh*$^\wp$*, do you play Halo too*$^\wp$*?*

37) *how'd*$^\wp$ *your parents get to Ohi*$^\wp$*o then?*

Late peaks also occur in threats. From a speech act perspective, threats are much like conditional offers. Both involve Speaker A promising to do some action depending on whether Speaker B performs or does not perform some other action.[14] Another commonality is that threats may also have late peaks.

Table 6.1 *Some speech acts that relate to future actions and are commonly realized with late peaks*

	who will act	who will benefit
suggestion	hearer	hearer
conditional offer	both (two reciprocal actions)	both
invitation	both (joint action)	both
unconditional offer	speaker	hearer
request	hearer	speaker
threat	hearer	speaker

38) *if you're not⁹ here in one⁹ minute, we'll leave without you!*

39) *say that again⁹ and I'll wipe that smile off your face!*

In threats the desired action may be left implicit but inferable. So, for example, if you hear

40) *you⁹ little twerp⁹*

it would be wise to make yourself scarce: you have been warned.

The late peaks seem to be essential to threats. If, instead of producing late peaks, the bully is aligning his pitch and intensity peaks, as in

41) *yôu lîttle twêrp*

then you're no longer being threatened – there is no longer an opportunity to back down. Rather, he's already tensing for action, and you should expect a blow, maybe landing in alignment with the last word.

Table 6.1 summarizes the functions of late pitch peaks discussed so far, an interesting subset of the familiar inventory of speech acts.[15] Three commonalities stand out: first, all involve a measure of consideration for the addressee, providing them with a choice. Second, these speech acts can all be face threats,[16] and the late peaks may serve to mitigate the possible offense. Third, all involve an element of *irrealis*, that is, all refer to a situation that does not currently exist. (In some languages *irrealis* is morphologically marked, so it's not outlandish to think that this is something important enough to merit a piece of the prosodic bandwidth of English.)

So far, everything has fit together nicely, but we've only covered half the meanings of late peaks. So stand up, stretch, and take a deep breath before we run through a dozen other uses. After that, we'll consider what they all have in common.

6.4   Grounding

Another common function of late peaks is "grounding." In conversation, each speaker comes in with their own knowledge and beliefs, and one by one, these can be introduced into the "common ground" of the discourse, to make them shared and available to be talked about.[17]

For example, at the start of a game, while introducing the characters and their abilities, the player with experience explained that

42) *Fireboy⸮, can touch the fire* [but not the water].

In grounding, people establish agreement about a referent, that is, establish what something is called or what it is. This is common in confirmation questions, and not only at the end.

43) J: *. . . Boondock Saints; have you ever watched that movie?*
      M: *oh, the first⸮ one, right⸮?*

Grounding is often associated with starting a new topic, as in

44) *umm⸮ I'm⸮ a trans⸮fer stu⸮dent, from EPCC⸮*

which served as an opening that led the conversation in a new direction.[18] Proposing a new topic is also a type of suggestion: a suggestion for what to talk about next.

This example is interesting for the density of late peaks: they occur on all the stressed syllables, and even the seldom-stressed filler *um* is recruited to serve. Especially interesting is the late peak on the last syllable, which might be called a case of "uptalk." Language mavens have criticized this usage on the grounds that final rises in English are for questioning, so it is inappropriate to use them for other functions. Among other problems, this criticism assumes that the only important feature in intonation is the distinction between rise versus fall, and that the only important aspect of prosody is intonation. In fact, there is much more to the prosody of questions and to the prosody of uptalk.[19] The latter seems to have smaller and later pitch rises,[20] and, I speculate, more tendency to creaky voice and lengthening.

The association between late peaks and grounding may underlie another common use, for marking proper nouns, as seen in this exchange:

45) I: *Masato is on Line.*
      S: *What do you mean, online?*
      I: *No, he's on Line⸮.*

Here the prosody distinguishes *line* and *Line*. Unlike tone languages, which pervasively use prosody to distinguish otherwise ambiguous words, English does this only occasionally. Textbooks always illustrate this with the same handful of examples – such as *billow* and *below*, and the noun *cóntest* versus the verb *contêst* – but in fact, with late peaks, prosody is a common way to distinguish proper nouns from the common nouns with the same phonemes.

Late peak on proper nouns is also common when introducing new referents. For example, on the news you may hear

46) *Today the Food ˤand Drug ˤAdministra ˤtion announced ...*

47) *the F ˤD ˤA ˤ intends to ...*

In read speech, just as commas and periods have their own traditional prosody,[21] word-initial capitalization often has its own prosodic reflex, namely late peaks on the stressed syllables.

However, not everyone marks proper nouns with clear late peaks. On the radio I once heard what sounded like

48) *NPR is supported by the main office of tourism*

but surely was intended as something different, which I would pronounce with a clear late peak on *Maine*:

49) *N ˤPR ˤ is supported by the Maine ˤ Office of Tourism.*

This illustrates how individuals differ, something that is also known from experiments,[22] where commonly a small minority does not produce late peak even in contexts that, for most speakers, reliably cue it.

More speculatively, another factor in the failure to distinguish *main* from *Maine* may have been the mental state of the voice talent: probably at recording time she was not thinking about how the listeners would hear her words. Perhaps after repeating this a dozen times, trying to get it right, for her the word *Maine* was not a new referent, though it would be for her listeners. Failure to use prosody appropriate for the context of presentation is a pervasive problem for amateur talent and amateur voice coaches, as illustrated by most airport announcements. Hopefully, such lapses will become rarer, as more people learn the techniques for producing good, context-appropriate recordings.[23]

6.5   Reaching Agreement

Life would be easy if we all could agree all the time. A good second-best would be if disagreements were always simple and pure. But, in real life, people often need to indicate partial agreement. Late peaks can mark this too, as in

50) S: *can you see yourself pretty good?*
   J: *yeah ˤ*

where the prosody, notably including a late peak and creaky voice, adds the meaning, "but actually not that well."

Another example of partial acceptance was already seen:

51) S: *it's still recording, apparently*
   J: *yeah, the light's ᵖ green*

in which J confirms that the recording indicator is on, but implies that she can't vouch for the laptop actually being recording. Here the late peak indicates partial agreement and invites the hearer to make an additional inference, for example that he might want to independently confirm the recording status.

Similarly, late peaks can be used when conceding a point, to agree with part of what the interlocutor has said before going on to disagree with the main point. For example, after S had disparaged a class, J conceded some problems with it

52) *it is ᵖ three hours long, and it's kind of late ᵖ, but*

before going on to say why it was still her favorite class.

Late peaks also occur when correcting misconceptions, as in

53) *well ᵖ, ac ᵖtually that's not a zebra.*

Correcting a misconception in this way is like making a suggestion: here a suggestion to consider an alternative view of the drawing. Without the late peaks, such a correction could sound rude – a direct contradiction can be a face threat[24] – but late peaks bring a softening nuance. In the same vein, people may use late peaks when venturing an opinion that the other may not share, as in

54) *I think ᵖ, in computer science there's not a lot of social ᵖ people ᵖ*

and, less tentatively but still courteously, in

55) *no, you didn't tag ᵖ me.*

The same can be seen in

56) *I'm just ᵖ kidding.*

This is commonly said to take back something that could cause offense: this retroactively marks an earlier comment as *irrealis* and playful rather than serious. It may also serve to apologize obliquely.

6.6   Imagining and Reminiscing

Martin Luther King's speech is not the only place you can hear a late peak marking an act of imagination. For example, it's present in the line from the song:[25]

57) *If I had ᵖ a million dol ᵖlars, I'd build a tree house in our yard.*

In contrast, in an imagination-free statement,

58) *If I had a million dollars to invest, I sure wouldn't put it in tech.*

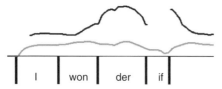

Figure 6.6 Pitch and intensity

the pitch peaks are aligned with the intensity peaks.

Another example of imagining and speculating occurs when a player remarks on an apparent anomaly in the logic of a game:

59) *oh, yeah, I was won˚dering if, if I would like kill you or something.*

Consider also

60) *I just need to get that lab done, and I'm done˚with that lab.*

While on paper it looks like the speaker is expressing a tautology or being gratuitously repetitive, when listening it is clear from the prosody that he is conveying two distinct messages: first a statement of what he needs to do after the recording session is over, and second a preview of his state after that, in particular, unstressed and potentially available to do something with his friend. The late pitch peak on the second *done* seems to indicate that in the last clause he's visualizing that future happy state.

The strength of the late peak can vary with the depth of the speculation. For example, if we're watching an event I may say

61) *I won˚der who'll go next*

with a slightly delayed, moderately salient pitch peak. The speculative element is rather weak: my question will be resolved as soon as the next speaker steps up. But if I'm pondering a great unknowable,

62) *I won˚der if the readers are a˚ctually listening to the examples*

the pitch peak can be shifted all the way over to the second syllable of *wonder*, as seen in Figure 6.6.

In these examples, late peaks are again marking *irrealis*: things that are not currently true. This can involve not only future situations but also past situations, as in the culmination of a story about a car crash:

63) *I'll tell˚you this right now: air˚bags hurt!*

and in an invitation to reminisce:

64) *do you remem˚ber that time we kayaked down?*

6.7 Assessing and Judging

Late peaks are also common in expressions of liking, approval, and admiration:

65) *I lov ˤed teaching*

66) *I like ˤ her style*

67) *I think she dresses so cute ˤ*

and also in expressions of disapproval

68) *her pro ˤjects are so ˤ ea ˤsy, it drives ˤ me nuts.*

Such assessments relate to suggesting, in that the speaker is usually implicitly suggesting that the listener also adopt a certain view of someone or something.

Incidentally, in my data this use of late peak seemed to be more common for female speakers, especially when strongly present.

Late peaks occur frequently in laughter and laughed speech, and often these are part of assessing something. Both participants may laugh together, thereby displaying shared feeling. This can create a form of social bonding.[26] Another case of laughed speech, from the games corpus, was expressing relief after a close call:

69) *oh, oh, I thought I was ˤ going to fall.*

In the gaming dialogs, late peak often indicates a playful feeling, sometimes relating to non-seriousness or losing control. This at times implies enjoyable distress, and at other times pure enjoyment.

70) *oh, no! I'm ˤ so ˤ scared!*

71) *whee ˤ!*

6.8 A Digression on Sarcasm

Although late pitch peak can convey liking, it can also appear in utterances conveying the opposite. For example,

72) *I love ˤ ethics*

said in the context of a discussion of classes and lecture topics, clearly meant the opposite: after this the speaker burst into laughter.

Sarcasm is a tricky thing.[27] Often the sarcastic intent is clear only given the context. In this example the other speaker had already expressed a negative sentiment, so when this statement appeared, with a strong late peak, it was obviously not meant at face value.

The So Dated Construction

Function: mock a fashion choice and the ephemerality of fashion

Form:
  <adjective>
  is
  so (with late peak)
  <temporal noun phrase>
Figure 6.7 The So Dated Construction

Another common way to convey sarcasm is with prosody that is incongruous with the literal meaning of the words.[28] For example, when words that express a positive sentiment are said with a narrow pitch range, suppressing the normal peaks for stressed syllables, sarcasm is likely present.[29] Consider the word *effective* in two renditions:

73) *I think that'll be effective.*

74) *well, that*⌐*'ll be effective.*

In the second example, the narrow pitch range on *effective* conveys a negative assessment, and the oddly placed late peak, on the word *that*, adds an incongruity that invites the listener to infer what is really meant.

As another example where late peak on a non-content word contributes to an impression of sarcasm, consider

75) *purple is so*⌐ *last year*

as might occur when commenting on someone's fashion choices. This is a conventionalized form:[30] a minor construction that I'll call the So Dated Construction. This construction exhibits both a grammatical peculiarity and a prosodic peculiarity. While the word *so* generally modifies adjectives of degree – *good*, *tall*, *weird*, and the like – here it precedes a temporal expression. The prosodic peculiarity is that the late peak is strongest on the word *so*, though in sincere uses the late peaks tend to be strongest on content words, as in the *so cute* example above. This construction, briefly popular for a time, had a complex, twisted meaning: mocking someone's style and simultaneously mocking the idea of obsessing about style and fashion. Figure 6.7 summarizes.

Sarcasm is an important part of English; in my data it is by far the most prevalent form of humor. This is, however, not universal. When my daughter went to school in Japan, she found that no one ever used sarcasm, and when she ventured to spice things up with a sarcastic remark or two, people were just confused.

The various prosodic forms of sarcasm are not yet well understood, and indeed may never be. Since sarcasm that's obvious is no fun, speakers tend to shave down the indications to the minimum, and they are always inventing new ways to be sarcastic, especially creative teenagers.

6.9   A Systematic Survey

Even discounting sarcasm, late peaks have so many roles that you may be wondering whether there's anything they can't mean. This section explains how I ruled out this possibility.

First, in order to get a grip on the range of uses of late peaks, I needed a way to automatically find all late peaks in a collection of dialog. This turned out to require a little innovation, as previous methods were not up to the task. For example, the method of Barnes et al. for identifying late peaks required speech with each phrase recorded twice, once with an aligned peak and then with a late peak. This enables measurement of how far a pitch peak is shifted relative to its location in the other production. Natural dialog, however, contains no matched productions: there are no neutral controls. So this method, like all previous methods for identifying late peaks, doesn't work for automatic processing of dialog.[31]

Fortunately, previous work has shown that late peak is a robust phenomenon, not overly sensitive to the exact methods used to find it: several researchers have found that pitch peaks are consistently late in certain pragmatic circumstances, regardless of exactly how "late" is measured.[32] Whereas Barnes et al. measured the time from a convenient landmark, namely the midpoint of the vowel, to a careful estimate of the peak's perceived location, namely the tonal center of gravity, other work has used different landmarks – including intensity peaks, voicing onset times, and pitch-rise start points – and different correlates of peak location, including pitch turning points and fall locations. Many experiments have found significant differences in peak timing for certain meanings, regardless of the exact metric.

Another thing that simplifies matters is the fact that the distinction between late and aligned peaks is only present on stressed syllables. While the exact nature of the stressed/unstressed distinction is complex,[33] in general, stressed syllables are loud, long, and high in pitch. These properties, are, conveniently, exactly those needed to support distinguishable pitch shapes: they make it possible both for speakers to produce different shapes and for hearers to distinguish them.[34] Indeed, it has been argued that the essential property of stressed syllables is exactly the fact that they can be realized in different shapes.[35] In an unstressed syllable, in contrast, the pitch is usually pretty flat; and even if it does have some shape, this usually comes from syllable-external factors, such as the effects of larger constructions. So, in order to detect late peaks, we only need to worry about the stressed syllables.

Accordingly, I built a disalignment estimator that does three simple things: it identifies intensity peaks across the data, it independently identifies pitch peaks across the data, and then for each pitch peak it computes a measure of how strongly it avoids aligning with an intensity peak.[36] This method, helpfully for integration with the workflow described later, is able to produce continuous estimates of the strength of the evidence for a pitch disalignment, computed every 20 milliseconds or so, throughout the data.

In spirit, this method is respectful of the uncertainty and complexity of real dialog. Earlier approaches to late peaks assumed that one can definitively identify whether a peak is present and definitively pinpoint where it is located. These assumptions are counterproductive if we care about real dialog: they drive researchers to acoustically clean data, and thus to laboratory-collected data. Further, to enable controlled comparisons, they drive researchers to collect data that is pragmatically simple, with each utterance conveying only one intent. This disalignment-based method liberates us from all this. Instead it works in terms of evidence, computing at every moment the likelihood of a salient pitch peak being there, and of there being a disalignment relative to an intensity peak. In this way, every aspect of late peaks is modeled probabilistically, avoiding discrete decisions. This also has the advantage of modeling stronger and weaker cases – times where a syllable seems somewhat stressed, or a pitch peak is somewhat present, or the peak comes somewhat after the intensity peak. (While there is work suggesting that perception of pitch alignment can be categorical,[37] more often it seems to be a matter of degree.)

This also brings practical robustness, in that this detector works even when the peak departs from the classic form of a mountain with a clear upslope and a clear downslope. For example, it works for the last syllable in Figure 6.2; such cases are common in spontaneous speech. To judge its reliability, I applied it to fifteen minutes of varied data, and then listened to a sampling of places where it found strong evidence for late peak. All but a small percentage of these were indeed late pitch peaks. (Many of the exceptions were *early* pitch peaks: places where a syllable's pitch peak was actually before the intensity peak. This may at times convey haste; however, early peaks are rare in my data, so I don't know if this a common pattern.) While my detector is not entirely trustworthy, since differences between measured and perceived peak positions can arise from pitch tracker errors, aerodynamic effects, microprosody, and so on,[38] it is still useful for locating likely instances of late peak. To be sure, I spot-checked many examples, including all examples in this chapter, both by listening and by plotting the pitch and intensity contours.

After this preparation I was ready to take a systematic look at the functions with which late peak appears. For this I took fifteen natural, unscripted conversations, with a total of thirty speakers and about an hour of conversation. This data was evenly distributed across three dialog types: face-to-face conversations, telephone conversations, and talk while cooperatively playing a two-person videogame. For each speaker I used the detector to find the ten places where a late peak was most saliently present. A patient research assistant listened to all 300 places and categorized the dialog functions happening at each, referring to a list of twenty functions (an earlier, cruder variant of the inventory presented in the next section). The vast majority of the 300 were clearly associated with one or more of these functions. There were only two new categories that she identified as necessary, distress-or-losing-control and telling a story, and with these additions, 220 of the 300 places exhibited one or more of the 22 identified functions.[39] Most of the exceptions were in the gaming corpus, where strongly disaligned peaks were rare, and where, since the dialog was mostly incidental to the game play, it was often not clear what pragmatic function, if any, was intended at any point.

So late peaks are indeed mostly associated with certain specific functions: they don't occur just anywhere or mean just anything.

6.10   A Family of Meanings and a Possible Core

In the literature, several other functions have been identified as associated with late peaks, including incredulity, persuasion, and new information,[40] all of which relate to one or more the functions already discussed. Putting everything together, Figure 6.8 summarizes the meanings commonly found with late

Figure 6.8 Some meanings of late peaks, with links indicating some of the closest relations

peaks, and some of the ways in which these meanings are related. These relations are quite dense, as seen from the fact that late peaks may simultaneously serve multiple functions. For example, back in Example 9, not only was *Drone Five* a proper name, it was also a new topic and also part of a suggestion. Similarly the *Boondock Saints* example, Example 43, was simultaneously grounding, reminiscing, and indicating liking. When multiple late-peak-inducing meanings are simultaneously present, it's likely that there will be multiple late peaks and that they will be strongly late. In a sense this is superposition, where the superimposed meanings are multiply activating the same prosodic form.

Now let's again consider the question of meaning. As in previous chapters, we face the question of how hard to work for a shared underlying meaning. On the one hand, we could just enumerate the various functions and their connections, as in Figure 6.8, and be done with it. We might also note that many of the functions are related to the overall commonalities noted earlier – namely displaying some kind of consideration for the interlocutor, allowing them some freedom of action, mitigating face threats, and marking some type of *irrealis*. That is, we could say that late peaks have a family of related meanings, with no single defining characteristic. Descriptions of this type are sometimes the best we can do, at least for lexical and grammatical meanings,[41] so we could certainly stop there. On the other hand, probing deeper may reveal a non-obvious commonality. Let's try.

Let's start with some lateral thinking, first considering the question of what *aligned* peaks mean. To some extent, alignment is the default: the human organism has a strong tendency to align actions. For example, to synchronize the intensity maximum and the pitch maximum is as natural as synchronizing gesture and prosody or synchronizing toe tapping with the beat of the music.[42] Further, the tendency to synchronize various actions and motions may be stronger in action-oriented situations. The battle cry in Figure 6.1 was followed a second later by a perfectly synchronized lunge and swing of the sword. If we're playing tag, my touch may synchronize with the stressed syllable of *you're ît* (76). Politicians thump the table as they speak to show that they are men of action. In tug of war, a team that synchronizes their pulls with a chanted *hâ, hâ, hâ* (77) is more likely to win. The general connection between language use and action coordination is so fundamental that, echoing the old yo-he-ho theory of language origin, Bangerter and Clark have argued that "dialogue has its origins in joint activities, which it serves to coordinate."[43] Be that as it may, synchronized action seems to evoke aligned peaks.

So, if aligned peaks are associated with action, disaligned peaks may conversely indicate "not action-oriented." This may be their primordial meaning, as summarized in Figure 6.9. This seems to subsume all the observed functions: a speaker who produces a late peak is indicating that they are not about to act right now, and that they're not cueing the hearer to act immediately either.

Late Peak Mapping

Function: indicate lack of orientation to immediate action

Form:

 one or more late pitch peaks

Figure 6.9 Late peak as a primordial prosody pragmatics mapping

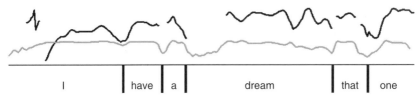

| I | have | a | dream | that | one |

Figure 6.10 Pitch and intensity of *I have a dream*

To speak expansively for a minute, if life is a game of tag, sometimes you need to run around and do things, and sometimes you need to take time to talk about things. The two modes naturally alternate. In one mode, the players are active, with their pitch and intensity peaks generally simultaneous, and often aligned also with physical action: jumps, turns, and touches. In the other mode, players back off and discuss things that might or might not have happened, or that may or may not happen next. This fundamental alternation in life is marked in our language, with aligned versus disaligned peaks.

This perspective allows us to more fully appreciate King's *I have a dream*. As seen by the intensity and pitch contours (Figure 6.10), there are strong late peaks on *I* and *dream*. This probably reflects multiple superimposed factors: King was making a statement that was a powerful imagining. It introduced a new topic, his hopes for the people of Alabama. It was a powerful suggestion. It was an invitation to work together to improve the nation. In addition, we can see a direct tie to the primordial meaning: at that point in history, there were voices inciting action in the streets, but King advocated non-violence, wanting thought to precede action. His late peaks helped to convey this rich message powerfully.

6.11   Distinguishing among the Meanings

If late peaks serve so many functions, how do people figure out which are present in any given utterance? Certainly context plays an important role, as do the words chosen. Superimposed prosodic features are also involved. As an example, let's again consider *I have a dream*. In addition to the late

Table 6.2 *Some other prosodic features likely contributing to some specific functions conveyed by late peaks*

Additional feature	Functions
harmonicity	offering, inviting, requesting, suggesting, expressing approval
low pitch	threatening
high pitch	suggesting, inviting, requesting, suggesting, laughing
creaky voice	threatening, correcting misperceptions, partial agreement, mixed feelings
consonant lengthening	threatening, correcting misperceptions
narrow pitch range	threatening, correcting misperceptions
wide pitch range	suggestions, laughter
nasal voice	appeal to shared knowledge or values
vibrato	warmth

peaks there are at least three other prosodic factors involved: a vibrato, as seen in Figure 6.10, which may convey a warmth of feeling; a high pitch on the unstressed word, which may mark an inspirational, liturgical style;[44] and nasal voice, which may convey appeal to shared values or sincerity.

While the details remain to be worked out, Table 6.2 lists some additional prosodic features that may be superimposed to add nuances, often based on primordial mappings, which may work with the lexical content to enable late peaks to serve specific dialog functions.

6.12   Late Peaks in Other Languages

The precise habitat of late peaks is language-dependent. In English they are bound to stressed syllables, but not all languages have lexical stress. Japanese, for instance, does not, but late peaks still occur, in remarkably similar ways, binding instead to syllables with pitch accent.[45]

As might be expected from the primordial nature of the core meaning, many of the more specific meanings of late peaks are also found across languages. In Japanese, late peaks are associated with suggestions, wishes, and invitations, as in English, but also with apologies and femininity.[46] In Swedish, late peaks serve several functions relating to non-assertiveness,[47] as in English. However, Swedes speaking English often correct misconceptions without using late peak. To me this feels like a display of a non-nonsense attitude, but perhaps it's just a meaningless random prosodic difference.[48] In German, late peaks serve some of the same functions as in English, such as questions, but not others, such as offers and invitations.[49] Germans speaking English thus tend not to use late pitch peaks for these functions, and can therefore appear impolite or too direct. In Spanish, late peaks have some of the same functions as in English, such as inviting inference, plus additional roles.[50] However, Spanish seems not to use late peaks for some functions seen in English, such as making suggestions. So if you have a Mexican on your team, pay a little extra attention, otherwise you may miss it when she proposes a great idea.

Thus, it seems that different languages have extended and adapted the primordial meanings of late peak in different ways. Some of these differences may also reflect differences in culture. Americans are stereotyped as always striving, ambitiously working to build a better future. Certainly, our language is well suited for planning and managerial functions, devoting a significant chunk of the prosodic bandwidth, that involving late peak, to offering, requesting, confirming, correcting misperceptions, and withholding full agreement. In some other cultures, at least by stereotype, people live in the moment. The travel industry promotes the idea that we need to occasionally escape the pressure, and that to truly relax we need to fly to a remote tropical island where the people are more skilled at properly enjoying life. But I wonder whether other cultures are really so different. Perhaps that's just a charming myth, with the real difference being in the means by which languages express those functions. Perhaps the real lure of visiting the tropics is hearing people whose language handles planning and control in ways too subtle for us to notice: perhaps they convey these meanings using lexical means, rather than in-your-face prosody. Personally, I think I need a research grant to do fieldwork on this question, for example in Bali, on the beach . . .

7   Expressing Positive Assessments

One of the true joys in life is saying something positive about someone, preferably to them directly. Prosody has an important role here: English has a specific construction for positive assessments.

7.1   The Positive Assessment Construction

Let's start with some clear cases:

1) *it gives me great plea#sure to present you with this year's staff # award*

2) *thank you for your ser#vice*

3) *good # job*

4) *go Cou#gars!*

5) *stay on it; there you # go*

directed, respectively, to an employee, a man in uniform, a student, a basketball team, and a novice player of a collaborative videogame. Positive regard takes many forms and can be expressed in many ways: praise, respect, admiration, approval, appreciation, encouragement, compliments, flattery, and so on. Prosodically, these examples share a configuration including relatively high pitch, then a lengthened, loud region with clear voicing, and finally a clipped end, that is, a sharp final drop in intensity.[1] Figure 7.1 summarizes these components, and Figure 7.2 illustrates.

The hash mark in each example indicates roughly where the high pitch ends and the loud region starts. To see that this is indeed contributing to the positive feeling, consider the final prosody of two utterances ending in the same words:

6) *there's # a good dog*

7) *what she wants is just a good dog.*

Figure 7.1 The three main components of the Positive Assessment Construction

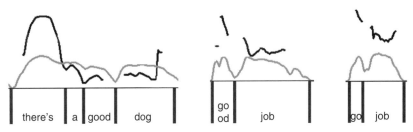

Figure 7.2 Pitch (black) and intensity (gray) for three positive assessments

While the first example, praising the dog, exhibits this configuration, in the second it is absent. The same difference can be seen between *mm* (8) used for positive assessment and an *mm* (9) lacking that meaning.

The strength of this pattern can, as for other patterns, be tuned to the occasion. In the context of an awards ceremony, over-the-top prosody may sound just right, but in a different situation the same prosody may sound condescending or ingratiating, as in

10) *wow boss, that # was great. I always learn so much just by watch#ing you*

11) *Dad#dy, next week, can I, um ...*

Let's take a closer look at the form. One thing to note is that the intensity is only *relatively* loud: the final syllable may not be loud in absolute terms. This prosodic construction, like the others, does not by itself fully determine the values of the features. Rather, its contributions are superimposed on whatever else is there in the prosody. In general, these often include the contributions of a turn end; this construction then adds some energy at the end and sharpens the final intensity drop.

A second interesting aspect of this form is that when the last sound is a consonant, it often includes a final release.[2] In English the usual pattern for word-final consonants is for the sound to end right after the tongue moves up and makes a closure: for example on the /g/ of *dog*. (This is not true for all languages. For example, a stereotypical Italian-accented pronunciation of *big dog* may sound like *bigga dogga*, with the final stops being released, following

---

Positive Assessment Construction

Function: express positive assessment

Form:

timespan	prosodic properties
−1600 to −800 ms	raised pitch
−800 to −200 ms	increased loudness, lengthened vowels
−200 to 0 ms	sharp drop in loudness (clipped end)
0 to 800 ms	silence or other low intensity

mnemonic: High then Loud then Quiet

Figure 7.3 The Positive Assessment Construction. The timings are typical for conversational uses; in stand-alone uses the initial raised pitch may be much shorter

the general pattern in Italian.) However, this construction can overpower the usual pattern, to cause the final consonant to be released. The final bit of air is, incidentally, why Figure 7.2 shows an apparent high pitch at the end of the first and third examples; this is a microprosodic artifact of the consonant release.

The third interesting aspect of this form is that the final syllable is strongly voiced. As a result, this site is suitable for the salient realization of other pitch-related features. These may include superimposed creaky voice to assert control or authority, or vibrato to convey warmth and encouragement.[3]

Figure 7.3 summarizes this construction. This is not the only way in English to convey positive assessment; there are several others: the Bookended Narrow Pitch Construction for grudging admiration; late peaks for liking and admiration; and high and wide pitch with fast rate for expressing happiness and giving good news.[4] Thus of English speakers have many ready ways to be positive in conversation.

7.2   Uses in Conversation

Now let's look at how this construction is actually used in conversation. Often it is used in simple positive assessments of something, such as a product, a situation, or an activity:

12) J: *I also really love the Boon#dock Saints*

13) E: *speaking of which, how do you feel about Monday:*
       Monday's exam?
    G: *I feel # good*

14) M: *it's really cool # like, coming up with # like, you know, a*
program, and then like being able to see # like that # program
on someone else's # phone.

Incidentally, for speaker M the loud part of this construction seems to have an affinity for the word *like*. While the word *like* does have specific pragmatic functions,[5] here it may serve mostly just as a docking site for the second part of this prosodic pattern.

This construction also seems to be used in avoiding conflict. Speakers sometimes say things that could be taken as a challenge or face threat, but in friendly conversations, they usually take care to mitigate these. One way is to use this pattern to convey positive regard of the other person, thereby taking the sting out of something that might otherwise cause offense. For example, in

15) L: *so, how's your semes#ter going?*
E: *um, pretty good. I'm getting As in all my classes.*

L's question is rather blunt and potentially a face threat, especially in a department where the students place great value on academic performance, but his final prosody makes this upbeat and positive-sounding. Similarly, in the following, J signals her positive regard and her intent to be non-judgmental. She uses this construction first on her words, faintly, then again more strongly in her laughter.

16) M: *I don't want to stereotype but, you know*
J: *you can # stereotype [haha#haha*
M: *[aha#haha*
      yeah, you just don't see a lot # of girls playing videogames,
      for some reason

Thus reassured, M goes on to verbalize what he'd hesitated to say. Interestingly, his words, which might have caused offense due to the politically incorrect term *girls*, went over smoothly; his use of this prosodic construction conveys respect for female gamers.

Conversational interactions, according to the philosopher Grice, generally respect certain "maxims":[6] people generally strive to say things that are informative, true, relevant, clear, and so on. Polite English conversation additionally follows more specific maxims. Sometimes these maxims come into conflict. The maxim "be interesting, not vacuous" may conflict with the maxim of "speak well of everyone." Some speakers seem to give absolute priority to one maxim, by never saying anything negative about anyone, although at the risk of seeming dull. A more common strategy is to make negative comments when necessary, but to mitigate them with this construction. Consider

17) *we all have our strengths and weak#nesses, and that's # hers*

where the speaker mentions something negative about a teammate but at the same time, with her prosody, conveys that overall she likes and respects her. In contrast, the same words, *and that's hers* (18), without this prosody may convey a much less positive feeling.

7.3   Considerations of Culture

Speakers of English know how to express positive assessment, but knowing *when* to do so can still be tricky. In my research group meetings, new members sometimes start out by showing great admiration and respect for everything the professors say. While this behavior may be appropriate in some groups, our group is minimally hierarchical and expects ideas to be praised or panned on their merits. New members usually adapt swiftly; after a stern look or two they learn this aspect of our microculture.

Positive assessment also ties in to broad cultural norms. This I realized in the course of some work for a Darpa project. Their need was for techniques to automatically discover sentiment towards various people and groups mentioned in news broadcasts: to identify who was being seen positively and who negatively. Naturally, I tried out using the High then Loud then Quiet pattern. Since we can automatically detect times when this occurs, we can automatically tag the entity mentioned at that time as being viewed positively. This generally worked, but not always; Positive Assessment prosody was also used for other purposes. One interesting case was mentions of recently deceased victims, for example of a stabbing or a traffic accident. Newscasters tended to use this prosody even though nothing praiseworthy had happened. I speculate that this may be a feature of our culture: our taboo on speaking ill of the dead. This dates back thousands of years, perhaps ultimately to some ancient tribal fear of vengeful ghosts.

Be that as it may, it is clear that the uses of this construction are complicated: positive assessment is done for various specific ends in various specific contexts.

7.4   Significance

This prosodic configuration does not seem to have been previously described in the literature. With its important social function, this seems strange, until we think about the history of prosody research.

Configurations like this have been completely off the radar for most lines of research, for reasons related to the traditions surveyed above. Although there is a lot of work on prosody and emotions, including positive affect, this mostly involves primordial prosody expressing emotions like joy, where independent features, rather than feature configurations, are the operative factors. More generally, most prosody research has examined prosodic features as independent streams, for example pitch in isolation or intensity in isolation, and this has led to the discovery of isolated correlations but rarely patterns. Research on the expression of sentiment has recently tended to handle every problem by feeding prosodic features into machine-learning algorithms, leading to models whose behavior is uninterpretable. Another problem is that most computational research in prosody focuses on one of two timespans: the prosody of individual words or the prosody of entire sentences; neither of which permits discovery of constructions like this one. Finally, research in interactional linguistics has primarily examined sit-down conversations, but in such dialogs this pattern generally occurs superimposed with other patterns, which makes it hard to identify.

Thus the limitations discussed in Chapter 5 are not just theoretical problems. Rather they have constrained what the field has been able to discover. Fortunately, we now have new, powerful methods. The next three chapters will explain how these can tease apart the separate contributions of superimposed constructions.

8   Superposition

Having now seen several prosody–meaning mappings, we're ready to consider examples of how these interact. Actually, the only reason why we've not yet seen such examples is that I have been deliberately choosing each example to illustrate just one prosodic pattern and just one salient function. However, in actual dialog, most utterances involve complex prosody and serve several functions at once. This chapter shows how this can be explained in terms of prosodic constructions: in essence, we merely have to recognize that constructions can be superimposed.

8.1   Examples with Downsteps

As seen earlier, the Minor Third Construction can be used to cue action. This section will illustrate how additional prosodic patterns can be superimposed to elaborate this basic meaning.

One feature that can be superimposed is late peak. Since this involves a pitch peak, it superimposes nicely on the Minor Third Construction, which already includes a syllable with high pitch, as in

1) J: *I love^{eth} ics*
    S: (laughter).

This, as already discussed, sarcastically conveyed mock appreciation, but in addition it explicitly cued the listener to laugh.

With the late peak added in a different place, the additional nuance can be different, as in

2) $^{Su-}$ *sa n*

where it conveys, like many late peaks, that there is an unstated implication. Thus, for example, if your child is moving towards water that's too deep for her, this prosodic combination can cue her to infer the danger and display awareness of it. Figure 8.1 shows how the pitch contours of the two patterns can add together to determine the composite pitch contour: a downstep plus a final upturn. Figure 8.2 shows the same process in terms of the pitch height gestures.

Figure 8.1 Pitch contour addition

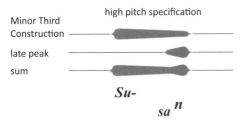

Figure 8.2 Prosodic gesture addition

These diagrams are of course simplifications. While they show only one prosodic feature, the other features also play various roles. For example, the intensity contour associated with the late peak pattern helps determine how it aligns with the Minor Third Construction, to get the pitch upturn in an appropriate location. Developing a model to account for such processes is an unresolved challenge. Nevertheless, we see that, when two prosodic patterns are superimposed, the resulting feature values, across time, may be simply the sums of the contributions of the two patterns. This is the most general form of superposition. The rest of this section will illustrate two special cases.

The first special case is when one pattern does not specify the value for some feature, leaving it free to be entirely controlled by the other pattern. Consider clipped ends. As noted earlier, syllables with an abrupt drop in energy are often used to establish control. A Minor Third Construction with superimposed clipped ends can thus make a strong reprimand, as in

3)   *bad* *dog*

and in

4)   *unh-* *uh*

where the glottal stops after each syllable turn the generic action-cueing effect into a more controlling one, specifically a cue for the listener to immediately stop whatever he is doing.

The second special case is when one pattern overrides some feature values of the other. Consider the superposition of creaky voice, as in

5) *bad* $dog*$

This brings a nuance of authority and distancing that again conveys a reprimand: a cue for your dog to act contrite. Here the Minor Third Construction calls for harmonicity, but creaky voice is physically incompatible with that: they require different laryngeal configurations. The result is that creaky voice overpowers and nullifies that property of the construction. Similarly, in

6) *you're* ^{it}

the superimposed feature is a final high pitch. This turns the utterance from a generic "chase me" cue into something more insistent. In form, this utterance has all the properties of the Minor Third Construction, except one: the pitch downstep has been flipped to a pitch upstep.

These examples illustrate three ways in which superimposed prosody can modify a prosodic form. It can: (1) modify some property of the original form, (2) add a new feature, unspecified in the original form, or (3) override some property of the original form.

8.2   Another Minor Construction: *I'm Good*

While patterns can be superimposed dynamically, as illustrated above, there are also conventionalized combinations of patterns. These often underlie minor constructions. For example, consider a fairly new one, which I first heard a few years ago after offering my daughter more dessert:

7) N: *There is another slice of cake if you want it.*

   D: $I'm^\varphi$ *good*

I was confused. Although I was making an offer, my teenager wasn't treating it as such. At a loss, I mapped it onto the closest thing that made sense to me and retorted *I know you're good; I'm asking if you want cake.* But later, after hearing this also on other occasions, I realized that this was not an error or a rudeness, but a fresh new way to decline an offer. Being highly specific in form, meaning, and contexts of use, this is clearly a minor construction. Eventually, this pattern found its way into my own speech.

From the pitch and intensity contours, as seen in Figure 8.3, it's easy to understand why this form has this meaning. Three constructions are involved: (1) the second syllable is lengthened and louder than the first, matching the Positive Assessment construction, (2) there is a late peak on the first syllable, and (3) there are several properties of the Minor Third Construction, including the downstep and harmonicity. Together these contribute three meanings:

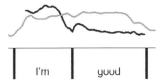

Figure 8.3 *I'm good*: pitch in black and energy in gray

I'm Good Construction

Function: casually decline an offer

Form: Superimposed: Positive Regard Construction
                             Late Peak
                             Minor Third Construction
                             the words *I'm good*

Figure 8.4 The I'm Good Construction

an implication that the current situation is fine already, an invitation to infer something (that no more cake is wanted), and a cue to move on to the obvious next action (to wrap up the cake for tomorrow).

While the superposition of prosodic forms is often fully compositional, here the meaning of the whole is more than the sum of the meanings of the superimposed constructions, as shown by my initial confusion. This is thus a construction in its own right, which we may call the "I'm Good" Construction, as summarized in Figure 8.4.

8.3   Examples with Bookended Narrow Pitch

This section gives a few more illustrations of superposition, all involving the Bookended Narrow Pitch Construction, including some multiply-superimposed cases. First one with a late peak:

8) *why^ᵖ would you do five^ᵖ, if you still have one left?*

which conveys simultaneously a meaning of suggestion and a meaning of contrast. Late peaks are superimposed on both bookends, which are convenient sites for this, being already high in pitch. Consider also

9) *hey, could you^ᵖ guys keep it down?*

which is simultaneously a complaint and a request.

Complaints can also be combined with "list prosody." While this can take many forms, often each item in sequence ends with a mid-level flat pitch,

10) *we need flour, butter, eggs, milk, sugar . . .*

When combined with a sequence of bookended narrow pitch regions, this turns the complaints into a litany:[1]

11) *first she tells me she wants to go, then she tells me she <u>doesn't</u> <u>want to go after all</u>, then ...*

suggesting that these are not isolated events, but are just samples from a much longer list of grievances.

Now let's consider a more complex case:

12) *if I fin�okⁱsh my⁹ classes⁹ this sum⁹mer, I feel wrong⁹ <u>graduating</u> <u>in</u> *May*.*

Here the speaker is imagining one possible future and speculating about what she'd do in that situation. There are three prosodic components, each contributing an element of meaning: (1) the late peaks mark this as speculative, (2) the creak at the end marks her certainty about her feelings, here regarding the idea of participating in the graduation ceremony before completing all her classes, and (3) the Bookended Narrow Pitch construction marks this as expressing a contrast with the alternative of participating in the December graduation ceremony.

Multiple superposition is also present in the following exchange, which occurred after R and J discovered that they were both registered for the same class next semester, Interval Computations, but that J wanted to drop it to take a different class, which was, however, full at the moment.

13) R: *just stay in Interval* (falsetto)
    J: *but I like Human Computer Interaction, like the interfaces,*
        and stuff like that. I like that.
    R: **you can't <u>get a waiver to try</u>⁹ and get in⁹*?*

In the first line R expresses the hope that J stays in the class so that they can be in it together, with the falsetto conveying a strong stance and that she's speaking from the heart.[2] After J explains that she has real reasons to change classes, R produces an utterance which does three things simultaneously: (1) with the Bookended Narrow Pitch Construction, she voices a complaint, that it's sad that the department won't let J take a class she really wants, (2) with the late peaks she makes a suggestion, to try to appeal this, and (3) with creaky voice she distances herself from the suggestion; since she would really prefer that J not actually do this.

Finally, consider

14) E: *let's get to the other topic, about your major*
    L: *these topics are ... we wouldn't talk about <u>this in</u>* <u>*normal#*</u> *life.*

Here E brings up one of the suggested topics of conversation,[3] but L, apparently remembering that the instructions also requested a "normal" conversation, objects. He does this first with a brusque interruption, and then states his reason. For this he uses the Bookended Narrow Pitch Construction to mark a contrast between "normal" and staged conversations. Superimposed on the final bookend is an appeal to the other's common sense, using the Positive Regard Construction to show that he's not putting the other person down, just pointing out a problem with the suggestion.

In general, people in dialog are often trying to accomplish many things at once, and the pervasive existence of prosodic superposition is thus unsurprising.

8.4   Implications

In a watercolor landscape you can add a little more gray, or blue, or white, to make the sky more menacing, more intense, or more ambiguous. Similarly, in an utterance you can mix in various prosodic components to get the exact combination of nuances you want to convey.

There are two ways to do this: concatenation and superposition. Concatenation is familiar: you convey one meaning and then the next. This can be done in separate utterances, or in different parts of the same utterance. Most prosody research has focused on concatenation.[4] This may be in part due to the popularity of symbolic models, as symbol sequences can be easily combined by placing one after the other. For example, Ladd speaks in terms of prosody as based on "strings of tones."[5] While convenient for discussing phenomena that fit this mold, symbolic models lack any obvious way to handle superpositional phenomena.

More applied work has also tended to consider concatenation to be the main form of composition. This can be appreciated when dealing with spoken dialog systems. These are usually designed so that each utterance serves only one purpose. You can't do more than one thing at a time; instead you have to wait until the right point in the utterance sequence. This is one reason why automated dialogs are so inefficient and tiresome.[6] This is partly due, in turn, to the fact that speech synthesizers have been optimized to produce speech that is highly intelligible, but not expressive (although some recent systems are able in addition to express one of a handful of emotions or intents[7]). Superposition has received little consideration.

Yet on the research side, there is a long history of prosody models based on superposition.[8] For example, Xu and Prom-on showed that sentences which combine the two functions of focus and questionhood exhibit pitch contours which are approximately the additive result of the intonational effects of these

A prosodic construction

i)   is a temporal configuration of prosodic features,

ii)   has a meaning,

iii)   is not necessarily closely aligned with words,

iv)   can be present to a greater or lesser degree,

v)   can share aspects of meaning and form with related (sister and daughter) constructions, and

vi)   can appear superimposed with other form–meaning mappings.

Figure 8.5 Essential properties of prosodic constructions

two functions.[9] Clearly, the potential exists for great improvements in speech synthesis and spoken dialog systems.

Be that as it may, for the rest of this book I assume that when constructions are superimposed, the observed prosody is the sum of the prosodic influences of all the constructions, and the conveyed meaning is the sum of the meanings of the constructions' meanings. That is, my working assumption is that prosodic constructions are entirely compositional. This is a simplification in leaving out not only non-compositional effects[10] but also complications such as hierarchical structuring and processes of aligning, warping, fitting, and smoothing.[11] Nevertheless, this simple model will take us a long way.

To summarize, people in dialog often do several things at once with their prosody. This means that we must augment our earlier list of properties of prosodic constructions, with one more, for superposition. Figure 8.5 shows the full list. Together these give us a huge benefit: a model of prosody in terms of such components is a model whose components can be directly inferred from data, as in the next chapter will explain.

9   A Big-Data Approach

Superposition, while wonderful for language users, makes things hard for analysts. Because of superposition, the prosody observed on a given utterance may reflect the contributions of many constructions. This challenge is magnified by the fundamental difficulty of effectively observing prosody in dialog, not least because it is so fast and involves multiple streams of diverse prosodic features.

So we need tools. Fortunately, using prosodic constructions makes superposition relatively easy to model: given sufficient data, they can support simple analyses and fast discovery. This chapter explains how we can do this, using Principal Component Analysis (PCA). The discussion will at times get technical, but mostly we'll stay at the conceptual level. Let's start with a parable.

9.1   A Parable

Imagine that the Cetian Science Foundation has sent you to Earth to study the inhabitants. Floating down from your spaceship, you are immediately fascinated by the fact that they have bodies, and that these are of many shapes and sizes. You start collecting them one by one and measuring everything you can think of, then wiping their memories and releasing them. Eventually you have a collection of data on hundreds of thousands: for each, their height, mass, foot length, upper arm circumferences, pupil size, cornea opacity, fingernail length, hair length, heart rate, blood volume, lung capacity, and much more.

That's good, but back home they want not data but a model: they want to know the underlying patterns behind the observed variation. So you start your analysis, beginning by computing correlations between the various measures. You find, for example, that height and mass correlate, and then surmise the possibility of some deeper factor underlying these two. You define a new composite variable, Factor 1 (F1), as height plus mass, and set out to see what it means. To do this, you realize you need help, so you collect a native informant. Showing him holograms of subjects along the scale, a mind probe reveals that he conceptualizes this as involving "age." Overjoyed, you freeze him for

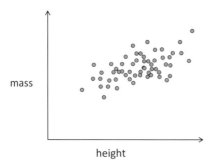

Figure 9.1 Measurements of a hypothetical sample of Earthlings

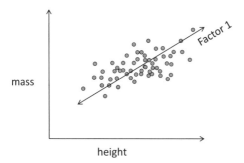

Figure 9.2 Factor 1

later use and beam a report back to Tau Ceti: "I have discovered an important underlying factor in human shape variation, which I call F1 or 'age.' This not only correlates positively with two important variables, but also relates well to a concept present in the Earthling mind."

To illustrate, you attach a diagram like Figure 9.1, where a few dozen humans are plotted on a graph of mass versus height. Clearly they are most stretched out from lower left to upper right. A line drawn along this axis of maximum dispersion (maximum variation) represents Factor 1, as in Figure 9.2.

You further notice that some other measurements also correlate positively with both height and mass, including arm length and leg strength. Others correlate negatively, such as heart rate. You revise your definition of Factor 1 to relate it also to these, and conclude that "Factor 1 (age) not only relates to height and mass, it also explains much of the variation in many other measurements." You would indeed have arrived at a deep understanding of something important about humankind.

While Factor 1 is a scale, the phenomena at the ends strike you as worth describing in their own right. You review holograms of examples of each

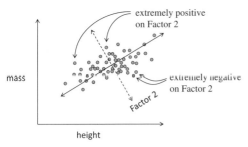

Figure 9.3 Factor 2

extreme: humans who have low F1 values, that is, who are short and weigh little, and humans who have high F1 values, that is, who are both tall and heavy. In the figures these are at lower left and upper right. Thawing the native informant, you find that he thinks of the first group as "babies" and the second as "adults." This seems important, so you spend a little time describing the common properties of cases that exemplify the negative-side pattern of Factor 1 (the babies) and the positive-side pattern (the adults). Both of these are interesting not only in terms of form, with their characteristic configurations of measurements, but also in their functions and roles in Earthling society.

But, of course, no single underlying factor can explain everything about humans. Indeed, this F1, age, doesn't fully explain even the observed heights and masses. In Figure 9.2, the dots don't form a line: some of them are above the Factor-1 line and some below. That is, some humans are heavier than one would expect for their age, and some are lighter. So some of the variance in mass is not yet explained: you need another factor.

There are infinitely many choices, but to maximize predictive power, you chose the second factor to be independent of the first, that is, fully non-redundant. Mathematically, this means that Factor 2 is orthogonal to (perpendicular to) Factor 1. To understand this new factor, shown as a dashed line in Figure 9.3, you again choose to examine two groups of exemplars: those rating highest on this new factor, and those rating lowest. Thawing the native informant again, a mind probe reveals that he thinks of the first group as "fat" and the second group as "thin." You beam back another message to Tau Ceti, announcing a second important factor underlying the observed properties of humans. Your evidence is again twofold: this factor is present, statistically, in the data, and the organisms themselves have a mental concept that aligns with this factor.

The observed mass of any specific individual would then be mostly explained by the additive (superimposed) effects of these two factors: that is, mass would depend on age and fatness. Considering a name for your factor, you might call it "thinness" or "fatness."[1]

You could continue. Although a graph on paper is limited to just two measurements, the math works for any number of measurements and factors. At every step, you choose the factor that (1) is orthogonal to the others and (2) explains as much as possible of the remaining variation, that is, accounts well for things that the factors so far do not. It's like taking apart an onion, where you can peel off the layers, one by one, examining each in turn. When you get to a lower layer, having cleanly removed all the higher layers, what you see is purely the properties of that layer alone. That is, the procedure guides you to then consider only the things that are unexplained by the model constituted by the previous factors.[2]

For example, imagine that you have already identified a half-dozen factors that explain many of the observed values. You would then turn to other, as yet unexplained, correlations. For example, hair length may correlate at best weakly with the factors found so far, but will correlate with things like leg strength and lung capacity (lower in both the very old and the very young).[3] This would give a new factor, Factor 7, say. A mind probe on this might reveal no correspondence to any simple adjective in the prisoner's mind, but weak activation of vague concepts such as "in the prime of life" or "needs a caregiver." Still, it explains something about the Earthlings, so you would announce the discovery of yet another factor.

As you work down into the lower factors, they will gradually tend to become more obscure: accounting for less and less of the variation and evoking ever weaker responses from your captive informant. Some may nevertheless have meanings: for example, your set of measurements could perhaps somehow encode information about such subtleties as "years in the army" or "hours until cold symptoms appear" or "mutation on gene 49287." Thus Cetian science could reveal things unknown even to the humans themselves.[4]

Eventually, funding runs out and you wrap things up. In your final report you point out that your factor-based model is "explanatory" in the sense that, "for any given specimen, simply knowing or estimating the values of Factors 1 through 12 explains much of the overall variation. From this low-dimensional representation, we can easily predict, without having to measure, the values for many other features, such as arm length, heart rate, and so on." You also include a footnote to acknowledge that your model is imperfect and incomplete, and to recommend that the next expedition to Earth include researchers with different skill sets than yours.

Finally, you return to Tau Ceti and an incorporeal parade in your honor.

So, what do you think: was this good science, or a sad story of paltry insight from a roundabout method? Perhaps it was both: since the Cetian had no ability to personally experience what humans feel or do, that is, he could not "get inside their heads," he had few alternatives.

In the same way, we who are curious about language use cannot get inside the heads of language users. This is true even though they are us: the knowledge and mechanisms that we use in the thick of dialog are simply not introspectable to our conscious minds. In particular, our prosody is fast, subtle, and often multiply superimposed. It's like riding a bicycle: while I can do it, I can't explain the force vectors, resonant frequencies, and dynamics, let alone the mental processes and neural mechanisms involved. So, like the Cetian, we need to use discovery methods that are systematic and quantitative.

9.2   Principal Component Analysis

Mathematically, the method in the parable is Principal Component Analysis (PCA).[5] This is a standard way to systematically reduce a large number of related variables to a smaller, more fundamental set: the underlying factors.

Each factor is defined by its weightings on the original variables. For example, if there are just two measurements, height, h, and mass, m, Factor 1 might be height plus mass, $F1 = h + m$, and Factor 2 might be the difference, $F2 = h - m$. In general, there will be weights on the features. For example, for estimating age, the height may matter more than the mass, so its weight might be 1.5, and thus $F1 = 1.5h + 1.0m$. Since the weights depend on the units – inches or centimeters – it's best to z-normalize each set of measurements, that is, to convert the values to units of standard deviations above or below the mean. This also prevents the bigger measurements from swamping out smaller ones, like thumbnail length.

The weights, such as the 1.5, also called loadings, are the heart of the model. Given the loadings and a new specimen with a new set of measurements, one can trivially compute the values of all the factors: F1, F2, and so on. Each factor has loadings on all the measurements, typically some positive, some negative, and many zero. Zero loadings occur when a measurement is irrelevant to some factor: for example, F2 (fat–thin) might have a loading of zero on the hair-length feature.

PCA also gives the amount of variance explained by each factor. For simple problems, like predicting miles per gallon, 90 percent of the variance may be explained by just a few factors, like engine size and car weight. For more complex things, like prosody in dialog, we need to consider many more factors.

There are software packages that do all the math: given a number of measurements for a set of data points, they find the correlations and output the underlying factors. Everything else, though, is up to the analyst: collecting data, deciding how to compute the measurements, and interpreting the resulting factors. Thus we still need significant work and human insight.

For our purposes, the input to PCA is various prosodic measurements and the output is factors that correspond to prosodic constructions.[6] The next section illustrates.

9.3   A Case Study

To apply PCA to a problem we need a population to examine and a set of things to measure. For dialog prosody, rather than captured humans, our population is points in time. For example, we may collect as a data point the time 23.34 seconds into the dialog between Steve and Janelle on November 3, 2014. Rather than bodypart lengths, we measure various aspects of the prosody around that timepoint.

To illustrate, this section will run through a simple example, using only measurements for intensity. Following signal-processing terminology, we'll refer to such measurements as "features" henceforth.

Intensity is an approximation to the perceptual quality of loudness. When people speak, they can be loud or quiet, all the way down to being silent. A single measurement of this is not too informative: for example, if we only know that Steve's intensity at $t = 23.34$ seconds was 68 decibels, then we really know nothing about what was happening in the dialog at that point. Accordingly, we take multiple measurements at different temporal offsets around our moment of interest. For example, if we're interested in the prosody around 23.34 seconds, we'll compute the intensity a little before that point, at that point, a little after that point, further after that point, and so on, as suggested by Figure 9.4. Specifically, we compute the intensity over small temporal regions, or "windows," that together tile a 6-second span of time. We'll refer to these as "time-spread" features: this is the key trick that enables PCA to find temporal configurations.

Further, since we're interested in dialog patterns that may involve both speakers, we take measurements for both Steve and Janelle's behaviors. In this case study we'll use 16 features for each speaker, 32 in all, as seen later in the first column of Table 9.1. Closer to the timepoint t being characterized, we use narrower windows to get finer resolution, and for regions further away we make do with coarser windows, as suggested by Figure 9.4.

Obviously there is a lot of redundancy in these measurements. For example, across many data points t, Steve's energy in the window from t to $t+50$ milliseconds will correlate highly with his energy in the neighboring window, from $t+50$ to $t+100$. This reflects the existence of inertia in speaking: sudden

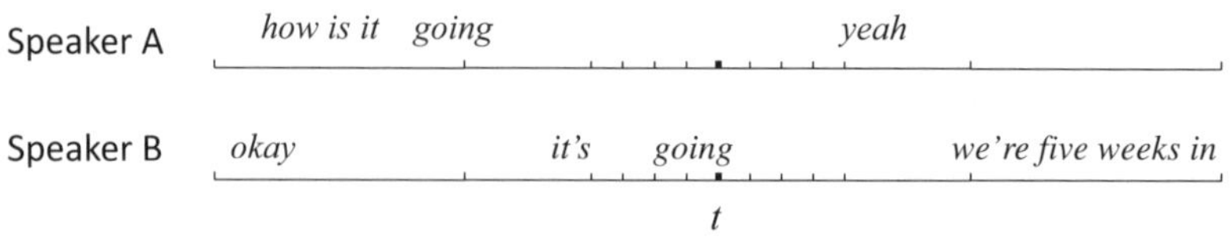

Figure 9.4 Illustration of intensity features across various windows. t is the point of interest, that is, the timepoint whose prosodic context is being described. The tick marks indicate the window boundaries

Table 9.1 *Loadings of the first four factors of an
intensity-only PCA*

Window	Factor 1		Factor 2		Factor 3		Factor 4	
(milliseconds)	A	B	A	B	A	B	A	B
−3200 −1600	−.11	.11	.05	.05	.20	−.20	.31	−.31
−1600 −800	−.14	.14	.05	.05	.25	−.25	.26	−.26
−800 −400	−.17	.17	.11	.11	.26	−.26	.10	−.10
−400 −300	−.18	.18	.16	.16	.21	−.21	−.01	.01
−300 −200	−.19	.19	.19	.19	.18	−.18	−.07	.07
−200 −100	−.20	.20	.22	.22	.12	−.12	−.11	.11
−100 −50	−.20	.20	.24	.24	.06	−.06	−.14	.14
−50 +0	−.20	.20	.25	.25	.02	−.02	−.15	.15
+0 +50	−.20	.20	.25	.25	−.04	.04	−.15	.15
+50 +100	−.20	.20	.24	.24	−.08	.08	−.14	.14
+100 +200	−.20	.20	.23	.23	−.12	.12	−.11	.11
+200 +300	−.19	.19	.19	.19	−.18	.18	−.05	.05
+300 +400	−.18	.18	.16	.16	−.21	.21	.01	−.01
+400 +800	−.17	.17	.11	.11	−.24	.24	.13	−.13
+800 +1600	−.14	.14	.05	.05	−.22	.22	.29	−.29
+1600 +3200	−.11	.11	.05	.05	−.17	.17	.34	−.34

changes in intensity are not common. But redundancy is not a problem for us, since PCA is good at cutting through the clutter of correlated measurements to find the underlying factors.

Together these 32 measurements give us a fairly comprehensive picture of the intensity in the vicinity of time t. We compute these features at every time-point, as t ranges through the data: at $t = 23.34$ seconds we get 32 values, then at time $t = 23.36$ seconds another 32 values, and so on. Since we want to find data on all behaviors, regardless of whether they're led by Steve or Janelle, we compute these features for each data point twice: once with A = Steve and B = Janelle, and then swapped so A = Janelle and B = Steve. For this case study I used 138,000 data points, sampled evenly across a couple hours of data taken from a half-dozen conversations involving various speakers[7] and fed this all to PCA. The output was a set of factors, each defined by its loadings on the features.

Table 9.1 shows the loadings for the first four factors. Since massive tables of numbers have little appeal for human readers, henceforth I'll present only graphs and qualitative descriptions, with the numbers relegated to the supplementary material.[8]

We'll start by looking at Factor 1. From the loadings, and also in Figure 9.5, we see that it is positive when A is silent and B is talking. While obvious from

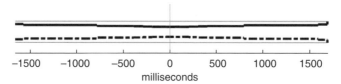

−1500   −1000   −500   0   500   1000   1500

milliseconds

Figure 9.5 Loadings of Intensity-Only Factor 1. Time is on the x axis; to save space, the loadings are shown only over +/− 1700 ms. The solid line shows the loadings on speaker A's features, and the dashed line the loadings on speaker B's features. The height of each line represents the loading on that feature, which can be positive (above the thin line) or negative (below it)

the loadings, it never hurts to verify, so let's look at an example, a timepoint whose F1 value is in the top 0.01 percent. This was at the point marked with a double dagger in the exchange:

1) *A: [your semester . . .] how is it going?*
   B: it's going.
   A: yeah?
   B: we're five weeks in ‡ I'm taking five classes, which is,
      a bit much . . .

Listening, it sounds like B clearly has the floor at the double-dagger point. Listening to other examples confirms that other timepoints that are strongly positive on Factor 1 generally also sound like this, so we may give this pattern a name, such as "Speaker B has the floor," as something more memorable than just "Factor 1 Positive."

Most of the interpretations of the patterns in this book were found using these two techniques: first, examination of a factor's loadings, and second, listening to timepoints where that factor's values are extremely positive (or negative) on a dimension.[9]

Like all factors, Factor 1 also has a negative-side pattern: the mathematical opposite. At times in the dialog when Factor 1 is strongly *negative*, it is A who is talking, with B quietly listening. Thus the positive and negative sides of Factor 1 happen to be symmetric: both describe the same behavior, just with the speakers reversed. While we could give a name to the factor as a whole, like "degree to which Speaker B, not A, has the floor," and speak of this as a scale, it's generally more useful to think of things in terms of two separate patterns, one for the negative side and one for the positive side.

In terms of the overall variance in the 32 intensity features, Factor 1 explains 35 percent of the variance in the six conversations. Plotting the distributions of its values, in Figure 9.6, we see that it is bimodal. This reflects the tendency in English, across any given 6-second interval, for one participant to be mostly talking, with the other mostly silent.

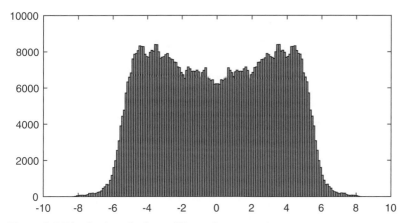

Figure 9.6 Distribution of values of Factor 1

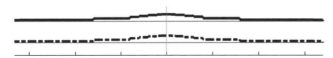

Figure 9.7 Loadings of Intensity-Only Factor 2

Another interesting property of Factor 1 is that the loadings vary over time. Specifically, for the windows further away from $t = 0$, out beyond 1600 ms in the past and in the future, the loadings are weaker. This suggests that pretty-much continuous speech of around three seconds is much more common than pretty-much continuous speech of longer times. While a tenuous inference, a little casual listening confirms that this is indeed true for this data set: in these conversations turns are usually quite short. This illustrates how PCA is good at suggesting patterns and tendencies, but also how we need other methods to confirm or disconfirm them.

Moving along to Factor 2, Figure 9.7 shows that the loadings are positive when both participants are speaking, and thus negative when both are silent. In informal dialog these two cases are not uncommon, and 13 percent of the variance is accounted for by this factor. Factor 2 nicely complements Factor 1. A value of Factor 1 near zero tells us only that neither speaker is clearly holding the floor, but it does not indicate whether both participants are talking or both are silent. Factor 2 provides exactly this information.

Moving on to Factor 3 (Figure 9.8), the loadings tell us that this is positive when A is speaking up to t and then falls silent, and B is, conversely, silent up to t and then starts speaking. Thus this represents a turn hand-off from A

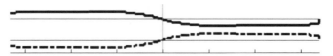

Figure 9.8 Loadings of Intensity-Only Factor 3

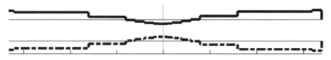

Figure 9.9 Loadings of Intensity-Only Factor 4

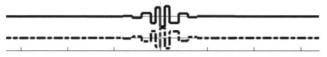

Figure 9.10 Loadings of Intensity-Only Factor 32

to B. Symmetrically, when negative, it represents a turn hand-off from B to A. Turn-taking is complicated, as we will see, but the substantial amount of variance explained by this factor, 7 percent, tells us already that turn-taking is a big deal in dialog.

When plotted, the loadings of Factor 3 look rather like intensity contours. There is no mathematical justification for viewing them in this way, but in practice it has never been misleading to do so. I speculate that this may reflect a fundamental property of language: the most consistently present components of a pattern are also those which are most strongly present.

Moving along, Factor 4 (Figure 9.9) is positive when A is mostly speaking but falls silent for a moment, and speaker B produces an utterance that neatly fits in that gap. This is most commonly a backchannel, such as *uh-huh*. This pattern is also common in dialog, with this factor explaining another 6 percent of the variance.

While some of the other factors in this analysis are probably meaningful, others are probably not, especially as we get into the lower-ranked features. Consider Factor 32, for example, which explains less than 0.2 percent of the variance. The loadings (Figure 9.10) suggest that it mostly serves to soak up the leftover "error" that the other factors cannot explain. Listening to exemplars, many involve microphone pops, breath noise, and the exact micro-timing of laughter bouts: all things without communicative significance. While a 100 percent-complete model of prosody would account for all that, this book is nowhere near that ambitious, and we'll leave many factors unexamined.

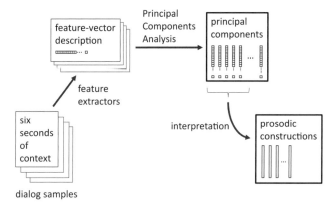

Figure 9.11 Workflow Overview: For hundreds of thousands of dialog samples, we compute many features, then apply PCA to discover the factors (principal components), each a set of loadings (weights) over the features. Finally, we interpret the top factors as prosodic constructions

In this case study we have seen how PCA can be used to analyze prosody, while noting some limitations.[10] It's possible to imagine data sets where PCA would give pathologically misleading results, but in practice this seems not to happen. I speculate that human language has evolved to be fundamentally organized so that the patterns will emerge even when the analysis method or learning technique is not bulletproof. Figure 9.11 overviews the process: I collect data, compute the features, apply PCA to get the factors, and interpret them.

9.4 PCA and Prosodic Constructions

Thus PCA is well suited to the discovery of prosodic constructions. The converse is also true: prosodic constructions are well suited for PCA-based analysis. This is because constructions embody a direct form–function mapping. While some linguistic theories are rich in rules, processes, and structures, a construction-based account dispenses with such intermediaries, instead relating form directly to meaning. Thus with constructions we assume that the ideal form of the construction is directly visible in the data at times when that construction is present. In other words, we assume that it is a fundamental property of language that the "mental representations" of constructions are essentially isomorphic to what we can observe in the data. This assumption is certainly an oversimplification, but does have some justification, as discussed in the literature on Construction Grammar and its relevance for dialog phenomena.[11]

To be used with PCA, the notion of prosodic construction must include two other essential properties: they must be superimposable, as discussed in the previous chapter, and they must be graded, in the sense of being not simply present or absent, but rather present to varying degrees. As illustrated in previous chapters, these fundamental properties seem to be generally present, so it is natural to model prosodic constructions in this way.

Thus constructions suit PCA, and vice versa, as we will see. Although a marriage made in heaven,[12] it wasn't an obvious match until the use of time-spread features made it workable.

9.5   A Couple-Hundred Prosodic Features

For PCA to do its job, it needs a good set of features. Based on the nature of prosodic constructions, these should be time-spread, multistream, and computed for both speakers. They should also have several additional properties. First and foremost, they should be fairly comprehensive. If you measured Earthlings with only a ruler – with no scale, no stopwatch and no blood pressure gauge – you'd get a shallow and warped view of humanity. The same is true if you examine only intensity features or only intonation features.

The rest of the section lists the prosodic features in my primary set and then explains them in more detail. If you're not interested, it's fine to skip this section; none of the subsequent descriptions critically depends on it.

This set has a single feature for *Intensity*, as a proxy for perceptions of loudness.[13]

The set includes four pitch-related features, all based on automatically computed F_0. Pitch height is represented by two features, one measuring generally how low the pitch is in the speaker's range, *Pitch Lowness*, and one how high it is, *Pitch Highness*. In essence, pitch is thus represented with a filterbank of two features.[14] Both of these are numeric, so for example, the pitch over some window can be strongly low or slightly high, depending on how high the pitch is there and how much pitch there is (since silence and unvoiced sounds contribute little or nothing to perceptions of pitch height).

Pitch range also is represented by two features, one for how narrow the pitch range is, *Narrowness*, and the other representing how widely the pitch varies, *Wideness*. Again these are numeric, so that, for example, if there is continuous pitch in a region and pitch height is nearly constant, it will be exceedingly strong on the narrowness feature.

There are no other explicit pitch features in the set. In particular, pitch slope is omitted. This is in part because pitch rises and falls are not something that most people can reliably perceive, except at utterance ends,[15] but mostly because pitch changes over time are something that PCA can discover for us. If, for example, in some dimension at time $t - 200$ the pitch tends to be high, and at $t + 200$ it tends to be low, then logically there must be a tendency for the pitch to be falling around t. Since the feature set includes pitch-height measurements over adjacent windows, PCA can find such patterns.

There is a feature for *Lengthening*. This is the only explicit timing feature; no others are included since PCA is also good at finding temporal configurations. Lengthening is computed by looking for evidence for stretched-out phonemes, that is, regions over which the sound changes little.[16]

Another important property is precision of articulation. This relates to intelligibility and to speaker effort. Although this can be measured for single phonemes, it generally seems to affect larger regions of speech, and in this sense is a suprasegmental phenomenon.[17] When articulatory precision is high, the speech is enunciated, with each phoneme distinct and clear. When it is low, there is articulatory reduction, or slurring, since the articulators only approximately reach the phoneme targets.[18] That is, in reduced speech, the tongue and lips never depart far from their neutral positions, so the phonemes may run together and be hard to distinguish. In this feature set, precision of articulation is represented with features for *Enunciation* and for *Reduction*, both computed by measuring, over voiced frames, how far the sound is from an average neutral sound.[19]

Finally, the set includes features for *Creaky Voice* and *Late Pitch Peak*, as described in Chapters 4 and 6.

9.5.1   Reasons for Using Many Features

In science, parsimony is a virtue: we don't want our models to be more complex than necessary. Traditional approaches to prosody take this to imply that observations should be done using a minimal set of adequate features. This has motivated the strategy of starting by identifying the obviously necessary prosodic features, using minimal-pairs contrastive methods, as discussed earlier.

But if we want a complete model, this is risky: premature parsimony in the selection of features can draw our attention away from factors that are actually relevant. In contrast, if one has a powerful downstream algorithm, such as PCA, it is generally wiser to use a large number of densely extracted features.[20] (Although for practical reasons we do not use an enormous number, to avoid exhausting the available memory on our computers, with the large data sets we're using.) This enables us to rely on the PCA to reveal which patterns are most important, and thus parsimony comes later, as we focus on the factors that explain most of the variance.

The use of a large feature set has another advantage: it helps compensate for the fact that any individual feature may inaccurately represent the perceptual reality, for example, by being vulnerable to noise.

In addition to the diversity of features, it is important that each feature is computed over multiple windows. This has two benefits. First, as mentioned above, adjacent-window features can in combination logically imply the presence of other features, such as pitch slope. Second, this enables implicit normalizations. For example, even a moderately loud syllable can be salient when it occurs in a region of generally quiet speech. With time-spread features, this pattern would show up in the PCA output as a factor with a positive loading on intensity over a few hundred milliseconds, with negative loadings on intensity windows outside that region. Including a high-resolution "foveal" region, that is, having narrower features towards the center of the span, helps such patterns to show up more clearly, and to account for larger fractions of the variance.[21]

Figure 9.12 shows the entire set of 212 features used in this analysis.[22] While this set certainly does not exhaust the acoustic and prosodic features that are relevant to dialog, of which there are literally thousands more that could be included,[23] together they probably capture most of the prosodic properties that are most important in dialog.

One reason for this is that English prosody is highly redundant. In this respect, prosody is very unlike phonology, which is fragile in that two different meanings might be distinguished by only a single feature, as in *pet* versus *bet*. In contrast, meaningful prosodic differences generally are richer. For example, the Minor Third Construction and the Giving-In Construction, although similar in some respects, differ in at least three features: duration, harmonicity, and consonant lengthening. Because of this redundancy, even if a feature set lacks one feature, its presence may be predictable in context from the values of other features. Thus PCA will still find patterns that include it, and when we listen to exemplars of that pattern, we may still hear that feature, even if it was not explicitly in the feature set. For example, for one data set, many extremes on one dimension were rich in noisy inbreaths, although none of the features were designed to detect this. It's interesting to note that redundancy helps not just PCA, but humans too. For example, it is known that pitch movements, up or down, are not something that most people can reliably detect in isolation. However, in context, thanks to co-occurring features, people do not have problems hearing the meanings that these pitch movements help convey.

Finally, use of multiple redundant features sidesteps a common issue: when choosing how to describe the properties of a construction, there are many descriptions that seem different but in terms of realization mean much the same thing. For example, flatness can be described in various ways: as a region of low standard deviation in pitch, as a region where the pitch is approximately linear with near-zero slope, and as a region where the pitch never changes by more than 1 percent per 10 milliseconds.[24] In practice, these definitions all correlate highly, making it hard to decide which to use. Including multiple

intensity	low pitch high pitch creakiness	narrow pitch wide pitch lengthening enunciation reduction late peak
(22 per speaker)	(12 each, per speaker)	(8 each, per speaker)
-3200 – -1600		
-1600 – -1200	-1600 – -800	-1600 – -800
-1200 – -800		
-800 – -600	-800 – -400	-800 – -400
-600 – -400		
-400 – -300	-400 – -300	-400 – -200
-300 – -200	-300 – -200	
-200 – -150		
-150 – -100	-200 – -100	-200 – 0
-100 – -50	-100 – 0	
-50 – 0		
0 – 50		
50 – 100	00 – 100	
100 – 150	100 – 200	0 – 200
150 – 200		
200 – 300	200 – 300	
300 – 400	300 – 400	200 – 400
400 – 600		
600 – 800	400 – 800	400 – 800
800 – 1200		
1200 – 1600	800 – 1600	800 – 1600
1600 – 3200		

Figure 9.12 One set of prosodic features used. Start and end times for each window are in milliseconds offset from the point of interest. These features are computed for both left and right speakers, giving 212 in total

redundant features avoids having to make an arbitrary up-front decision; again we can leave it to the PCA to find the correlating set.

9.5.2   Reasons for Using Unaligned Features

The topic of this book is dialog prosody, but prosody also has many other functions. Thus the prosodic features used here also relate to marking lexical accent, showing syntactic structure, conveying emotion and attitude, and so on. Interesting as these are, for the study of dialog-related prosody, these are distractions that we wish to avoid.

This is one reason why all our prosodic features are computed "unaligned." That is, features are computed over fixed time windows, without regard to where these fall relative to words, syllables, or phonemes. In the world of prosodic feature set design,[25] this is an unusual choice. Most features are usually computed in alignment with some kind of unit or anchored to some kind of event.[26] For example, there may be a feature for pitch slope over the last 200 milliseconds of a turn, that is to say, anchored at turn end, or a feature such as the pitch slope over a word, that is, aligned with a word. However, prosodic features which are anchored to or aligned with other linguistic units tend to relate more to lexical and syntactic functions than to dialog. Hence for our purposes, unaligned features are more appropriate.

More specifically, the features were computed at timepoints sampled uniformly across the dialogs, typically every 10 or 20 milliseconds,[27] without relying on any segmentation of the input. In particular, there was no segmentation into turns or utterances, no identification of words, and no identification of syllables. Thus our method considers prosody as it appears everywhere in the conversations. This is in line with Chafe's idea that "It is futile to limit our attention to isolated sentences. The shape a sentence takes can never be appreciated without recognizing it as a small, transient slice extracted from the flow of language and thought, when it has not simply been invented to prove some point,"[28] Indeed, data points were taken even during silent regions, another uncommon analysis choice, but appropriate in that silence is also a dialog phenomenon, and, as we will see, silence can be part of prosodic constructions.

Unaligned features are not only more relevant to dialog, they also have processing advantages. In spontaneous (unscripted) speech, units such as turns or even words are hard to identify automatically, and the data-hungry nature of PCA makes it impractical to annotate sufficient data by hand. Unaligned features enable fully automatic computations.[29] Even if it were possible to hire enough annotators, all units come with some theoretical baggage. Unaligned features help us see what can be learned from the data directly, unfiltered by preconceptions.[30]

Unaligned features also serve as a way to deal with microprosodic variation.[31] For example, the measured intensity in any small window will reflect the intrinsic intensity of the phoneme at that time, with vowels having more energy than consonants. While these differences may not affect perceived loudness, they do affect the automatically computed intensity feature. Similarly for pitch features:[32] different vowels and consonants have different intrinsic F_0 heights and contours, as a result of momentary changes in the airflow due to the aerodynamics of producing some sounds.[33] In graphs of intonation contours these often show up as tiny bumps and wiggles, as seen many times before. Although sometimes visually salient in graphs, these are not perceptually salient when heard. As these are not intentional, their only communicative role is in the low-level function of helping confirm the identity of the phonemes. They are not perceived as affecting the pitch. Instead, hearers subconsciously compensate for such small dip and rises, applying their knowledge of the regularities of language.[34]

Microprosodic pitch variation is not a problem for controlled speech: one can use sentences carefully designed to minimize them, such as *Marianna made the marmalade*, or otherwise preselect the words that the speakers say, but for dialog this is of course not possible. In work which uses data with transcriptions, either human-provided or given by speech recognition, the prosodic features can be conditioned on the phonemes, but this again requires a lot of extra work.

The strategy here is instead phoneme-blind: the phonetic and lexical content of the utterances is simply not considered. This works out okay for two reasons. First, the feature set computes values not at points but over windows, which are mostly wide enough to span several phonemes, which reduces the effects of any single sound. Second, and more importantly, the method uses a large amount of data, so microprosody-induced individual inaccuracies effectively cancel each other out when patterns are aggregated across many timepoints. Thus the use of large data sets enables us to discover the larger patterns: the general shapes of the ridges and valleys, regardless of the rocks and trees that may complicate any specific hillside.

Using unaligned features, however, is not an unalloyed benefit. It means that caution is required in interpreting the loadings. For example, Figure 9.8 suggested a gradual fade in loudness at turn ends.[35] While this is generally true of English, we wouldn't want to conclude it from this graph alone, since it only shows the fuzzy "average" behavior over many imperfectly aligned cases. Thus a possible distinction between fade-out turn ends and abrupt turn ends may elude a PCA analysis with unaligned features.

9.5.3 Normalization and Robustness

A good set of features should address many desiderata in addition to those already discussed. Each feature should be perceptually valid, that is, it should represent what people actually perceive. The features must be automatically computable, so that we can process large data sets. And, since we're working with real conversations, not laboratory-collected speech, the features should be robust to noise and invariant to extraneous influences. Sadly, no feature set can fully satisfy all these criteria, so we have to make compromises. In fact, no standard set even comes close, so I had to build my own. This section describes some technical issues relating to normalization and robustness.[36] For full details on the exact implementation I used, please download the source code and documentation.[37]

Regarding the intensity feature, two issues arise. The first involves normalization. Since the raw intensity reflects not only communicative intentions but differences in recording conditions and individual speakers' voices, to compensate, the intensity is normalized within each track so that the typical intensity during silent regions is 0.0 and the typical intensity during voiced regions is 1.0. The second issue involves the treatment of silence. Based on the observation that very quiet speech can be nearly indistinguishable from silence, I treat loudness as a single continuum, from loud speech to silence. Thus this feature set does without an explicit feature for silence. Representing silence in this way is an unusual choice in feature-set design, but works well, although with one drawback, as we will see.

Regarding the pitch features, all are computed after converting the raw F_0 values to per-speaker percentiles. This compensates for inter-speaker differences in typical pitch height and range.[38] Like some other normalization techniques,[39] this has the advantage of robustness to many kinds of noise. While it does have the theoretical disadvantage of losing the exact pitch information, this would be an issue mostly if the aim was to process music, where perceptions of pitch are closely tied to log F_0. However, the perception of pitch in speech is generally different, and, in particular, less accurate.[40] This is also why, unlike in many feature sets, pitch values are not directly used as a feature. This is appropriate also because many speech sounds are unvoiced, that is, without pitch. Missing pitch values are a problem for downstream algorithms that need everywhere-meaningful features, including PCA.[41] This well-known problem is commonly addressed by linear interpolation or curve-fitting. While workable for some genres, such as read speech, this can give results that poorly reflect human perceptions. In this feature set the paired features – highness and lowness, and narrowness and wideness – deftly handle missing values. For example, at a time with no pitch the evidence for high pitch is zero, and so is the evidence for low pitch; and these two statements together fully represent the situation.

9.6   Data Selection

In addition to features, PCA also needs data points. These were mostly taken from one primary corpus, of casual dialogs in American English.

These were recorded in El Paso, Texas, in 2013 by my student Steve Werner. In terms of dialect, El Paso English has no real distinguishing features, and in particular none of the typical properties of an East Texas or Southern dialect. In terms of conversation culture, El Pasoans are stereotypically unpretentious, patient, and considerate, and those qualities are often evident in these dialogs.

El Paso is a bilingual city, with Spanish as common as English, but all of the speakers in the primary corpora were native or highly proficient speakers of English.[42] The primary corpus also includes a few speakers from outside this region

As the main genre addressed in this book is casual conversation, these recordings were of conversations among university students, all in the Computer Science Department at the University of Texas at El Paso, and thus all having many things in common to talk about. Steve had them come in to the lab for recording, and most were friends or acquaintances, with one pair of strangers.[43] Wanting spontaneous, everyday conversations, we gave them no constraints, although for some pairs we did suggest possible topics to start with. While the dialogs were induced, rather than freely occurring, they were all among people who might have had a conversation anyway that day, so in that sense, at least, they were natural.

From the nineteen conversations collected, I selected six to work with. This was because I wanted the total to be no more than around 80 minutes, for ease of processing.[44] I chose these six primarily on the basis of perceived quality: I wanted conversations in which the participants were clearly interested and enjoying the interaction. While conversations among people who are tired or unengaged are also part of the reality of human existence, in this book I wanted to focus on the behaviors of engaged people having good conversations.

The rest of this book relies heavily on this corpus, processed by PCA with the 212 features described above.[45] Most of the examples are also taken from this corpus. In addition, the discussions are informed by four similar studies, done earlier with different feature sets and different data sets, namely (1) a set of task-oriented dialogs, again recorded in El Paso, in which the speakers were playing videogames together,[46] (2) another set of casual conversations in El Paso,[47] (3) a collection of telephone conversations, recorded mostly in East Texas,[48] and (4) a collection of puzzle-solving dialogs recorded in Edinburgh, Scotland.[49] These data sets are diverse in dialect, speaker aims, dialog activities, and situations, but across all, most of the top few PCA-derived dimensions were similar. Overall, the fact that similar findings are seen across these sets suggests that the prosodic constructions described here may truly be properties of American English in general, and probably also of other dialogs.

9.7   Summary

This chapter has illustrated how PCA can find interesting configurations and interesting examples, automatically. To summarize, I apply PCA to data points, each a point in time in a conversation, with each point described by various observed prosodic features. The output is then a set of dimensions, which are configurations of features that occur frequently together.

The features are a critical ingredient. The set adopted here works well because they are robust, time-spread to tile a span, varying in duration to give a foveal region, unaligned, inspired by what is known about the human perception of prosody, and numerous. As long as these criteria are met, PCA can be productive, with the exact details being less critical. I say this because, in my experience, using different feature sets causes the picture to change slightly, but the highly ranked factors include mostly the same patterns regardless.[50] This robustness suggests that the patterns described in this book are not linked just to this feature set, but are truly general patterns of American English.

Previous chapters having illustrated how prosodic constructions are useful for *describing* dialog prosody, this chapter has begun to explain how they are also useful for *discovering* things about prosody. The next chapter will complete the explanation.

10 From Patterns to Meanings

Principal Component Analysis, as the previous chapter explained, can find patterns in the data and direct our attention to places that exemplify these patterns. That's what the mathematics provides. After that, it's up to us to examine the patterns and listen to the exemplars, to figure out what they mean. Applying PCA with 212 features to the primary corpus gives us 212 dimensions. Eventually we'll examine all the top dozen, but this chapter will cover just a few selected to illustrate how the PCA-derived patterns relate to meaningful constructions.

10.1 The Minor Third Construction, Revisited

Let's first consider Dimension 12. Figure 10.1 shows the loadings on the negative side. From this point on, all the loading lines are smoothed, to hide the meaningless discontinuities that otherwise appear where feature windows abut. The A speaker features are above, with solid lines, and the B speaker features below, in dashed lines. This may look complex, but we can understand it piece by piece.

First, the intensity line for A indicates that this involves two regions of speech, separated by an intensity dip, such as silence.

Second, the loadings for A's pitch highness decrease over time, and those for A's pitch lowness increase. This is clearer in Figure 10.2, which shows, across each time window, the difference between the loading of pitch highness and pitch lowness. (An additional advantage of looking at plots of differences is to avoid the potential confusion that arises due to spurious correlations between the various pitch features and loudness; the drawback alluded to earlier.)[1] Thus we see that the pitch of the first speech region is higher than that of the second.

Third, the other A-side pitch feature loadings indicate that both regions tend to have pitch that is more narrow in range than wide. This tendency is seen more clearly in Figure 10.3, which shows across each time window the difference between the loading of pitch wideness and pitch narrowness. This indicates that the first region tends to be fairly flat in pitch, with this tendency fading out during the second region. In future figures, for readability, we won't

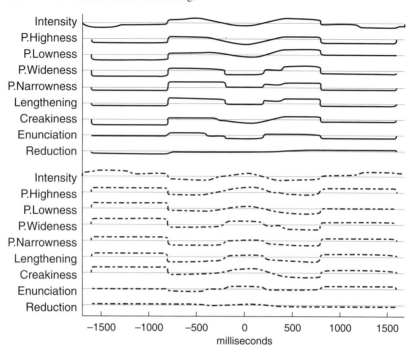

Figure 10.1 The loadings of Dimension 12, negative side (the Action Cueing / Minor Third Construction)

Figure 10.2 "Pitch Height," namely the differences between the loadings on Pitch Highness and loadings on Pitch Lowness, for Dimension 12, negative side

Figure 10.3 "Pitch Range," namely the differences between the loadings on Pitch Wideness and loadings on Pitch Narrowness, for Dimension 12, negative side

look at all four pitch features; rather just the two difference-based lines, namely "Pitch Height" and "Pitch Range."

Fourth, the loadings for lengthening suggest that both regions tend to have lengthened syllables.

Doesn't this all sound familiar? These aspects include all the most salient properties of the Minor Third Construction, as discussed in Section 3.5: two words separated by a syllable boundary, both lengthened and flat in pitch, with a pitch downstep between the two.

Action Cueing Construction (Final)

Function: cue the hearer to do something
    1) when there is single obviously appropriate action
    2) when doing this action is required by a social norm
    3) when this action is easy to do, and
    4) when this action should be done immediately

Form:

timespan	prosodic properties
–800 – –200 ms	O: region of high, flat pitch
–200 – +200 ms	O: short intensity dip, a word or syllable boundary
+200 – +800 ms	O: region of mid-range, flat pitch, about 3 semitones below the first
+1200 – 1600 ms	N: high-pitched response

mnemonic: Minor Third

Figure 10.4 The Minor Third Construction, Final

This is kind of amazing. A purely mathematical procedure, done without reference to words, meaning, or function, reveals a form, and this form turns out to match one discovered by researchers who used completely different methods. Is this just a coincidence? Perhaps not. There are two additional reasons to think that this dimension really does correspond to the Minor Third Construction. First, in the loadings for B, the interlocutor, the intensity line jumps up about a half second after the end of the Cueing Construction. This is no surprise: as discussed in Chapter 3, this construction serves to cue a response. Second, many of the extremes on this dimension exhibit not only this form but also the meanings earlier identified for this form. Such exemplars include Examples 3.27 and 3.28 above.

Interestingly, the loadings also suggest two other properties for this construction, neither reported in the literature: a decrease in articulatory precision from the first region to the second region, and a tendency for the interlocutor's response to come in high pitch. These are indeed often present, as seen in many of the examples in Chapter 3.

The loadings also show the typical temporal configuration of these features. The timing properties differ from those reported earlier, which were based on scripted performances, and thus apparently slower in pace. Figure 10.4 is a revised summary of this construction, using time values inferred from the Dimension 12 loadings. It's worth stressing that is really just a summary: the true form of any pattern is fully described only by the loadings on all 212 features. However, for readability, summaries will mention only some of the features, and only at times when their loadings are strongest. Incidentally, while I earlier described this as a construction used by one person to cue a response or action by the interlocutor, here the loadings suggest thinking of it as a joint construction, collaboratively performed by both participants.

10.2   Attributing Meanings to Patterns

Before examining more dimensions, let's step back for a minute, to consider how we can know that a prosodic form has a specific meaning. While a hoary philosophical question, intractable in the general case,[2] it's usually actually not that hard.

10.2.1   Qualitative-Inductive Methods Work Well

Starting with PCA puts us ahead of the game, because the patterns that it finds are guaranteed to represent collections of features which occur together more often than they would by chance. Therefore, they are prime candidates for being meaningful prosodic constructions. Moreover, for any factor output by PCA, it is an easy computation to locate where in a corpus it is highly positive or highly negative. Such extreme points are exemplars: places where a construction, if one indeed exists, will be strongly present, and its meaning is likely to be especially visible.[3]

From this starting point, my method for determining the meaning of a dimension side is a three-step process, with nothing original about any of the steps.

The first step is to identify the functions present at exemplar times, that is, when the dimension is present either strongly negatively or strongly positively. Following common practice in Conversation Analysis:[4] I listen and consider the context holistically, including the prior and follow-on behavior of the speaker and of the interlocutor. I pay attention both to the prosody and to the words, especially the words immediately surrounding the exemplar time-point. I do this without transcriptions or prosodic annotations, since it's usually better to do analysis based on direct listening. I make and record observations impressionistically, using any suitable descriptive terms, traditional or not. There may be many descriptors, since at any given moment in a dialog typically many things are simultaneously happening, and they can be described at various levels.

The second step is to sift through the lists of descriptors to identify those shared by many exemplars. These are then candidate generalizations for the shared meanings or functions. This is thus a bottom-up, qualitative-inductive approach.[5] Coming up with a candidate generalization can be tricky, as the initial observations may have been recorded using different terms for essentially the same function. For example, three examples described variously as "challenging," "correcting," and "contradicting" may all involve essentially the same dialog activity. To find the best-fitting generalization, I often have to go back and listen to the exemplars again.

The third step is to determine which of these candidates is valid. To do this I examine new extreme examples, not considered in the first step, and usually taken from different dialogs. I consider an example to support a candidate generalization if it matches the description, and one to falsify it if the functions observed are incompatible. My policy is to accept a generalization if it is supported by a large fraction of the examples and contradicted by none. If a generalization does not meet these criteria, I go back to step one and examine more exemplars to find a new generalization.

Incidentally, it is not unusual to see examples which neither support a generalization nor falsify it. There were a few common reasons for this. First, even though the computed features are fairly accurate generally, at any specific timepoint some feature value may not accurately reflect what the ear hears, due to the effects of microprosody and robustness issues. Thus some extreme points found for a factor may not actually exhibit the general prosodic pattern. Second, creative and non-literal uses of prosody, for example, in sarcasm and reported speech,[6] often flout the general tendencies. Third, there are differences among speakers in their prosodic behavior. Fourth, a few dimensions included examples of more than one function; this was the case for Dimensions 5 and 12, as we will see. More fundamentally, since the pragmatic force of any individual construction depends on the local context, including other constructions simultaneously present, and since my working assumption, that meaning is compositional, is only approximately true, it is easy to see why a pattern's general meaning may not be observable in some instances.

This process generally went smoothly, with a couple of hours' work usually sufficient to understand both the positive and negative sides of a dimension.

10.2.2 The Possibility of Bias Is Slim

Each decision here – whether an example supported a generalization, falsified it, or neither – was ultimately a judgment call, so it's important to consider the possibility of bias. In many situations, people hear what they expect to hear, so it's not impossible that my judgments were contaminated by my expectations. However, this does not seem likely, for three reasons.

First, many of the interpretations were done while working in pairs, with a student and I constantly comparing perceptions. We spent a lot of time examining the details of specific examples, frequently listening to them many times, and sometimes listening to several minutes of context to really understand what was going on.

Second, the functions associated with constructions are fairly specific, and so it was almost always easy to tell whether an example supported or contradicted a generalization, for example, of "showing authority" or "giving factual information." Ambiguous cases certainly may exist, but at the exemplar times it was generally obvious whether or not a candidate function was present.

The third reason to believe that such judgments were solid was an inadvertent experiment. My code originally output timepoints in terms of seconds, but the audio player took inputs in minutes and seconds, so we always had to do a little mental arithmetic to convert, for example, from 823 seconds to 13:43. Since this was error prone, one day I modified the code to do the conversions for us. The next morning, Yuanchao and I resumed our examination of some dimensions of Mandarin and found it very hard going. Unlike the day before, we were unable to find any good generalizations for the meanings of constructions, or even to confirm those we had identified earlier. I ended the analysis session early, quite depressed. While taking a long walk to recover, I remembered that I had changed the code. The problem was a bug that had made half the timepoints wrong: 80 seconds became 1:20, but 100 seconds became 2:40 instead of the correct 1:40.[7] After fixing it, the next day we revisited the dimensions, and as usual, found clear commonalities in meaning. The moral of the story is, while you may have a bias towards fitting data into patterns, if the examples really don't fit, you can't force them.

10.2.3   Confirmation Is Often Possible

While this PCA-based workflow is the mainstay of the results presented in this book, it is not the whole story.

In particular, I looked to other sources of information to check the interpretations it led to. One source is native-speaker intuitions. Sometimes it's useful to know, for example, what contrastive prosody would mean if produced on words not implying contrast, as in Example 2.5. Even if the corpus included an utterance like this, it would be enormously time consuming to find it, but it's quick to make up an example, say it out loud, and see how it sounds, that is, hear what it might mean. Since this can be risky – linguistics has seen more than one theory built on the shaky ground of examples made up according to the principles of the theory itself – such evidence is used sparingly in this book. The second source of confirmatory evidence is observation in daily life. For example, many of the Cueing Construction and Late Peak examples were observed in the wild, with the observed meanings always fitting well with the functions inferred from the corpus data. The third source of confirmation is informal production studies. These were a side-effect of my attempt to reduce the gender imbalance in the audio illustrations by occasionally asking one of my daughters to produce an utterance to illustrate some pattern. For this, I took care not to instruct her in the prosody to use; rather I only described the situation, the intent or function to convey, and sometimes the words to use. So she had no bias to use any specific prosodic form, yet the result always matched the corresponding pattern from the PCA. The fourth source of confirmation is evidence in the research literature. While seldom available – most reported observations and findings are irrelevant to dialog, and irrelevant in particular to the prosody–meaning mappings identified here – when present this is the best type of confirmation.

Thus there are many ways to independently verify insights suggested by the PCA-based workflow. Much more of this should be done, and at present the possibility of error is not zero, but each attribution of meaning to a pattern in this book is supported by good, diverse evidence.

10.2.4 Examples Are Chosen Carefully

The final step of the process is documenting and explaining the findings. My strategy has been to explain briefly and use carefully chosen examples to evoke the reader's own intuitions. Thus the examples are critically important, so it's worth saying a few words about where they come from.

Most of the examples in this book are from the primary corpus. These were selected, from among many examples, as ones that clearly illustrate the general meaning without requiring lengthy explanation of the context, and in which the prosodic pattern was clearly evident, without being obscured by superimposed patterns. In the interest of conciseness, each example is presented with only enough detail to illustrate the points, with no attempt to follow consistent transcription conventions, since the audio is always available as the complete, veridical record.

Some of the other examples are taken from other corpora. When the rights are unavailable, I re-enact them in my own voice. There are also some re-enactments of utterances observed in the wild, by me or a daughter. (In terms of dialect, I am originally from Southeast Michigan and my daughters are El Paso natives.)

Finally, as noted above, there are some made-up examples. To reduce the risks alluded to earlier, in this book most of these are simplified versions of actually observed uses, and no claim is based only on made-up examples.

10.3   Three Patterns Revisited

This section looks at three more PCA-derived dimensions that also happen to match up with a pattern already described, further illustrating the utility of the method, and then discusses a few more aspects of the discovery process.

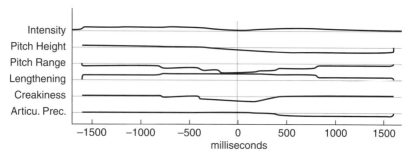

Figure 10.5 The loadings of Dimension 11, positive-side (the Bookended Narrow Pitch Construction)

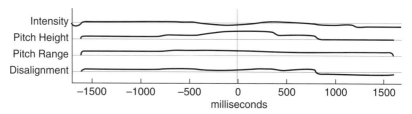

Figure 10.6 Some loadings of Dimension 10, negative side (Not Action-Oriented / Late Peak)

10.3.1   The Bookended Narrow Pitch Construction

Figure 10.5 shows some of the loadings of the positive side of Dimension 11. (Here and henceforth I'll only show loadings that are relevant, for conciseness. Full diagrams for all of the top dimensions, plus the numeric loadings are available at www.cambridge.org/ward. Also for conciseness, I'll henceforth show a line for "articulatory precision," representing the difference between enunciation and reduction.)

Clearly, the strongest loadings here are for pitch range: it is strongly narrow for a second or so. This is reminiscent of the Bookended Narrow Pitch Construction, although the bookends are missing.[8] Listening to some extremes, the most common clear function is contrast, so this really does seem to be the same construction. Indeed, Example 9 of Chapter 2 was identified by examining extreme examples of this dimension.

10.3.2   Late Peaks

Dimension 10 negative has the loadings shown in Figure 10.6. The strongest loadings are for pitch height, so this dimension relates to a pitch peak.

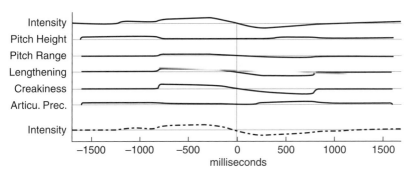

Figure 10.7 Some loadings of Dimension 6, positive side (Positive Assessment)

Atypically, the pitch peak occurs aligned not with an intensity peak, but with an intensity dip.

Again, this is something familiar: such disalignment is the key characteristic of late peaks. The loadings further suggest that late peaks tend to occur in the midst of a region of wide pitch range. Examining some exemplars of this pattern reveals that many have the functions discussed earlier. Indeed, Examples 6.43 and 6.68 were found in this way. Curiously, the loadings on the disalignment feature itself, designed to capture late peaks, are only mildly positive. This may be because that feature does not suffice to capture very delayed late peaks, occurring several hundred milliseconds after any energy peak, so PCA discovered another pattern which does capture those cases.

10.3.3 The Positive Assessment Construction

Figure 10.7 shows some of the loadings for Dimension 6 positive. This shows a region of increased pitch, followed by a region of lengthening and increased intensity, then silence. In addition, the loadings on the pitch features are generally high, indicating the presence of clear voicing. These are all properties of the Positive Assessment Construction; once again, PCA succeeds in delivering us a meaningful pattern.

10.3.4 Dimensions and Patterns

The process of identifying constructions from dimensions is not always trivial. Depending on the configuration of loadings, the same 212 features can represent constructions of many types. Some span several seconds, while others are mostly about what's happening over a second or two. Some represent

Table 10.1 *Dimensions discussed so far*

	Function (form)	Type
6 pos:	Positive Assessment (High-Loud-Quiet)	either speaker
10 neg:	Non-Action-Oriented (Late Peaks)	one speaker (B)
10 pos:	ditto	one speaker (A)
11 pos:	Consider This (Bookended Narrow Pitch)	either speaker
12 neg:	Action Cueing (Minor Third Downstep)	joint pattern (A leads)
12 pos:	ditto	(B leads)

joint behaviors, with both participants involved. These can be of two types. In the first, both participants are doing the same thing, and in the other, they are doing opposite but complementary things. Other patterns represent two independent actions, at the two extremes, which either speaker may perform.[9] Others involve two unrelated patterns, such as Dimension 6, which conveys positive assessment by either the A speaker or the B speaker on the positive side, but conveys something else on the negative side, as we will see.

Table 10.1 summarizes the examples discussed so far.

Incidentally, most of the dimensions seem to exhibit some kind of symmetry in their loadings, being either symmetric, the same for both speakers, or antisymmetric, opposite for the speakers. There is no mystical power here. For one thing, few of these symmetries are as perfect as they seem in the graphs. For another, they are partly an artifact of the use of PCA, which often results in dimensions with some form of symmetry.[10]

10.3.5   Stories of Discovery

For convenience of exposition, earlier chapters presented evidence without regard to the order in which it was found. This subsection describes the actual order of discovery, to document what PCA contributed in each case.

For the Minor Third Construction, I first became aware of the pattern in an earlier exploration with PCA, on a different data set using a different feature set.[11] In that analysis, examination of Dimension 37 led me to the example used as the opening illustration in Chapter 3, which I naively characterized as illustrating a "sing-song" pattern that could function as an "adjacency pair start." Later I found the connection to what Day-O'Connell had identified as the Minor Third pattern, with ties back to earlier work on the calling contour.[12] The same pattern showed up in a PCA-based analysis of videogame play,[13] and I initially wrote Chapter 3 on the basis of these findings. Finally, the same pattern showed up as Dimension 12 of the present analysis.

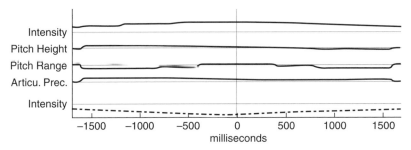

Figure 10.8 Some feature loadings of Dimension 1, negative (A is speaking)

For the Bookended Narrow Pitch construction, I similarly noticed it first during an earlier PCA-based exploration,[14] and then made the connection to the contradiction contour and related forms in the literature. I initially wrote Chapter 2 on that basis, before the construction showed up again on Dimension 11 of the present analysis.

Late peaks were something I first became aware of from the literature. I then wrote a feature detector for them, and wrote Chapter 6 based on the examples it led me to, before finding them also revealed by Dimension 10 negative in the present analysis.

The Positive Assessment Construction was discovered purely as a result of the present analysis. For this, PCA was truly indispensable, as explained in the next section.

Thus in each case the PCA contributed something. This was true also for the other constructions in this book. For some, PCA helped more precisely identify the form or better understand the functions conveyed, and some constructions were discovered entirely thanks to PCA.

10.4   Disentangling Declination

Across the sciences, PCA is often used for its ability to tease apart independent factors, when each individual data point messily embodies the combination of multiple superimposed factors. PCA also does this for us; this section examines declination as a case study.

First let's consider Dimension 1. Figure 10.8 shows some of the negative-side loadings.[15] The intensity loadings tell us that this is associated with one speaker talking for a few seconds while the other is mostly silent (just as we saw earlier in the first dimension of the intensity-only analysis). Looking at the pitch height of the active speaker, we see an overall tendency for the pitch to be higher towards the beginning of an utterance and lower as it progresses.

The fact that pitch tends to drop over time is well known, but it is still a pleasant surprise to see this phenomenon show up here without any special analysis: it's directly visible in the first dimension given by PCA.

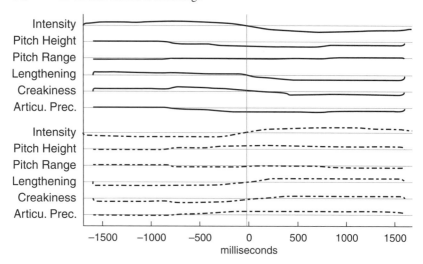

Figure 10.9 Some loadings of Dimension 3 (Turn Yielding)

Now let's consider an old question in intonation: whether declination is attributable entirely to physics (pitch dropping as the speaker runs out of air), or whether it is something that speakers deliberately control (for example to signal turn ends). Looking through the dimensions, the intensity loadings indicate that Dimension 3 relates to turn exchanges (Figure 10.9). The loadings also show a tendency for the pitch to drop about a second before the speaker ends his turn. Because Dimension 1 already accounts for the effects of declination, this implies that the pitch decrease of turn ends is an orthogonal, independent factor. This gives an easy answer to the classic question: it implies that pitch declination is partly deliberate. This is by no means a new finding,[16] but it nicely illustrates how PCA can separate out superimposed factors.

This also helps with an associated practical problem: the way declination complicates analysis of prosody. Instrumentally, we can measure the height of pitch peaks in Hertz, but what matters to listeners is instead how high the pitch is relative to the declination. Thus, for example, an objectively small pitch peak near the end of an utterance can be perceived as equal in magnitude to a larger one early in an utterance.[17] Since human listeners subconsciously compensate for declination, models of prosody must do so also. The usual way to do this is with explicit preprocessing, typically fitting a line to the pitch across an utterance, then subtracting that from every value.[18] However, with PCA no such mechanism is required. Since the model is based on superposition, the pitch patterns handled by Factors 1 and 3 do not affect the other factors. Thus analysis of the properties of other factors can proceed without considering declination: those layers of the onion have already been peeled away. Thanks to this helpful property of PCA, the Positive Assessment Construction, Dimension 6, positive, emerged clearly, separated out from the clutter of other reasons why pitch and intensity go up and down.

10.5   Implications

This chapter has shown how we can use PCA-derived dimensions, very directly, to identify meaningful constructions.

It amazes me, every time, when a dimension output by PCA, a purely mathematical procedure, corresponds to some phenomenon uncovered by great effort by researchers over the years. We've seen this so far for three constructions and two aspects of declination, and in the next three chapters we will see many more. In fact, it turns out that there are meaningful constructions associated with all the top dimensions. Why? Although not an inevitable result of PCA as a mathematical procedure, it can't be just coincidence. I think this is likely due to some fundamental properties of language use. In particular, configurations of features which co-occur more often than they would by chance are likely to be meaningful prosodic constructions, and the most statistically important dimensions of variation in observed prosody are likely to be the dimensions that are the most meaningful to speakers of the language.

Such fundamental questions aside, in practice PCA is very useful: indeed its use is the critical innovation that led to this book. Previously, each fact and insight about the prosody of dialog has been a hard-won triumph by a dedicated researcher or team. Research on prosody, especially on the prosody of dialog, has been slow going. PCA enables much faster progress.

Of course, PCA does not do all the work for us. It serves to identify interesting patterns and exemplars of them, but the rest still requires human effort. This is not unique to this method: all methods for identifying prosodic meanings rely, in one way or another, on observation and subjective judgments. What PCA does is help make the process of observation more efficient and effective, especially for analysis of large data sets. Overall, this workflow can be said to combine strengths from all the major approaches to prosody research: with signal processing it shares the ability to obtain insight from large data sets, with Conversation Analysis it shares the focus on what people are actually doing in dialog and the practice of patient listening, and with phonetics it shares the ability to uncover the significance of barely perceptible detail.

Well, now that we see how PCA can be useful, let's use it. Onward! The next three chapters will examine the prosodic patterns associated with the top 12 dimensions, thereby covering a large chunk of English prosody. We'll start in the next chapter with the prosodic constructions of turn-taking.

11   Turn-Taking Constructions

In dialog, when one person stops talking and someone else starts up, the hand-off is often surprisingly fast, with gaps between one turn and next often just a few hundred milliseconds.[1] Though we take this for granted, in fact it involves superlative feats of coordination. To appreciate this, consider voice user interfaces, the kind you may get when you call a bank or an airline. These typically take at least a half second to even realize that you've done speaking. Only then do they start recognizing your words and deciding what to say, so there can easily be a full second of silence before the response arrives, as suggested by Figure 11.1. We've grown used to such behavior, but if a human were to act like this we'd consider them dim-witted, inattentive, or obnoxious.

In contrast, human turn-taking is generally swift and smooth. How is this possible? Human conversationalists, like computers, still need to understand speech and formulate responses, and these things take time.[2] But humans have in addition the subconscious ability to produce and interpret subtle signals that enable them to predict what will be happening soon, for example, when the interlocutor will end her turn. Prosody is an important part of this.[3]

This chapter presents some of the prosodic constructions involved in turn-taking. It starts with the main construction, an intricate joint pattern. It then discusses some between-turn and within-turn phenomena, including fillers, supportive overlaps, meaningful silences, and rhythm. It then takes a deeper look at backchanneling, and finally considers how turn-taking varies across situations and cultures.

11.1   The Basic Turn-Switch Construction

Figure 11.2 shows the loadings of Dimension 3. From the intensity loadings it is evident that this relates to turn-taking: the A-track speaker is talking up to a point and then silent, and conversely, the B-track speaker is quiet and then speaking.

The loadings of the other features reveal the typical prosody before the turn hand-off. About a second before ending a turn, the speaker typically produces a

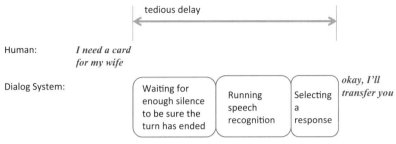

Figure 11.1 Some components of turn-taking delay in voice user interfaces

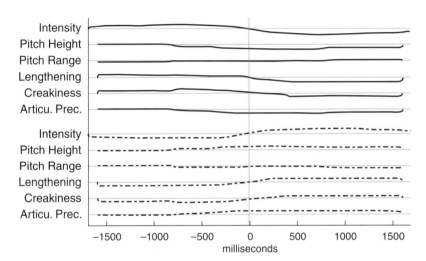

Figure 11.2 The loadings of Dimension 3, positive side (Turn Hand-Off)

bundle of characteristic features, including higher pitch, narrower pitch range, and lengthening. This is followed by a region of lower pitch and increased creakiness, and then a half second later by the turn end.

This pattern is summarized in Figure 11.3: I'll refer to this as the Basic Turn-Switch Construction.[4] An example is seen in the last two lines of the following exchange, where M explains why he plays Halo online only when he's mentally in top form:

1) M: *so, it's really competitive, but like, I can't play Halo*
   if I'm not like, at my game.
   J: <sil:0.3> *oh, I know, huh.*
   M: <sil:–0.2> *'cause I, I don't wanna, otherwise I'm just gonna get*
   like, ⌜*wiped all* ⌝ ∟ *over the floor*⌟ *and*
   J: <sil:–0.4> *and you're just gonna feel horrible abut yourself.*

Basic Turn-Switch Construction

Function: perform a change of speakership

Form:

timespan	prosodic properties
–1600 ~ –800 ms	O: louder, higher, narrower, lengthened
–800 ~ 400 ms	O: lower pitch, creaky voice
–400 ~ 0 ms	O: quieter falling to silent
0 ~ 400 ms	N: silent or a quiet, tentative start
400 ~ 800 ms	N: loud, high pitch, creaky, reduced
800 ~ 1600 ms	N: continued speech, with prosody reverting to more typical values

Figure 11.3 The Basic Turn-Switch Construction. "O" is the old speaker and "N" the new speaker. 0 ms is the point halfway between the original speaker's end and the new speaker's start

where <sil> indicates silence, with times in seconds; for example <sil:1.3> indicates 1.3 seconds of silence. Negative numbers indicate overlap.

As M approaches the end of his utterance, the words *wiped all* are loud and slightly high in pitch, as indicated by the upper corner quotes, and as he continues, his pitch goes lower and his voice becomes creaky on *all over the floor*, as indicated by the lower corner quotes. Consider also:

2) E: *seriously, give me* ⌜ *five, actually five*⌝,⌞ *that you actually do every day*⌟
   L: <sil:0.1> *you can do Xbox like you said ...*

3) E: *where, uh,* ⌜*where do you live*⌝, ⌞*by the way?*⌟
   R: <sil:0.3> *uh, just* <sil:0.8> *um,* <sil:1.0> *Florence and Schuster, almost*

Although the incoming turns here are semantically diverse – a completion of the other's thought, a response to a demand, and an answer to a question – the prosodic cues before the turn-switches are similar. Further, the timing of the incoming turns is also similar: the new speaker comes in at a timing appropriate to complete the Basic pattern. This can happen even when the incoming speaker doesn't have the words ready in time, as in the last example, where the incoming speaker preserves the pattern by starting with some *ums* and *uhs*.

Returning to the topic of prosodic cues, in addition to the early yield bundle, later prosodic markings are also common, some as late as the final syllable before silence. Low pitch is common, as in the Halo example, where the pitch drops very low on *floor*. Other common turn-final features include slowing

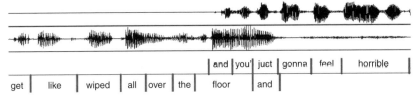

				and	you'	juct	gonna	feel	horrible	
get	like	wiped	all	over	the	floor		and		

Figure 11.4 Overlap at a turn-switch

and low intensity on the last syllable or two. Many discussions of turn-taking consider only such final prosody.[5] Final prosody is certainly easier both to hear and describe than the early bundle. However, it usually has no causal role in turn yielding. For example, in the Halo exchange it could not have had any role in J's decision to launch a turn; since she started before M had stopped speaking, as seen in Figure 11.4. Even when there is a gap between the speakers, the final-syllable prosody can have a causal role only if the gap is longer than human reaction times, which are typically at least a couple-hundred milliseconds. Thus for most turn exchanges, final prosody can play no role in the turn-start decision,[6] and the idea that it does so is just a popular myth.

So far I've been focusing on pre-switch prosody, but the prosody afterwards, as the new speaker takes the turn, is also significant. As the loadings suggest, this commonly is high in pitch, and also loud, reduced, and creaky. These do not always show up on the first word, but this package of features often occurs with appropriate timing anyway; for example, in the Halo example, J comes in a little early, but by the time she's in the clear, with M fully done with his utterance, her pitch is high, on *just gonna*, clearly staking her claim to the turn.

11.2 Fast, Slow, and Disrupted Turn-Taking

Turn-taking is not always swift and smooth, but when it is, it often involves signals in addition to prosodic ones.[7] In the Halo example, from the context and the first half of M's utterance it's easy to predict what his point will be, and to roughly project how much longer it will take him to complete it. Moreover, M ends with a cliché; from the words *wiped all over*, J can infer that he will end with *the floor*. In addition, beyond the prosody and the words, multimodal cues may also pre-signal turn yields. Gaze is one: outgoing speakers often look at the interlocutor.[8]

Why so many cues? A helpful analogy may be the signals to the runners on the starting block. They often get three: *Ready, Set, Go!* The first cues them to get in position and tense up their muscles, and the second establishes the rhythm that enables them to predict accurately the last, so that they can launch simultaneously with the *Go!* Speakers in dialog similarly need early signals to give them time to prepare. Producing a sentence is a complex activity:[9] speakers need to decide what to say, to formulate it in words, to mentally queue up the words, and to put the tongue in motion. Evidence for this difficulty is readily observed: people tend to look away from their partner as they start a turn,[10] probably in part to reduce the stimulus load, helping to prevent information overload. Multiple cues, staggered in time, help the incoming speaker more accurately predict and plan ahead for when they should start their utterance. Statistically, when fewer cues are present, the new turn tends to come later, or not at all.[11]

Thus people often have many cues to help them achieve tight synchronization at turn-switches. When they do, it can give the impression of two minds thinking as one. More specifically, people can behave as if they are following one joint construction, relying on a shared prototype for how to behave together. This amazing feat seems trivial only because our brains have specific mechanisms that enable us subconsciously to achieve tight coordination in communication.[12] Further, to digress briefly, it seems as if overhearers' brains are comfortable with hearing both sides of a joint pattern, but when only half is heard, as when overhearing a mobile phone conversation, it's incomplete and jarring.[13] Yet tight coordination is not always present: when dialog participants are not really on the same wavelength, possibly even having conflicting turn-taking intentions, their behavior will diverge from this ideal.

Turn-taking is usually less than ideal also in limited-bandwidth conversations. This is clearly true for text-only channels, like texting or emailing, where people often misunderstand feelings and intentions,[14] often because the prosodic signals are absent. Even most telephone channels are limited-bandwidth in many ways; for one, most fail to reliably transmit inbreaths, although these play important roles in coordination between speakers.[15] Videochat systems are also problematic. While they have the advantage of transmitting gestures, the disadvantage is that the delays often prevent the participants from effectively coordinating their actions. You may find yourself clashing with the interlocutor at turn starts, and then compensating by backing off to a more primitive style of turn-taking, with long delays between turns. Interestingly, while people can adapt to communicate effectively anyway, they tend to misattribute the resulting patterns of behavior not to channel deficiencies but to the attitude of their conversation partner.[16] This is unsurprising, given the general meaning of delay in turn-taking, as discussed in the next section. Such problems will hopefully decrease with the growing availability of wideband and low-latency telephony, although sadly, most consumers are unaware of the importance of good channels for good communication,[17] and so may not even ask for it.

11.3   Delayed Turn Starts

Let's now consider Dimension 2 on the negative side. As seen in Figure 11.5, the loadings suggest that this involves a region where both speakers are silent

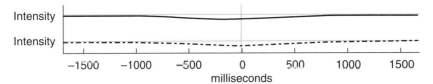

Figure 11.5 Intensity loadings of Dimension 2, negative, for Speakers A and B (Delay/Reluctance)

Delayed Response Construction

Function: indicate reluctance or reservations

Form:

timespan	prosodic properties
over about 1 second	both speakers silent, or one producing very quiet speech

---

Figure 11.6 The Reluctance (Delayed Response) Construction

for a second or so. Among the many ways this can happen – in topic exhaustion, during distractions, and so on – let's consider delayed response, as in

4) M: *what are your hobbies outside of school?*
   J: <sil:1.2> *videogames* (laugh)
   M: *videogames. that's cool, that's really cool.*

Here J displays a momentary reluctance to respond, and when she does, uses a quiet voice and follows it with a quiet, slightly embarrassed laugh. In the hierarchy of hobbies, playing videogames is low in prestige, and thus not the sort of thing one is eager to mention. Consider also

5) J: *it was ridiculous, they put me into pre-engineering; they didn't*
      put me into Computer Science
   M: *mm* <sil:0.9> *yeah, it's, uh, you always deal with that kind of*
      stuff when you transfer

Here J does not respond immediately. When he does, it's not with an easy display of empathy, but rather with a more nuanced assessment that leads into a larger discussion.

We can loosely consider this little pattern to be a construction, as summarized in Figure 11.6.

The connection between delay and reluctance has also been shown experimentally. When the gap between a request for a favor and a positive response,

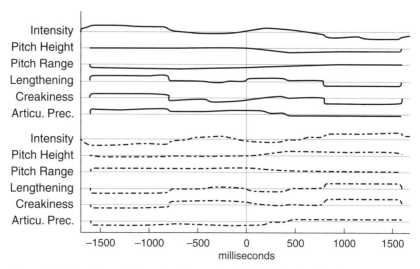

Figure 11.7 Loadings of Dimension 9, negative side (Particle-Assisted Turn-Switch)

sure, was artificially manipulated, lags of over about 700 milliseconds were more often interpreted as indicating a lack of willingness to do the favor.[18]

11.4   Particle-Assisted Turn-Switches

While many turn-switches are remarkably swift, following the Basic pattern, others take more time. Sometimes these slower switches follow their own pattern, as suggested by the factor loadings for Dimension 9, negative (Figure 11.7).

Looking first at the intensity loadings, initially Speaker A, at top, is speaking and B is silent, but by the end, B is speaking and A is silent. Thus this pattern involves a turn end by A and a turn start by B. Unlike the Basic Construction, however, the hand-off is not immediate: between the two turns there's about a second and a half of silence or quiet things. Consider for example

6) J: *I really like the instructor and his style of teaching. So it's not*
   ...that bad.
   S: <sil:0.6> *that's good*
   J: <sil:0.5> *yeah*
   S: <sil:0.1> *What's uh, what's the instructor's name?*

This occurs after J has been holding the floor, as she comes to the end of what she had to say. As seen in Figure 11.8, the speakership then oscillates

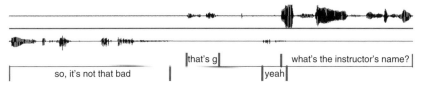

Figure 11.8 Timeline view of Example 6 The vertical lines mark the temporal extent of each phrase.

before coming fully to S. His *that's good* seems to indicate that he's getting ready to take the turn: prosodically, this has fairly wide pitch range, is clearly articulated, and is rather creaky. His words are ambiguous – it's not clear what *that's good* actually means, if anything – but they do provide a vehicle for prosodic features that fill out the pattern, as he positions himself to take a turn. Then comes J's *yeah*, a "postcompletion" particle. It's not clear what this sound means either, but with its low pitch and its temporal position, it confirms that J is completely done with her turn. After this little bit of dancing around, all in low intensity, S comes in with a full turn, starting strong with high pitch.

The same pattern is seen in

7) J: *it's not too bad. It doesn't feel like five classes; it just feels*
      like four
  R: <sil:0.3> *really*
  J: <sil:0.2> *yeah*
  R: <sil:0.3> *I'm just scared . . .*

In general, this pattern is a turn exchange with a longish gap in the middle, where the silence may be partially filled with one or more little "particles." Like tugboats, these help position the larger contributions, the full turns. Figure 11.9 summarizes the overall pattern, which I'll call the Particle-Assisted Turn-Taking Construction. Compared to basic turn-switches, particle-assisted switches may invite longer turns. That is, this construction can be used to transition from one speaker strongly holding the floor to the other strongly holding the floor. Further, in terms of form, compared to the basic pattern, the yield takes more time, and in particular the early yield bundle comes earlier, relative to the turn end. This gives the new speaker an extra moment to marshal his thoughts, although it still may not be enough, as in

8) L: *you were going to ask me something; I told you to wait,*
  E: <sil:0.4> (tongue click)
  L: <sil:–0.1> *until the conversation*
  E: <sil:0.1> *uuuh, oh oh oh, yeah, yeah, yeah; I was saying . . .*

Turn-switches with this pacing may give you the chance to think about what you want to say and then express it in full. In job interviews, noticing this can

The Particle-Assisted Turn-Switch Construction

Function: perform a more relaxed change of speakership

Form:

timespan	prosodic properties
−1600 ~ −800 ms	O: louder, higher, narrower, lengthened
−800 ~ −400 ms	O: falling silent
−600 ~ 0 ms	N: short, quiet, low pitch, wide pitch range utterance
0 ~ 600 ms	O: quiet, lengthened, short utterance
600 ~ 800 ms	N: a quiet, high-pitched start
800 ~ 1600 ms	N: loud, high pitch, creaky, disaligned

Figure 11.9 The Particle-Assisted Turn-Switch Construction

be important: if you give a short answer to a prompt that was intended to elicit a long one, you may seem unintelligent or disengaged.[19]

While speakers have the choice of whether to perform a basic or a particle-assisted turn-switch, in actual dialog the outcomes may not be so clear-cut. In

9) G: *what position do you want for ACM?*
    S: <sil:0.8> *oh, I don't know*
    G: <sil:−0.2> *are you going to run?*
    S: <sil:0.1> *not mm, not president though*

the interaction starts out looking like a particle-assisted turn-switch, but G uses his yielding-particle slot to interpolate a full question, transforming the end of this sequence into something more like a basic switch. However, S goes on to answer the first question, not the second, as if he's still following the particle-assisted construction. Thus speakers may change their intentions as they go along, or operate at cross-purposes, following different constructions. Other complications also arise, including the involvement of other prosodic features and the effects of factors such as the participants' genders and the conversation topic.[20]

11.5   Turn Metaphors and Myths

So far, we've considered only the most classic kinds of turns, where one person at a time has the floor and the turn exchanges are well marked. There is much more to turn-taking, but before examining other phenomena, let's look at some myths about turns.

While I have been using the word "turn" informally, this word is sometimes used with a more specific meaning, as in the claims that that "turns are the basic unit of conversation"[21] and that participants in conversation are "constrained

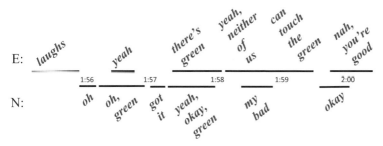

Figure 11.10 Timeline view of Example 10

to issue their utterances in allocated turns, and enlist various mechanisms to obtain them."[22] Taking this perspective, much early research aimed to specify rules for turn-taking, but there was always something strange about this endeavor. The philosopher John Searle put his finger on it in a famous debate with the sociologist Emanuel Schegloff. Searle imagined someone noticing a chandelier about to fall on his interlocutor's head: clearly he'd say something immediately, without worrying about whether he had the turn or how to get it.[23]

While my corpora lack examples of falling chandeliers, there are others that illustrate this point. Consider an example from our collection of game play,[24] where pairs of students played Fireboy and Watergirl, a maze game where they run and jump and coordinate actions to overcome obstacles, such as the fatal green mud. In this example, the expert player, E, cues the novice, N, to jump, but N lands in the green mud. N realizes what happened and apologizes, and E reviews the relevant game rule.

10) Expert: *you first*
    Novice: (jumps and lands in the green mud)
    E: (laughs)
    N: *oh. oh, green.*
    E: *yeah.*
    N: *got it, yeah, okay, green.*
    E: *there's green, yeah, neither of us can touch the green*
    N: *my bad. okay.*
    E: *nah, you're good, you're good*

When written out like this, the interaction appears to be comprised of turns. Indeed, any interaction can be represented on paper so as to respect the claim that turns are fundamental to dialog. Yet this is really just a myth, as can be seen here when the words are shown on a timeline, as in Figure 11.10.

Here each person's speech at each moment seems to reflect his understanding of the situation at that moment. This rapidly changes as E realizes

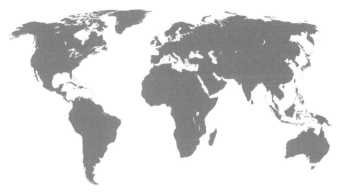

Figure 11.11 A simplistic view of the world

what's happened, then N realizes it, then N quickly diagnoses the problem with *oh, green*. Then E and N both speak, E to make sure that N understands what went wrong, and N to clarify that he already understands it. Their speech actions are a real-time reflection of the state of the game play, and of what each player understands about the other person's understanding of the situation, and of what they think the other person is attempting to communicate.[25]

While this is an extreme example, dialog is in general a continuous process.[26] Participants can continuously monitor the state of the dialog, continuously deciding whether in the next moment to be speaking or silent,[27] depending on the estimated appropriateness of each possible behavior.[28]

Clearly the word "turn" should not be taken too literally.[29] Thinking of conversations as "made up of" turns is like thinking of the world in terms of maps like that in Figure 11.11,[30] where the continents are monotone gray with nice sharp shorelines where they meet the monotone white oceans. But real continental margins are much more interesting, with two plates grinding together at the California coast, and in the east, hundreds of miles of continental shelf stretching out under the sea. Similarly, turn boundaries, though they look simple on paper, are in real life full of complexity. Rather than thinking of turns as building blocks, it is helpful to think of them as emergent,[31] arising from the process of interaction, as people use prosodic (and other) patterns to serve their own purposes, not just top-level goals, but also "micro-intentions"[32] that can appear at any time, and may then be satisfied, disappear, combine, overlap, or evolve, moment by moment.

Along with the metaphor of turns-as-units, there is a metaphor of turn-as-possession. In some models of conversation, "the turn" is something that, at each moment in time, is owned by one speaker or the other. This is a rich metaphor: some scholars speak of people not only of "having" the turn, but also "holding," "giving," "assigning," or "taking" it. Sometimes this metaphor is spot on. Consider riddles.

11) I: *why did the ⌜ chicken cross⌝ ⌞ the road⌟?*
    D: *I don't know; why ⌜ did the chicken⌝ ⌞ cross the road⌟?*

Here the requirement for a response is absolute: the teller will not continue on to the punchline until she gets a response, the response has to be long and full-form, and neither speaker can say anything until the other has clearly yielded the turn. Incidentally, perfect prosody is easy to achieve here, since the joke teller doesn't need to think, having the prompt and punchline well rehearsed, and the receiver doesn't need to think either, beyond the minimal processing needing to recognize and echo some words, with the rest of the response entirely formulaic. Thus it is easy for the exchange to perfectly display the prosody of a basic turn-switch. Perhaps this is a reason why riddles are addictive for second-graders: they help them not only to develop humor but also to rehearse and perfect the prosody of turn-taking.[33]

More often this metaphor, of turns as things that can be possessed, is misleading: "having" the turn is not all or nothing, nor does "a turn" belong exclusively to one person at a time; these are myths. The idea that hearers wait passively until the speaker yields the turn is another myth. In real life, people can have the turn to different degrees, and in different ways, as the next sections discuss in detail.[34] Consider, for example, how a listener can support an ongoing turn with backchannels or undermine it with "incipiency" markers, such as hand and facial gestures, posture shifts, fidgeting, blinking, inbreaths, or specific words, as he signals decreasing interest in listening and strengthening intention to say something himself. [35]

Where did these myths come from? One source is the salience of turn-final prosody, as already discussed. Another source is social norms about proper turn-taking, including some imported from non-conversation situations, of which more later. Another factor is that much of the early work on turn-taking was done on paper, by examining transcripts, with little direct examination of the audio. Another cause is that, until recently, researchers were not equipped to model turn-taking at all points. Needing to select locations on which to focus, they unsurprisingly chose to look at pauses, and then to begin by classifying them into turn-hold and turn-yield pauses. Looking at turn-taking in this way was also helpful for dialog-systems builders trying to reduce the tedious delays alluded to at the start of the chapter, and this has fostered a minor industry in training discriminative models using machine learning techniques.[36] Such models are finely tuned to make one specific decision in one specific context of use. While sometimes useful for practical purposes,[37] such models have not much helped with the discovery of the actual patterns involved in turn-taking.

Has-Turn Construction

Function: be the primary speaker

Form:

timespan	prosodic properties
varies	one participant speaking, with gradual declination the other speaker quiet

Figure 11.12 The Has-Turn Construction

Overall, it seems to be more productive to view turn-taking patterns not as constraints that speakers follow, but as resources that they employ.

11.6   Overlap

Turning now to behaviors that don't fit with simplistic notions of turns, let's start with Dimensions 1 and 2. As noted earlier, Dimension 1 is positive when speaker A has the turn, and negative when speaker B has the turn. We can consider this loosely to be a construction, as summarized in Figure 11.12.

Looking next at the loadings of Dimension 2, positive (Figure 11.13), we see from the intensity loadings that this relates to both speakers talking at once: that is, overlapping. (This is of course the opposite of what happens when Dimension 2 is negative: as discussed above, when both speakers are silent, sometimes indicating reluctance.) At positive extremes, the loadings suggest that these overlaps typically involve wide pitch range. This is illustrated by an exchange which happened at the end of the semester, where R had expected G to be all done with his classwork but in fact:

12) G: *I've got to finish the automata project.*   *[we did not*
     R: *[oh, still,*
     G: *[finish it last night; [we worked very late; we've been here …*
     R: *[oh,   that's so [big.*

Here the left brackets mark the same timepoints across the two speakers' utterances. Wide pitch is also seen in Example 13.

13)   J: *when she had her, her arm in the scarf,*
           oh like that's [cute
        R: *[oh yeah, I have a little   [sling*
        J: *[I wouldn't have*
           thought of [that, I would've just held my [arm like,
        R: *[that was cute   [laughing*

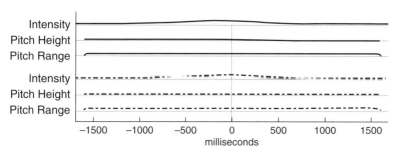

Figure 11.13 Some loadings of Dimension 2, positive side (Shared Enthusiasm / Wide-Range Overlap)

Shared Enthusiasm Construction

Function: display shared feeling

Form:

timespan	prosodic properties
over 500 ms	both speakers: speaking or laughing, wide pitch range, speaking rate slightly reduced

mnemonic: Wide-Range Overlap

Figure 11.14 The Wide-Range Overlap Construction

In these examples, the overlap is supportive, as it was above in the green mud exchange, Example 10.[38] In general, overlapping speech with wide pitch ranges is a common way to display a shared feeling, such as sympathy or liking.

The Dimension 2 loadings show also that the region with high intensity is relatively short, corresponding to the fact that most overlaps are brief. This pattern, the Wide-Range Overlap Construction, is summarized in Figure 11.14.

A common special case is shared laughter, as in the next two examples, both of which involve sarcasm.

14)   J: *I love ethics* [laughter
       S: [laughter

15)   E: *where do your relatives live?*
       G: *the only ones I care about* [*live in Ohio (laughing)*)
       E: [laughter

To digress for a moment, laughing together is something special; a powerful way to help establish rapport. Cowley has noted that people laughing together are engaged in an activity that "were they birds, would be regarded as finely-timed duetting."[39] One known property of laughing together is the tendency to higher pitch than in non-overlapped laughs.[40] The prosody of laughter is complex. While it exhibits some of the same prosody-meaning mappings seen for words,[41] in other ways the prosody of laughter is characteristically different from the prosody of speech. There is even evidence that laughter is partly governed by a vocal system separate from that of speech, one that shares much with the vocalizations of nonhuman animals.[42]

Returning to the topic of overlap, there is a common belief that polite people don't do this: that speaking in overlap is an unpleasant, aggressive thing to do. For dialog, at least, this is mostly a myth. When people think of overlapping speech, they probably mostly think of competitive overlaps, where one speaker interrupts to challenge another for the turn.[43] Although these are very salient when they do happen, these are rare in most conversations.

The Wide-Range Overlap Construction often occurs superimposed with other constructions. The Halo example (Example 1) illustrates this. As seen in Figure 11.4, in the final line J times her response so as to overlap M's for a half second. Thus at this point the Basic Turn-Switch Construction and the Wide-Range Overlap Construction are superimposed.

Stepping back for a moment, imagine a species that is like humanity in every respect except that in conversations both organisms can talk simultaneously. Among other benefits, every conversation would be over twice as fast, or else be twice as informative. Human brains, however, are not able to process incoming speech and outgoing speech at the same time.[44] But sometimes we overlap anyway. During overlap, there is little content conveyed: not much more than the information that the other person shares your feelings. But when that's all we want to convey, this kind of overlap is effective, appropriate and often the polite thing to do.

Of course, there are also times where overlap is really not wanted, and in such cases speakers may coordinate to avoid this. One way to do this is by suspending declination: pitch that stays high indicates that a turn will probably not end soon. The next four sections consider other ways in which a speaker can clearly hold the turn.

11.7   Turn Holding with Lengthening

Probably the most common way to hold the turn is with a lengthened sound or word, as in

16) J: *would you ever want to teach?*
    R: <sil:1.3> **umm**[0.7] <sil:1.3> *sometimes I would. Well . . .*

The Filler Construction

Function: hold the floor

Form:

timespan	prosodic properties
–400 ~ +400 ms	lengthened, loud, narrow pitch range, slightly falling pitch

mnemonic: Lengthened Loud Narrow

Figure 11.15 The Filler Construction

Such fillers hold the turn and may also serve related purposes, such as indicating that the speaker is looking for the right word.[45]

17) R: *except for math, I'm done with* **theeee**[0.4] <sil:0.9> *the left side of the degree plan*

18) G: *press* **uh**[0.4] *stop on it* <sil:0.6> *and then press stop on the* **uh**[0.5]
     S: <sil:0.1> *this?* (pointing)

19) S: **he**[0.7] *came to talk with us during our,* **um**[0.5]
     J: *security [class]?*
     S: **nooo**[0.8] <sil:1.0> *for software [class]*

Since lengthenings are important in turn holding, I'll indicate durations in this section, for example, *um*[0.7] indicates an *um* lasting 0.7 seconds. While lengthening is also associated with turn yields, in this pattern the lengthening typically spans one word, not several words, and does not necessarily involve an intensity reduction.

While this behavior holds the turn, it does not preclude all contributions by the interlocutor. Indeed, in two of the examples above, the hearer offered a completion for the word or concept the speaker was looking for, but they did so deftly, as a small suggestion that did not challenge or interfere with the original speaker's ongoing turn.

In addition to being lengthened, fillers are usually fairly low in pitch and often somewhat louder than the surrounding words. Figure 11.15 summarizes the construction. While this prosody can probably be applied to any word, it has affinities for a few words and non-lexical items, such as *the, a, yeah, uh,* and *um*.[46]

Incidentally, non-lexical fillers, such as *uh*, are rather stigmatized: there is a myth that intelligent people don't use them.[47] While avoiding fillers can give a good impression in interviews and in public speaking, in dialog they are

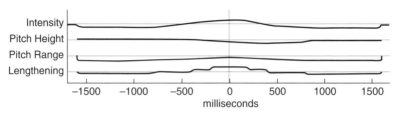

Figure 11.16 Some loadings of Dimension 8, negative side (Fillers)

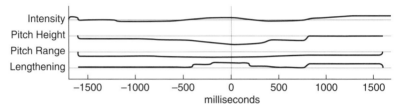

Figure 11.17 Some loadings of Dimension 10, positive side (also Fillers)

essential. Speakers often need time to decide how to express something, or recall some fact or find a word. When the course of speech directly follows the speaker's thought process,[48] fillers can directly reflect his instantaneous mental state, of thinking, remembering, deciding how to say something or describe something, and so on. They can also convey the speaker's confidence in what they are saying, their attitude about the topic, how long a turn they intend to take, and so on, depending on the details of their phonetics and prosody, based on various primordial mappings.[49] Fillers can show awareness of the context, such as whether the speaker needs to respond to some question raised by the interlocutor or is free to let his thoughts take him where they may. Finally, fillers often serve to help the listener, by providing them with a moment of extra time to catch up and assimilate some information, or to ready themselves to receive some critical new information.[50] Non-lexical fillers are especially flexible: *um*s and *uh*s, as mere dollops of sound, are readily shaped prosodically to such constellations of nuances.[51]

Returning to the dimensional analysis, many fillers are simultaneously extreme on Dimensions 8 and 10. As seen in Figures 11.16 and 11.17, these both involve lengthening and a tendency to increased intensity and low pitch. However, they differ in the exact loadings. Thus, when combined with different strengths, these two may help determine the exact duration and intonation contour of a filler, and thereby the nuances conveyed. The longer, lower ones, with stronger weightings on Dimension 10, may be more common turn-initially, for example when stalling while thinking of an answer to a direct question. In contrast, the shorter ones, often with strong weightings on Dimension 8, may be more common in the middle of an ongoing utterance. However, these tendencies are weak and not consistent across speakers.[52]

11.8   Pausing without Yielding

Silences in dialog can have many meanings. While sometimes silence just happens, it is often significant:[53] as Cowley notes, "a reader will be not the wiser if a writer has a cup of tea in midsentence," but during talk, even a momentary delay can greatly affect the interpretation.[54]

Many silences, if not most, are specifically framed, which helps the listener avoid inferring the wrong meaning.[55] Filler-associated pauses, as seen above, are one example. A very different use of pauses is in a construction used for dramatic effect.

Dimension 8, unlike most others seen so far, corresponds not to one joint behavior but rather to two separate, unrelated constructions, one for the negative side, just discussed, and one on the positive side, with the loadings seen in Figure 11.18. These suggest that the speaker tends to have wide pitch range and creaky voice, then a short pause, and then more speech, again in wide range and with creaky voice. In addition, not shown in the figure, all pitch features are positively loaded during the two speaking regions: thus both regions are heavily voiced, rather than being, say, breathy or rich in lengthened consonants.

In addition to the features visible in the loadings, exemplars of this pattern often also have a clipped end to the first part. Consider the roles of the silences in:

20) G: *the sun was actually up before I went to sleep*
     E: *ooo, I hate that, like when it's coming up, like right there, and*
         you're like <sil:0.6> *I should probably not go to bed right*
         now, 'cause <sil:0.3> *I'm going to be groggy all day*

21) R: *so, like, it's been ten minutes. Because I have class.*
     J: *oh, yeah. We can stop, I guess.*

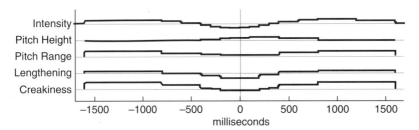

Figure 11.18 Some loadings of Dimension 8, positive side (Bipartite)

The Bipartite Construction

Function: hold the floor; have a dramatic effect

Form:

timespan	prosodic properties
−1.5 −.4 s	heavily voiced, creaky voice, wide pitch range, ending with sharp decrease in intensity
−.4 s +.4 s	pause
+.4 s 1.5 s	heavily voiced, creaky voice, wide pitch range

Figure 11.19 The Bipartite Construction

> R: *yeah?*
> J: *yeah.*
> R: *okay* <sil:1.0> *bye*
> J: *bye* (laughs)

22) R: *So how's your semester going?*
    L: *Pretty good, I'm* <sil:0.6> *getting 'A's in all my classes.*

Overall, this configuration of prosodic features, which I call the Bipartite Construction, as summarized in Figure 11.19, is well suited to holding the floor and adding a little build up-for rhetorical effect, since it relates to three primordial mappings: the mapping between wide pitch range and getting attention, the mapping between clipped turn ends and taking charge, and the mapping between creaky voice and distancing, here distancing from the ongoing interaction to create some space to perform something noteworthy. While this construction occurs in dialog, it can be equally at home in monologue, where pauses framed like this are often denoted with colons.

The function of this construction is diametrically opposite to the function of fillers. Whereas speakers use fillers to hold the floor while they decide what to say or what words to use, they use this construction when they know what they want to say. Thus we can see Dimension 8 as embodying a scale, from the negative side where the speaker needs more time to think before he can complete his utterance, to the positive side where he knows exactly what he will say for the next second or two.

11.9   Turn Holding with Rhythm

A third way to hold the turn is to set up a rhythm, alternating strongly stressed words and silence or quieter words, as in

23) *it îs three hours, ând it's kindâ late, bût I really lîke
    the instrûctor, ând his stŷle of teaching*

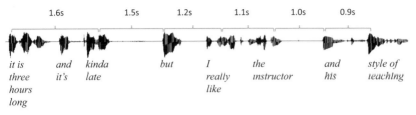

Figure 11.20 Holding the Floor with Rhythm, with the intervals between stresses marked

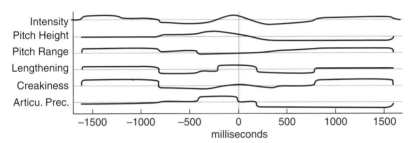

Figure 11.21 The intensity loadings of Dimension 14, positive side (Elocutionary Rhythm)

where each caret, ˆ, roughly marks the most stressed syllable in each phrase. The rhythm here is more evident in the timeline view in Figure 11.20. It's certainly not a strict rhythm – she's not rapping – but there is a repeating pattern. This is seen in the intensity loadings of Dimension 14 positive, in Figure 11.21. While the feature set is not fine-grained enough to be sure, it looks like the typical interval between stresses may be around 1.3 seconds. Further, the loadings around 0 ms, where the resolution is highest, suggest that there is also a tendency for the stressed phrases to start enunciated and high in pitch and to end with lengthening.

The function of this rhythm seems to be mostly to hold the turn. The example above occurred right after the speaker had been repeatedly interrupted by her interlocutor; and with her rhythm here she's tightly holding the floor, shutting him out so she can make her point. Another example is

24) *my last job with tûtoring* <sil:0.6> *I lôved teaching* <sil:0.2>
   I lôved helping kids . . .

In this example, already seen above, the speaker is not only expressing strong feelings but also flagging her intention to hold the floor for quite some time, so she can explain how she's conflicted about the idea of teaching as a profession.

As this pattern has a deliberate, formal feel, let's call it the Elocutionary Rhythm Construction. Figure 11.22 summarizes.

The Elocutionary Rhythm Construction

Function: hold the floor for some time

Form:

timespan	prosodic properties
–1.3 s	a stress
0 s	another stress
1.3 s	another stress
and so on	

Figure 11.22 The Elocutionary Rhythm Construction

To digress briefly, this pattern reminds me of Duck Duck Goose, the preschool game. Small children learn various rhythm-based games, including *eenie-meenie-minny mo* and jump rope songs, but for me I think Duck Duck Goose came first. I remember it as quite a thrill: perhaps the first time in my life when everyone else had to listen while I was the only one allowed to speak. Indeed you are required to speak, but it is easy: you only have to say *duck, duck, duck* ... and the walking and head patting help you keep the rhythm. The other challenge in this game is not to reveal who you plan to tag as the goose. In ordinary life we are constantly "leaking" signals about our intentions – about when the list will end, about how soon we'll finish our turn, and so on – and this enables people to predict what we'll do and comfortably interact with us. But in this game you have to *prevent* others from predicting the tag: you have to suppress any leakage before that final *goose*.

As a final note on rhythm, there also seems to be a weak tendency for speakers to engage in shared rhythms, sometimes even spanning turn boundaries.[56]

11.10   Backchanneling

The fourth behavior involved in turn holding is our old friend, the backchanneling construction. As discussed in Chapter 1, this involves the listener interpolating some small contribution, like *uh-huh*, in the midst of ongoing talk by the main speaker.

As a listener, following this pattern conveys that you're paying attention to the speaker, at least to some extent, and that you're interested in what he will say next, at least somewhat.[57] As such, you're encouraging him and making it easier for him to deliver the next increment of information: that is, with active listening you help to advance the conversation.[58]

As a speaker, with this pattern you enable the listener to predict that something important or interesting will be coming up in a couple of seconds, and encourage him to signal that he realizes this with a backchannel. This may help prepare his brain to be maximally receptive at exactly the moment when you're delivering the important information. Consider

25) R: *so, I don't know. It, it'll come.*
    J: *yeah*
    R: *I can't believe it's in a year.*

Here R has been talking vaguely about career plans, but after receiving the backchannel, she reveals that she has more immediate concerns about her future, and this then expands into a new, more personal, topic.

There is a myth that people can become good listeners – active listeners – just by adjusting their attitude. In fact, active listening requires the mastery of very specific skills. Let's look at this one in detail.

The loadings of Dimension 4, as seen in Figure 11.23, indicate, as previously noted, a short region of low pitch not long before the backchannel, typically lasting around 150 milliseconds. This is the main feature identified by previous work as a cue for the interlocutor to backchannel.[59]

The loadings tell us more: that this pattern involves a slightly increased pitch for about a second, followed by a short, somewhat louder region (often a content word), rather enunciated, then the short low-pitch region, with reduced loudness, and then the backchannel. The loadings also indicate that disaligned

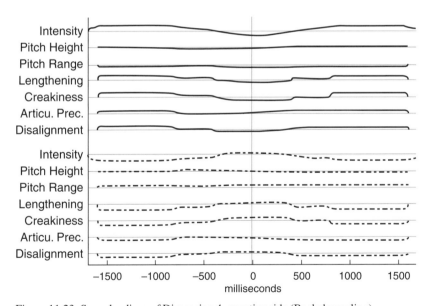

Figure 11.23 Some loadings of Dimension 4, negative side (Backchanneling)

Backchanneling Construction, Refined Description

Function: encourage continued listening; encourage continued talk

Form:

timespan	prosodic properties	
	Speaker A	Speaker B
–600 ms	loudness, creakiness, and articulatory precision increase	
–400 ms	pitch drops and stays low	
–300 ms	loudness decreases	
–100 ms	silence	
0ms		backchannel, lengthened, quiet, flat pitch
800 ms	resumes speaking, loud, fast, high pitch	

Figure 11.24 The Backchanneling Construction, in more detail

pitch peaks are relatively common around 1.2 seconds before a backchannel, which likely reflects the role of late peaks in grounding, in that establishing shared knowledge of some referent commonly occurs with a backchannel cue. After the backchannel, the speaker resumes, typically with a momentarily faster rate, bringing a feeling of renewed energy.

Pre-backchannel behavior somewhat resembles the pre-switch behaviors of the Basic and Particle-Assisted Constructions: they all have an early bundle involving intensity, creakiness, and lengthening. However, before backchannels the bundle seems to be generally weaker, which can be seen as correlating with the short duration of the "turn" that it cues. In particular, the bundle quickly leads to a drop in pitch, around only 400 ms after the bundle starts. In turn yields, in contrast, the low pitch usually comes later, and the response much later after that.

Pre-backchannel behavior also has similarities with the Minor Third Construction, in that the pitch is high and then much lower. However, the pre-backchannel pitch drop tends to be more gentle, and to end much lower in the speaker's pitch range, among other differences.

Figure 11.24 summarizes what Dimension 4 tells us. I must add two caveats here: there are many other factors also involved in backchanneling,[60] and, as always, this is just the most typical pattern: actual behavior varies greatly.

One type of variation is the strength of the cue. People may include more or fewer of the components of this construction, or make them weaker or stronger, which affects the probability of receiving a backchannel in response.[61]

The strength of the backchannels also varies, from fairly loud, as in

26) M: *he, like, literally brought me an* ⌜*Xbox, so I could*
          play⌝ ⌞*Halo with him*⌟
     J: *lucky!*
     M: *yeah, and he got me, like, the Halo edition too*

to quieter, such as a typical *uh-huh*, to completely silent, such as nods and blinks.[62] The longer and louder backchannels approach full turns, and may be briefly acknowledged by the main speaker before continuing:

27) M: *I saw Boondock Saints before it was even in America, like;*
          [*because*
     J: [*really?*
     M: *yeah, I think it was released in Canada first.*

Another type of variation is in the speaker's behavior after cueing a backchannel. In general, as the loadings suggest, intensity drops. Sometimes it drops all the way to silence, creating a little pause for the backchannel to nestle in. At other times the intensity drops only slightly. In such cases, the backchannel may therefore come in at an overlapping position,[63] as seen in

28) J: *are you going for your Masters?*
     R: *it depends on the day; how I feel*
     J: (laughs)
     R: *sometimes it's yes, and sometimes I'm okay with*
     J: [*yeah*
     R: [*a Bachelors.*

However, correctly-timed backchannels seldom overlap with anything important: only rarely does the backchannel come in so late that it clashes with the speaker instead of supporting him.

Other aspects of backchanneling prosody also vary. While backchannels are prototypically flat in pitch and slightly creaky, additional prosodic features can add nuances of meaning, generally following primordial mappings.[64] There are also variant uses in varying contexts. Indeed, "backchannel" is a natural kind, shading off in various directions into related phenomena such as "continuers," "assessments," and "acknowledgments." These usually involve the Backchanneling Construction, but generally with additional prosodic properties superimposed.

Today the world's best listeners are not humans but computer programs, at least in terms of backchanneling. Gratch and colleagues have developed a family of virtual humans that specialize in attentive listening.[65] These systems follow patterns like the one described above, although honed by training on a large corpus of people listening to retellings of one specific story When subjects are brought into the laboratory and asked to retell the story, they generally feel more rapport when the virtual human follows the learned behaviors than when its backchanneling is controlled by a hidden human operator.

Other experiments in automatic backchanneling confirm the role of prosodic cues, and suggest that they are more important in backchannel timing than the actual words being said.[66] Looking only at short time frames, backchannel production seems to be almost a reflex, and in fact a dialog system that responds immediately to prosodic cues can keep up its end of the conversation for a dozen seconds, although after that things break down unless the interaction is carefully staged to prevent the user from doing things that will expose the system's limitations.[67] In our experiments we also found that successful backchanneling requires some degree of unpredictability: a system that responds at all opportunities (for example, after all regions where the pitch goes low for 110 milliseconds) starts to sound robotic very quickly.

The past four sections have discussed four ways to hold the floor: fillers, dramatic pauses, elocutionary rhythm, and backchannel invitations. While our focus has been on their roles in turn-taking, all serve additional communicative purposes. We have also seen that good turn-taking involves fast, partly automatic responses to low-level cues, and that it can lead to rapport. In general, interacting cooperatively with someone in tight rhythm is an effective way to form social bonds, something which happens to be true of many species.[68]

11.11   Multiparty and Regulated Turn-Taking

The legendary Prince Shotoku, early ruler of Japan and font of Buddhist wisdom, had a superpower. Running the empire, he constantly needed to receive provincial administrators who came to the palace with issues. Cleverly, he would have them come before him in groups and all report at the same time. His superpower was the ability to understand up to eight people at once.

I wish I had this power: then semester-end presentations would be over in an hour instead of a day. Unfortunately, the human condition is different. Apart from cheering your team, there are few situations in which we can reasonably all vocalize at the same time.[69] I think of this sometimes during committee meetings, wishing my co-workers all had Prince Shotoku's superpower, so we could be all done in minutes. While some committee chairs skillfully allocate turns very effectively,[70] more often committees fumble around, following the standard turn-taking patterns learned on the playground, modified by some elements of performance and guided by an overlay of formality inspired by noble ideas about fairness and politeness.

Another interesting environment is the courtroom, where the turn-taking is strictly controlled by the judge, who herself follows strict rules. These ensure, among other things, fairness and enough time for everyone to say what they need to. These also limit the opportunity for dominance displays disguised as turn-taking signals. News interviews also have a specialized turn-taking system.[71] Classrooms are also interesting. While not as strict as a judge, the teacher is still in control. She needs to make her expectations unambiguously clear at every moment. In conversation it's fine to be vague in your signals, but when teaching, you must always control who has the turn. Questions are a good example: the students must always be able to sharply distinguish your real questions from your rhetorical ones.

Multiparty interactions mostly follow implicit rules.[72] Think of the old timers' table at the coffeeshop or a construction crew on site. Picking up these rules is a big part of becoming accepted. But sometimes the rules are explicit. Children in class are trained to follow specific rules and maxims: "one at a time," "wait your turn," "don't interrupt," "be ready to answer when you're called on," "speak so everyone can hear," and so on. Thus, in the classroom, many of the myths of turn-taking actually match the reality.

11.12 Polite Turn-Taking across Cultures

Across many languages, parts of the turn-taking system are similar.[73] For example, the early yield bundle, foreshadowing a turn end, is similar in English, Spanish, Mandarin, and Japanese.[74] Nevertheless, there are differences,[75] and these can have a disproportionate impact in cross-cultural interactions. This is because many of the prosodic elements of turn-taking also have roles in conveying respect, dominance, involvement, and politeness in general. Small differences in turn-taking styles can therefore lead to serious misunderstandings.

One well-noted difference between languages and cultures is in the preference for overlap.[76] Both Greek culture and French culture are reported to use it more than American culture, and its use also varies among English dialects.[77] My friend Eric the New Yorker can seem pushy, even disrespectful, to people in El Paso, although when you get to know him, you realize that he's a very considerate person. It is unfortunately easy to misattribute differences in turn-taking style to personality defects or attitude issues.

Another example comes from the prosody of turn starts. In recordings of Mexican students conversing in English, Paola Gallardo and I found that, whereas the initial words of a turn tend to be fast for native speakers of English, for these non-native speakers this tendency was much weaker.[78] It is interesting to speculate how such differences may relate to perceived cultural differences. American businessmen often perceive Mexicans, it has been said, as being leisurely and disinclined to rush.[79] While there may be real cultural differences, such perceptions may be clouded by misattributions of such minor differences in prosodic behavior.

Table 11.1 *Summary of Turn-Taking Constructions*

Basic Turn-Exchange Construction
Delay Construction
Particle-Assisted Turn-Exchange Construction
Minor Third Construction
Wide-Range Overlap Construction
Filler Construction
Bipartite Construction
Elocutionary Rhythm Construction
Backchanneling Construction

Backchanneling provides many more examples. Wataru Tsukahara and I found that Japanese speakers not only backchannel typically twice as often as English speakers, but also produce the backchannels much faster after the cue.[80] It is easy to see how in cross-cultural interactions this could lead to misperceptions of one side being shallow and the other being stand-offish and unsupportive. Backchanneling in Arabic is different again. Yaffa Al Bayyari and I found that its most common cue for a backchannel is a sharp pitch drop.[81] While this is merely a turn-taking cue, it resembles the prosody of angry accusations in English, and is generally perceived negatively by American listeners.[82] Since backchanneling happens about four times a minute in Arabic, this is not an unlikely outcome. Happily, we also found that the negative perception can be significantly alleviated by a little bit of explanation and exposure.[83]

11.13   Summary

Turn-taking seems like a simple thing, something that you could model with a few simple rules, like the rules of a ball game or a card game.[84] But the needs of people in interaction are far too varied and multifaceted for that. English has many prosodic constructions that together provide a rich inventory of turn-management resources for speakers to use, alone or in combination, to achieve their goals. At the same time, these constructions are not just about turn-taking: participants deploy them to achieve other goals too.

As an example of an often-intertwined goal, consider the goal of establishing dominance. Stretching or flouting the general patterns of turn-taking is a common way to show dominance.[85] This can be done in many ways: withholding backchannels, interrupting, not yielding the turn, not taking the turn when offered, taking the turn after a delay, not signaling intentions, and so on.

Spoken dialog systems cleverly exploit this connection. As a way to help users comprehend why a system's turn-taking abilities are limited, designers often write their scripts in slightly formal language and give them slightly dominant voices. While this makes them somewhat tiresome to deal with, at least the turn-taking quirks are then more understandable and less jarring.

Be that as it may, Table 11.1 lists the constructions relating to turn-taking. Together they form a complex ecology, filling a set of niches that range from fast to slow, automatic to deliberate, short to long, and so on. Turn-taking also relates closely to the processes of managing topics, as the next chapter will explain.

12 Topic Management Constructions

The last chapter discussed how people manage who should talk when; this chapter addresses another major realm of functions: how people organize what they are talking about. Thus it examines the five main constructions involved in topic management.

12.1 Topic Closing

When people tire of a topic, their pitch tends to go low and they tend to use reduced forms: to speak less clearly.

Consider the following, coming after a long discussion of a class project, considering it from every angle:

1) S: _they might be able to add it_   (tongue click)   _or something_
   I dunno how that works
   J: _hm_ _that's good_
   S: _yeah_   ⌐We've been talking for seven minutes⌐.

Here the underscores (_) mark utterances in low pitch, and the overscores (⌐) the new topic start. S goes low in pitch, and additionally signals his declining interest by many pauses and by decreased loudness, dropping all the way to a whisper by *that works*. His words are reduced, and he once clicks his tongue, a common signal of topic exhaustion.[1] J then shows that she has nothing to add, with a low-pitched *hm* and *that's good*, both barely audible and flanked by long pauses. The topic thus having been declared dead and buried, metaphorically speaking, S starts a new topic, brightly announcing that they are well on their way to finishing the allotted ten minutes, which then leads to a new topic, that of the purpose of the recording.

Similarly, in the context of discussing the best semester to take the Networks class,

2) R: _I don't think it's right now_
   J: _I don't think it is_
   R: _it's with Romero_

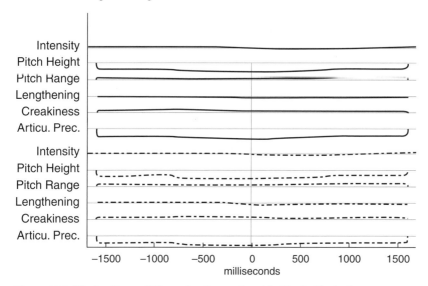

Figure 12.1 The loadings of Dimension 5, negative side (Topic Closing)

> J: _I don't know him_
> R: _I've never had a class with him_
> J: _me neither_
> R: ⁻There's a lot of professors I haven't had a class with⁻

both speakers are continuously in low pitch for several seconds, bringing the topic to an end, and then in the last line R jumps to a related but new topic.

Figure 12.1 shows the loadings of Dimension 5 on the negative side. These suggest that such topic closings typically have low pitch but no tendency to narrow pitch, which can distinguish this pattern from the low flat pitch of negativity. These closings also weakly tend to creaky voice. As noted earlier, this can contribute a nuance of distancing: here distancing from the current topic. Critically, this is a joint construction, with the same loadings for the features of both speakers. Thus, both speakers may contribute a few low pitch utterances in order to display joint readiness to move on to a new topic.

As these examples illustrate, another factor involved in topic closing is low intensity: the speakers say little, and what they do say is quiet. In terms of the dimensions, this is often a superimposed contribution of Dimension 2, negative, as seen back in Figure 11.5.

Incidentally, this topic closing pattern seems to have affinities for repetition, for shared laughter, and for certain words and phrases,[2] like *um, yeah, anyway, you know, I dunno*, and

> 3) _so that's basically how it is_.

Topic Closing Pattern

Function: indicate willingness to move on to a new topic

Form:

timespan	prosodic properties
over about 3 seconds	both speakers: low in pitch low in articulatory precision with slightly creaky voice somewhat wide pitch range

mnemonic: Low-Quiet-Reduced

Figure 12.2 The Topic Closing Pattern

Figure 12.2 summarizes this construction.

12.2   Topic Starting and Continuation

The opposite of topic closing is topic continuation, and, unsurprisingly, this involves the opposite features, including high pitch rather than low pitch, and enunciation rather than reduction. Figure 12.3 shows the loadings of Dimension 5, positive: these are, of course, the exact opposite of the negative-side loadings seen in the previous section.

Thus when Dimension 5 is positively present, the speakers are usually engaged in the topic. The major prosodic indications, high pitch and precise articulation, are often especially salient at the beginning of new topics,[3] as already seen in the examples in the previous section. These can be informally described as having a "bright" feel, and in a novel they might be flagged with exclamation marks. This could be done for example in

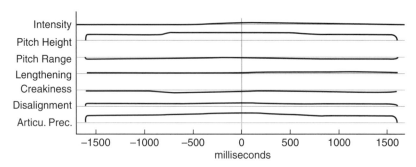

Figure 12.3 The loadings of Dimension 5, positive side (Topic Starting/Continuation)

4) M: *do you want to stay in school, or do you want to, like*
        try to get a job as a ... programmer
    J: ⁻*oh, I want to go into industry!*⁻   *yeah*
    M: *okay, so*
    J: *I didn't want to do a Masters*

where, after a minute of faltering conversation and repeated failure to find a topic of mutual interest, the participants at last found something engaging.

Sometimes both speakers participate in marking the jump to a new topic. After S had been saying how uninteresting his classes are, and had driven home the point by saying that the class he likes best is the one that's least demanding, J forcefully proposes a new topic, and S with high pitch accepts this.

5) S: _*it's nice to have a class that I can not care about*_
    J: ⁻*okay, well what's the favorite class that you do learn*
        something in?⁻
    S: (laughs) ⁻*um*⁻
    J: *content-wise, what's your favorite class?*

Sometimes speakers have to suddenly shift gears, jumping to a new, high-priority topic. In

6) S: _*we're making a project for, our project is for him*_   ⁻*Move*
        that thing?⁻

S notices that the screensaver has launched, and interrupts himself to ask the other person to move the mouse. As a priority request, this is in high pitch. Experiments with realistic interruptions have also found this connection, showing that the more disruptive the priority task, relative to the previous dialog activity, the higher its pitch will be.[4]

Another common correlate of new topics is late pitch peaks, as discussed in Chapter 6. This is also seen in the loadings in Figure 12.3, and is hearable in the previous two examples.

Figure 12.4 summarizes this pattern. Overall, the features mentioned in these two sections match up with those identified by previous research as marking "discourse boundaries" in monologue,[5] in both English and Dutch. The oppositional nature of Dimension 5 suggests that topic boundaries involve not a discrete choice but rather a scale: that topic closing versus continuing is a continuum.

12.3   Topic Development

One might think, logically, that there are only two topic-related activities available to speakers: continue a topic or change it. In real data, however, we can observe three more behaviors. The first is topic development, also known as

Topic Start/Continuation Pattern

Function: show interest; start or sustain a topic

Form:

timespan	prosodic properties
over about 3 seconds	one or both speakers high in pitch high in articulatory precision non-creaky voice somewhat narrow pitch range one or more late peaks

mnemonic: High-Enunciated

Figure 12.4 The Topic Start/Continuation Pattern

topic progression and topic elaboration. In this the focus shifts as a topic develops or evolves over time.[6] A pattern commonly associated with this is the negative side of Dimension 6, as seen in Figure 12.5.

This involves a short pause, then a rather sudden increase in intensity with creaky voice. Consider the following, in which J is responding to a question about her favorite movies, but after listing a few, turns the tables to ask whether M likes a movie:

7) J: ... *Harry Potter, Lord of the Rings*
    M: *yeah*
    J: *but I also really loved the Boondock Saints.*† *Have you ever watched that movie?*

Here the dagger, †, marks the point of topic redirection. This particular conversational move, switching from one person's perspective to the other's, is a common gambit in topic development, but there are many others.

Consider also

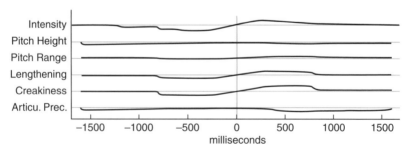

Figure 12.5 Some loadings of Dimension 6, negative side (Topic Progression)

Topic Development Construction

Function: shift to a new subtopic

Form:

timespan	prosodic properties
a brief pause	one or both speakers
$0 \sim 800$	increased intensity
$400 \sim 800$	low pitch, creaky voice, lengthening

mnemonic: Creaky Low Start

Figure 12.6 The Topic Development Construction

8) G: *she'll put our names on the sheet, so that we can turn it in*
      at the beginning of class†
   S: *okay*
   G: *I mean we'll all have worked on it, but*
   S: *at different times*

where on the third line G pivots from the logistics of turning in the assignment to the new subtopic of whether the team members all contributed.

Figure 12.6 summarizes this construction. While some theories of discourse make a sharp distinction between topic change and topic progression, in conversation there is again a gradient.[7] As the transition from one topic or subtopic to another is larger, the superimposed contribution of Dimension 5 may become proportionately stronger.

12.4 Digressions

During one topic a speaker can briefly digress to take up another topic, often marking this with reduced pitch range,[8] as in

9) M: *he's being hailed as the JR (JRR, JRR Tolkien, is that it?*
   J: *JR Tolkien, yeah*
   M: *just JR Tolkien, right.) He's being hailed as*
      the Tolkien of this era.

and

10) E: *so, how'd you do on the assignment?*
    G: *(assignment, which one?*
    E: *uh, the one for AI, creating the rooms.)*
    G: *uh, I did alright, except ...*

where the parentheses indicate the region of reduced range. Figure 12.7 summarizes this pattern, the Digression Construction. It may involve one speaker or two.

Digression Construction

Function: introduce a time-limited small topic

Form:

a sudden shift to a narrower pitch range

mnemonic: Shift to Narrow

Figure 12.7 The Digression Construction

In terms of the dimensions, digressions are associated with Dimension 12. Indeed, the examples above were both extremes on this dimension. While Dimension 12 is also associated with the Cueing Construction, with quite different prosody, the PCA analysis does not distinguish the two. This may be due to the limitations of the current feature set or to the lack of enough examples of both in the data.

12.5   Interpolated, Meta-, and High-Priority Utterances

The final pattern in this chapter marks utterances as standing outside the normal topic structure. This corresponds to the negative side of Dimension 11. As seen in Figure 12.8, the loadings indicate a slow rise in pitch, rather low intensity, and fast speaking rate. Listening to the exemplars, two additional features seem to be generally present: a subsequent silence, and breathy voice.

In this book we have not yet talked about breathy voice. Perceptually, breathy voice is a mild case of whisper. In a full whisper, the vocal folds flutter as the air passes by, never fully closing. Breathy voice is a milder case, with irregular or incomplete glottal closings, as the air passes through the glottis in a disorderly flow, rather than in neat, discrete pulses.[9] In whispering we use this effect to be quieter so as not to be overheard. Breathy voice is not so extreme, but still tends to be quiet. Many speakers use slightly breathy voice as a default, but in the examples here the breathiness is relatively stronger.

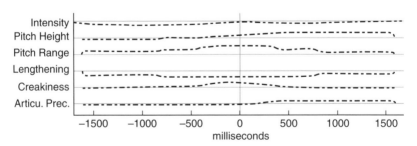

Figure 12.8 Some loadings of Dimension 11, negative side (Interpolations, Meta-Comments, and Priority Topics)

As a technical note, while our set of 212 features lacks a feature for breathy voice, fortuitously it appears here in a pattern anyway. This is because it has slight correlations with a high rate of change in the sound (and thus low values on the lengthening feature), with high pitch, with intensity that is lower than would be otherwise expected, and with the creaky-voice feature.[10] This shows the value of using a large number of prosodic features, even if some are mutually redundant in most contexts.

Now let's examine some times that are low on Dimension 11, starting with

11) R: *which one's your favorite?*
     J: *Programming Languages, because it's the only*
        hope I ⊔have (laughing)
     R: (laughs) <sil:0.3> *I'm taking five classes . . .*

where the square cup, ⊔, marks roughly the start of the pitch rise. However, since these features in this pattern have fairly wide temporal spans, the exact position is not that significant.

In this example, J jokes that only in one class does she have a chance of earning an A. This is clearly not intended to advance the topic. In response, R laughs briefly but does not otherwise acknowledge the comment, and she then immediately moves on. This pattern frequently involves laughter or laughed words, as in

12) J: *I love ethics* ⊔(laughs)
     S: ⊔(laughs)

Here again, this comment and the resulting laughter are not connected to the previous topic nor to an upcoming one. It's an off-topic throw-away line: an irrelevant little interpolation of levity, after which the speakers return to their main topic.

However, this pattern does not always involve laughter. In

13) E: *let's get to the other topic, about your major*
     L: *these topics are . . . we wouldn't talk about these topics in*
        normal ⊔life
     E: *fine, I'll just leave it on the table*
     L: *alright, what would you do with your major?*

L throws out a swift protest in the second line, and his use of breathy voice and the other properties of this pattern shows that this is a kneejerk reaction rather than something intended to be taken seriously. Indeed, two seconds later he's abandoned his objection and is back with the suggested topic.

The use of this pattern to mark a lack of connection to the ongoing topic can also be seen in

14) L: *you can go out with a friend, and go get some food, you can*
     E: *but you're not even answering my ⊔question*

where the speaker steps outside the flow of the conversation to make a meta-comment about his interlocutor's conversational behavior, with the strong breathy voice also conveying exasperation. Another example is

15) *how much time do ⌐we have?*

where the speaker steps outside the conversation to ask about the duration of the recording session.

This pattern can also be part of openings and closings. It may appear at the start of a dialog, here as the participants verify that the recording equipment is functioning:

16) L: *alright, we're live ⌐man*
    E: *we're ⌐live*

Again, this is not proposing or continuing a topic; it lacks even the weak topic connection seen in digressions. Rather it is outside the normal flow of dialog. Similarly, at conversation end, as in

17) S: *well it's like Bejewelled, but better*
    (timer beeps)
    G: *is that the timer?*
    S: *I don't know*
    G: ⌐*yep*

and in an example already seen, where the first *bye* exhibits, superimposed on an action-cueing downstep, strongly breathy voice:

18) J: *we can stop I guess*
    R: *yeah?*
    J: *yeah*
    R: *okay. ⌐bye!*
    J: *bye*

Breathy voice can occur in self-directed speech, as in the game corpus when one player said

19) ⌐*whee!*

as she made a bold jump; her prosody indicating, among other things, that this utterance was not connected to any larger topic. Also in the game corpus

20) M: *alright, here, let's do this together*
    H: *okay*
    M: *one . . .*
    H: ⌐*jump, jump, jump!*

illustrates an urgent command using this construction. M had proposed a plan which they were about to jointly execute, but they lose their balance and H sees that they now need to jump right away. In the same way,

Interpolation/Meta-Comment Construction

Function: mark something as unconnected to the ongoing discourse

Form:

timespan	prosodic properties
−1500 to 1000 ms	lower intensity, quick, often breathy
−800 to +400 ms	pitch rise, often breathy

mnemonic: Breathy Rising

Figure 12.9 The Interpolation/Meta-Comment Construction

21) ⌴*look out!*

is probably also breathy in general. This relates back to Searle's observation about the so-called rules of turn-taking:[11]: when the situation calls for an immediate warning, people will do what they need to do, without thinking to obey any putative rules. While certainly true, even high-priority exclamations are not done haphazardly; rather, speakers tend to use the specific prosodic construction that English provides for this purpose.

In general, the meaning of breathy voice seems to relate to three related things. First, there are meta-comments that step outside the flow of the conversation, for example to say something about the appropriateness of a topic, the behavior of an interlocutor, the recording quality, the amount of time left, or to open or close the conversation. Second, there are one-offs, to make an in-passing protest or say something funny, without much connection with what's come before or what will come after. And finally, there are priority topics, things that must be said immediately. Figure 12.9 summarizes this construction.

Just for fun, let's speculate about what primordial mapping might underlie the common occurrence of breathy voice in these uses. The dialog uses of breathy voice have not been systematically studied in English, but Ishi's work on Japanese offers a clue.[12] In addition to some roles that sound strange for English speakers, such as marking with politeness, breathy voice is, as in English, used when laughing and talking to oneself, and when showing surprise. The latter is easy to understand: when a speaker needs to produce a sound all of a sudden, as in *look out!*, there is no time to prepare the glottis, so the voicing may start out weak and unstable. This may underlie the other meanings: given the commonality between sudden starts and a lack of connection to the previous activity or topic, it is easy to imagine how the inevitable use of breathy voice for the one could have become extended to conventionalized uses for the other.

13   Stance-Related Constructions

The third main realm of functions of prosody in dialog, after turn-taking and topic management, is stance. Stance refers, very broadly, to the attitude of the speaker towards what he or she is saying.[1] We've already seen two patterns that express stance: the Consider This Construction and the Positive Assessment Construction. This chapter presents four more, relating to seeking empathy, asserting independence, appealing to shared knowledge, and being factual.

13.1   Seeking Empathy and Agreement

Sometimes people really want to be understood. In the corpus, this often arises when they talk about personal preferences or feelings.

1) *I'd feel wrong graduating in May and still having a ◇class left over*

2) *I really want to do a Masters, and probably a Ph.D., but ◇um*

Dimension 7, positive, as seen in Figure 13.1, typically involves several seconds over which the speaker articulates their words and uses high pitch and a slightly reduced pitch range. In addition, within that span there may be a short region with lengthening and slightly louder than the rest, with a late peak. In the examples the center of this pattern is marked with a ◇; however, of course this pattern is not just about the prosody at a single point.

This pattern serves to bid for empathy or understanding of the speaker's specific situation or perspective. Figure 13.2 summarizes this construction, which I will call the Empathy Bid Construction.

This is used, for example, to seek empathy for personal tribulations and triumphs, as in

3) G: *he's a good professor. he's tough. I love that look that he*
        gives you, like, 'you're an idiot' ...
    S: *you ask him something and he's like*
        (mimics the professor giving a quizzical stare)
        'are you retarded?' and you're like
        'but I ◇asked, like, really nice'
    G: (laughs)

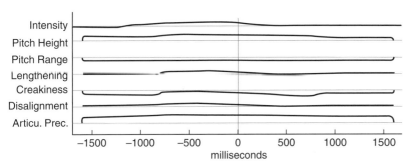

Figure 13.1 Some loadings of Dimension 7, positive side (Empathy Bid)

4) *uh, pretty ◇good I'm getting ◇'A's in all my classes*

As a special case, people use this pattern when telling stories, often to signal ahead that they will recount something that may deserve empathy. Examples include description of the situation leading up to a car crash,

5) E: *well I didn't see the stop ◇sign . . .*

6) E: *this was a tree; this was not an El Paso ◇small tree . . .*

the situation leading up to an embarrassing experience,

7) E: *they had two ◇costumes; they had a pink unicorn ...*

and the situation where the speaker keeps getting teased:

8) J: *when I ◇play online, I get so many 'get back to the kitchen's*
    M: *what is that?*
    J: *you know, 'get back to the kitchen and make me a sandwich,*
        because you're a girl'
    M: *oh*

It also occurs when seeking agreement about a negative assessment of something, as in an example already seen:

9) *L: but these topics ◇are . . . we wouldn't talk about this in*
        normal life, like why are we talking about these topics?
    E: *fine, I'll just leave it on the table*

This pattern is also used when seeking agreement about a positive assessment, as in

10) G: *she knows we're ◇enjoying the class*
     S: *well, that's true too*

where S had suggested that the professor probably thought of them both as goofballs, but G suggests a more positive spin.

Empathy Bid Construction

Function: seek empathy

Form:

timespan	prosodic properties
−1500 to +1500 ms	articulated speech, raised pitch, little or no creakiness, narrow pitch range
−600 to −200 ms	increased loudness, lengthening, late peak
−200 to +400	gradual decrease in loudness

mnemonic: High Articulated

Figure 13.2 The Empathy Bid Construction

This pattern also occurs when suggesting a word, to seek confirmation that it's correct,

11) M: *I haven't learned anything in um ... what's the other one?*
    J: ◇*programming?*
    M: *Programming Languages. well, Programming Languages maybe.*
       I learned ...

when trying to get someone to understand your point of view,

12) L: *is the Walking Dead good?*
    E: *dude, you know it's good*
    L: *dude, I've never seen it; that's why I'm asking*
    R: *whaaat?* (skeptically)
    L: *I've never ... all these ◇people talk about it and I've never ...*

and when seeking agreement on a course of action, for example, instead of just putting everyone's names on an assignment,

13) S: *we should, we ◇should get like that, work scheduled, kind of like,*
     we should honestly do the homework on Monday or something

This example also exhibits superimposed late peaks and a bookended narrow pitch. Such superimpositions are common, as people often seek empathy or agreement when complaining or when bringing up a point for consideration. In terms of form, the Bookended Narrow Pitch Construction is highly compatible with the Empathy Bid Construction as both involve narrow pitch.

Incidentally, listeners respond to empathy bids in various ways, with an interesting special case being "upgraded assessments."[2] In these, one speaker assesses something as good or bad, using moderate language, and then the other agrees strongly. For example, I might observe that the weather today is *nice,* and you might say *absolutely beautiful,* or *truly delightful.* Consider an example that occurred while discussing a class. R has said that it had been easy for him because a key technology had fortuitously already been covered in another class. Unfortunately, when G took that class, the coverage had changed. He says:

14) G: *I would have loved to have been able to do that ◊before going into the class; I figure it would have helped a lot*
   R: *oh, yeah, it would have; you would have been set*

In the corpus dialogs, the bids for empathy are all relatively mild, but more intense bids can also follow this pattern. Consider a childish whine

15) *Mommy, ◊Jimmy's bothering me!*

and a heartfelt plea

16) *could you help me out with some ◊money for food?*

Such empathy bids can become very finely tuned. A speaker who says this hundreds of times a day has ample opportunity to learn what works and what doesn't. In a sense, his plea undergoes "natural selection," where the better prosody gets rewarded, and over time, the plea evolves into something maximally effective for the circumstances.

Speculatively, the use of this prosody to bid for empathy may be rooted in a primordial mapping: infants crying for comfort will often use high pitch and a narrow range, and listeners by instinct are moved to empathize and infer what the baby needs.

13.2   Expressing Independence and Indifference

Empathy is partly automatic: listeners have a general tendency to come to share the speaker's affective state.[3] But empathy is also context-dependent, and in conversation, speakers can cue listeners to temporarily increase their empathic sensitivity. The opposite also happens: sometimes speakers disclaim any desire for empathy, and instead proclaim their independence and self-sufficiency. This is the opposite of seeking empathy, and its prosody is the opposite of that of empathy bids. Figure 13.3 shows some loadings of Dimension 7, negative. It involves a broad span of reduced speech, low pitch, mostly creaky voice and fairly wide pitch range, and in the middle of that a region of quiet, fast speech. This is marked with triangles in the examples below. Figure 13.4 summarizes the key properties of the construction.

While not common in the primary corpus, an example occurred where the speakers were discussing bugs in their programs. After S describes the nature of his bug,

17) S: *mine was off by one*
   G: *that was mine too, but I managed to △fix it in the session, so he only took off one point for that*

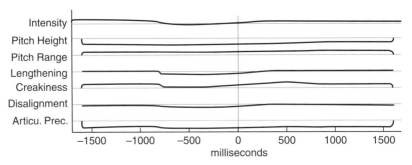

Figure 13.3 Some loadings of Dimension 7, negative side (Indifference Construction)

Indifference Construction

Function: take an independent stance

Form:

timespan	prosodic properties
–1500 to +1500 ms	reduced speech, low pitch, creaky voice, wide pitch range
–600 to –200 ms	quick, quiet speech

mnemonic: Mumble Fast

Figure 13.4 The Indifference Construction

G reveals that he had a similar problem but a different outcome. His prosody conveys that he was okay with that: he certainly is not playing for sympathy. Consider also, an utterance after a long explanation of why *Walking Dead* is such an interesting show:

18) L: *so I should watch it*
    E: *yeah, you should definitely watch it*
    L: *alright, I'll probably △watch it then*

L accepts E's suggestion, but probably only for the sake of ending the topic: his prosody blatantly proclaims a lack of commitment.

Incidentally, the A-speaker loadings of this dimension are similar to those of Dimension 5, negative, the Topic Closing Construction. In both cases there is reduced speech and low pitch; both convey a lack of interest and usually serve to end a topic. This construction, however, seems to connote more of an emotional sign-off on the part of one participant. In the loadings, the main difference between the two constructions is that in the Topic Closing Construction the loadings for speakers A and B are identical, but for this construction the loadings are opposites. The difference is seen in the following example, which is an exemplar of indifference but not of topic closing:

19) S: *but then, if they changed it in midstream. It depends.*
   △*I dunno.*
   J: ◇*yeah, but, don't you do most of the coding in Software 2?*

Here S wants to drop the topic, but J has something more to say. S's prosody exhibits the Indifference construction, and J's the Empathy Bid Construction: together they exemplify both sides of Dimension 7.

13.3   Appealing to Shared Knowledge with Nasal Voice

Speakers often refer to things that the other person is already aware of. This is commonly marked by using nasal voice. Consider a phrase used by counter workers to call forward the next customer:

20) ≻*can I help who's next?*≺

Here the slim angle brackets indicate nasal voice. In terms of content, what the speaker is saying here includes nothing new or surprising;[4] indeed the customer has already heard it several times while waiting in line. In contrast, a similar phrase that does convey new information

21) *can you see who's next?*

exhibits less nasal voice. Similarly,

22) ≻*since this is on sale, there are no refunds or exchanges*≺

is appealing to shared knowledge – customers generally already know the rules regarding sale items – and anticipates ready agreement and acceptance. In contrast, nasal voice is generally absent when conveying new information, as in

23) *it's under the sign that says no refunds or exchanges*

Since the 212 features do not, alas, include a feature for nasal voice, I was unable to examine this systematically. However, some of the previously presented examples exhibit a strongly nasal voice, and in each case they refer to or appeal to shared knowledge. This is seen in

24) *I know what you mean. I have the same class.* ≻*It's annoying,*
   how much homework is given.≺

and in Examples 6.10, 6.50, 6.72, and 13.15 above. Nasal voice also characterizes requests to do or not do something based on an appeal to shared knowledge of what's appropriate and inappropriate.

25) *hey, could you guys* ≻*keep it down?*≺

Nasal Voice Pattern

Function: appeal to shared knowledge or values

Form:

timespan	properties
–1500 to +1500 ms or more	nasal voice

Figure 13.5 The Nasal Voice Pattern

and on cues to do or refrain from doing something:

26) ≻*unh-uh*≺

We also saw nasal voice as a component of the Awww of Cute Construction, in which it is appropriate since that construction is used not to convey an individual opinion, but to express a presumably shared feeling.

Finally, consider again King's *I have a dream*. His dream was not some personal fantasy, but something that he wanted us to participate in; and the nasalization reinforces the appeal to norms that his listeners presumably all shared. Figure 13.5 summarizes this pattern.

Incidentally, the articulatory process behind nasal voice is quite interesting. A little way down your throat, just behind the dangling uvula, is the velum, a flap of tissue that guards the passage from the throat to the nasal passages. This can be fully open, fully closed, or in any position in between, and this can be true across different timescales. At the fastest timescale, in English the velar port is open for sounds like /m/ and /n/, where the lips or tongue completely block any air from escaping through the mouth. In French it also opens for nasal vowels. For these, air simultaneously passes through the mouth, but the nasal contribution changes the sound and distinguishes these from the oral vowels. This distinction is as fundamental to French as it is hard for Americans to master, since English does not use nasalization to distinguish phonemes in this way. At the slowest timescale, some people tend to keep the velum generally partially open, and this articulatory setting is said to be typically American: American English is said to be more nasal than British English. Our interest here, however, is in the use of nasal voice at intermediate timescales, lasting over a few words: it is on this timescale that it can be deployed meaningfully in English.

13.4   Explaining

Finally, let's take another look at Dimension 5, negative, with the loadings shown in the previous chapter (Figure 12.1). As noted there, this pattern most saliently involves low pitch, and it is often associated with closing a topic.

Low Pitch for Explaining Pattern

Function: mark a technical explanation

Form:

timespan	properties
−1500 to +1500 ms or more	low pitch

Figure 13.6 Low Pitch for Explaining

However, this pattern also has another role: it is common for explaining. Consider some technical talk about a software system,

27) _a temperature sensor, it's located in Antarctica, and for
        this time frame_

some talk about the picky details of choosing courses to complete the requirements for the degree,

28) R: *oh, because that one is JPO*
      J: *oh, I see*
      R: *_because I haven't taken it. So that's going to be the fifth one_*
      J: *you really don't have a choice*
      R: *no, I don't*

and some talk about what to choose as topic for the next tutorial in the series

29) S: *_I want to bring back the Android_*
      G: *the Android development?*
      S: *_I like Android development_*

In this last example, the words *I like* suggest an individual preference, but the prosody makes it clear that this is not about the speaker's personal feelings; rather he's starting a dispassionate review of the reasons why this would be a good topic for the next tutorial.

Figure 13.6 summarizes the connection.

This style of explaining can be overused. Doing so is a major symptom of "geekiness": appearing obsessed by knowledge and facts to the point of forgetting whether they are relevant in the current situation or of interest to the listener. If you're a teacher, this style of speech has to be in your repertoire, but this brings the occupational hazard of overusing it and appearing geeky.

The use of low pitch in explaining connects with the primordial functions of low pitch (Section 4.5), but is not universal. Once I was responsible for overseeing a systems administrator from Mexico. He was knowledgeable and sharp and kept the systems running flawlessly, but I always had trouble following his explanations. He gave me lots of information in small chunks, always checking my knowledge and understanding as he went along, but I never felt that I'd received a proper explanation. Later, I discovered this pattern, and the fact that many native speakers of Spanish seldom use it in explanations.[5] Some appear not to use it at all, and others tend to use it when talking about personal topics, such as family background, habits, intentions, and likes and dislikes. This prosodic difference may contribute to a general cross-cultural misunderstanding: American businessmen often perceive Mexicans, it has been said, as prone to bring personal and emotional considerations into business discussions, rather than rationally sticking to facts,[6] but this perception may in part be due to these differences in how often and when low pitch is used. Had I understood this difference earlier, I might have better appreciated my systems administrator's explanations.

14 The Rest of English Prosody

This book has presented a couple dozen constructions and other meaningful prosodic patterns. But there is a lot more to the prosody of English. This chapter briefly overviews the rest.

14.1 Other Functions

Our focus so far has been on the prosodic patterns most directly related to dialog, but there are many other relevant aspects of prosody.

First, prosody in English is important at the lexical level. For one thing, it helps mark lexical identity. Most words have prosodic tendencies,[1] most obviously, as dictionaries tell us, their stress patterns. For dialog, these provide sites for prosodic constructions to link to and manipulate. The prosody of individual words can also be manipulated in many ways.[2] We can add intensity and increase the pitch to add "emphasis" or "prominence," which can serve to convey "focus" or mark something as being new information,[3] or to draw the listener's attention to any aspect of the word or what that word refers to. This interacts in non-trivial ways with the meanings conveyed by prosodic constructions.

Second, prosody in English is pervasively used to indicate structures and boundaries, including word boundaries, rhetorical structures, and syntactic structures, including phrase and sentence boundaries.[4] These also provide sites for prosodic constructions to align with.

Third, prosody in English is used for social functions. Beyond prosodic constructions, this involves longer-term processes, most notably accommodation to the interlocutor's speaking patterns.[5] Such convergence can convey affection, liking, respect, empathy, and so on, and can also serve the purpose of changing the interlocutor's mood, opinions, or behavior. While some of these processes operate at the level of raw prosodic features (for example, if you speak faster, I may too), these effects are more often mediated by prosodic constructions: speakers may adapt to each other in terms of which constructions they use more often and their exact forms.

A complete, unified account of English prosody would of course cover these aspects and many more. I think the analysis methods used here might help, if the feature set was extended to have finer resolution, wider temporal span, and include features aligned to syllables, words, and phrases. But in any case, there is still a lot of work needed to connect up all the dots.

14.2   Fluency and Self-Presentation

There is often a trade-off between lexical fluency and prosodic fluency. Most people can produce perfect grammatical sentences only with effort, which typically results in stiff or choppy prosody. Conversely, most people can produce truly rich, flowing prosody only by sacrificing grammatical sophistication, like my undergraduate housemates from Sacramento whose utterances were largely composed of four-letter words.

Different people make different choices. Consider

1) A: *I just need to get that lab done, and* ⌐*I'm done with*⌐ ∟*that lab*⌟
   B: <sil:-0.2> *what, what about, where did you guys get in the homework?*

Lexically, B's turn-start is disfluent; on paper it looks awkward. However, the prosody is exemplary: a great match to the Basic Turn-Switch Construction. With a perfectly timed start, a nice clear turn-claim package, and a smooth resolution into a fluent utterance, the prosody is very natural.

Consider also

2) L: *it's like Buckwild*
   E: *yeah*
   L: *you know what that is, right*
   E: *no, I have no idea what that* [*is*
   L: [*it's on MTV,*
      [*you know, right?*
   E: [*uh*
   L: *you've never seen MTV? It's this . . .*

In terms of lexical content, this dialog fragment is quite goofy, as is much of the conversation it came from: ten minutes where the speakers have been deliberately misunderstanding each other, flouting politeness expectations, and generally teasing each other. But in terms of turn-taking and the deployment of prosodic cues, their behavior was fluent and coordinated, and they clearly enjoyed their interaction.

In general, appropriate prosodic behaviors may matter more, for achieving social effects, than lexical fluency or even the meaningful exchange of information.[6] Speakers may also choose different prosodic styles for purposes of self-presentation: to appear clever, dominant, appealing, polite, and so on. This is an important part of making a good first impression, but as yet, very little is known about how people actually manage it.[7]

14.3   Individual Variation in Prosodic Skills

In this book I have pretended that all speakers of American English use the same prosodic constructions, and use them in the same ways. But every speaker of English probably has his or her own particular model of prosody,[8] even within in the same dialect.[9] Nevertheless, our individual models have enough overlap that, with a little patience and persistence, at the end of a conversation we can at least get on the same page.

Probably every speaker of English also has his or her own set of prosodic skills. Sometimes we are tested on these. Consider job interviews. First comes the greeting phase, where you will need to display confidence and deference. Then comes some small talk, testing your ability to take turns with appropriate timing, to answer questions with replies of appropriate length, and to develop and end topics. There will be puzzles, requiring you think on your feet and use appropriate prosody to signpost your thought process and indicate how confident you are in your answers. There will be a description of the job, requiring you to backchannel to show you're interested and that you can quickly perceive what's important. There may be some misunderstandings, opportunities to show that you can mark contrast and make corrections. You'll need to show that you have the ability to empathize and are generally agreeable, but also that you bring solid expertise and a new perspective. You'll need to show that you have deeply held values, which coincidentally you share with your interviewer, and that you feel respect for your potential new co-workers. Deeper into the interview, you may need to demonstrate your ability to explain things and make suggestions. Finally, you may get an opportunity to negotiate terms and establish a commitment. All of these things involve prosodic constructions.

While no one deliberately plans a job interview to test prosodic skills, that would not be an entirely crazy idea. Prosody is an important part of communication ability, and people with better prosodic skills tend to have greater empathy.[10] Good prosody may also correlate with intelligence and other desirable traits. However, judgments based on prosody are not always correct. The "appropriateness" of prosodic behavior is cultural, and when the interviewer and the interviewee have different language or cultural backgrounds,[11] "small interactional differences and difficulties feed into larger scale judgments" regarding competence and attitude. These may be inaccurate and set some candidates at an unnecessary disadvantage, unrelated to their ability to actually do the job.

Be that as it may, the normal range of prosodic behaviors and abilities is vast.[12] Some speakers, for example, can produce utterances finely balanced between two forms. This is needed for successful punning and ambiguity-based jokes. This skill can also be used subversively. A few years ago, *whatever* (3) was in fashion as an all-purpose phrase for teenage girls. My daughter was able to produce a downstepped *whatever* that was perfectly ambiguous between the Cueing Construction and the Giving-In Construction, and was thus on the borderline between, on the one hand, sullenly accepting my parental authority on some issue, and on the other hand, cueing or demanding me to perform the "obviously appropriate" next action, namely dropping what she felt had become a tiresome topic.[13] As a parent, I found this vexing: I never knew how to respond. Fortunately, this was just a phase, gone after a couple of months.

Wide as is the normal range of abilities, there are also clinical populations with significant prosodic limitations, both in production and in comprehension. The deficits are diverse, and involve both innate and acquired conditions, such as amusia (tone deafness), autism, and conditions resulting from alcohol abuse and many other issues.[14] Children, of course, have different prosodic competencies, and specific abilities develop at different ages.[15] On these topics much remains to be discovered.

Larger questions aside, speaker differences were the main reason for stopping the PCA-based analysis after about twelve dimensions: it became gradually harder to see the commonalities across exemplars, as they were more often masked by the variations among speakers.

15 Envoi

If dialog is a garden, the words and grammar are the flowers and flowerbeds, and prosody is the lawns and trees, the paths and streams. The flowers get most of the attention, and books about language have mostly discussed words and how they combine to form meanings. For the man in the street too, language is mostly about the uses of words; and no wonder, since he's had thousands of hours of schooling on this, but nothing on prosody, except perhaps for giving speeches and reading poems.

But prosody is also part of the garden: it frames the words and meanings, tying them together and giving them social significance. Like the paths in the garden, prosodic patterns are easy to use without noticing. Even when you do notice, it's hard to pin down their contributions. But without prosody, words lack impact. This book has attempted to reveal what prosody means and how.

15.1   Summary

My goal for this book was to describe most of the prosody of English dialog. How far have we come? In terms of the dimensions, we've covered the top twelve, as seen in Table 15.1, and these together account for 44 percent of the observed variance. In terms of roles, we've inventoried around twenty general constructions that handle many important dialog functions. We've also covered a sampling of minor constructions and primordial mappings.

This book also explored the utility of a new model of dialog prosody, in which the key elements are prosodic constructions, that is, multistream temporal configurations of prosodic features, and the key combining principle is superposition. Building on insights from previous work, this enabled the systematization of many previously disparate findings, and the discovery of heretofore unsuspected patterns.

Nevertheless, this is far from the whole story. The descriptions need extension, refinement, and elaboration, and they need to be better connected to the other components of prosody. The model itself has inadequacies and limitations. I hope that others will improve the model and the methods, and will go on to discover many more marvels of prosody.

Table 15.1 *The top twelve PCA-derived prosodic dimensions*

1	14%	n:	Has Turn, speaker A
		p:	ditto, speaker B
2	6%	n:	Reluctance (Delay)
		p:	Shared Enthusiasm (Wide-Range Overlap)
3	4%	n:	Basic Turn-Switch, B to A
		p:	ditto, A to B
4	3%	n:	Backchanneling Construction, B as listener
		p:	ditto, A as listener
5	3%	n:	Topic Closing (Both Low)
		p:	Topic Continuation, Involvement (High Articulated Wide)
6	3%	n:	Topic Development (Creaky Low Start)
		p:	Positive Assessment (High then Loud then Quiet)
7	2%	n:	Empathy Bid (High Articulated)
		p:	Indifference (Mumble Fast)
8	2%	n:	Fillers (Lengthened Loud Narrow)
		p:	Bipartite Construction (Creaky Wide)
9	2%	n:	Particle-Assisted Turn-Switch, A to B
		p:	ditto, B to A
10	2%	n:	Non-Action-Oriented (Late Peaks)
		p:	Fillers (Lengthened Loud Narrow)
11	2%	n:	Interpolation/Meta-Comment (Breathy Rising)
		p:	Consider This (Bookended Narrow Pitch)
12	1%	n:	Action Cueing (Minor Third Downstep), A to B
		p:	ditto, B to A

The second field is the amount of variance explained by the dimension. The third field lists an associated construction when this factor is negatively or positively present, that is, "positive-side" and "negative-side" constructions.

15.2   The Advantages of Imperfect Understanding

I dream of a day when prosody is all figured out: the general constructions, the minor constructions, the primordial mappings, and everything else, plus the exact details of how they all combine. We would then have a fully adequate model of prosody: a stunning scientific achievement. This should of course be done not only for English but for all languages.[1]

At the same time, I don't think we'll ever understand prosody completely, and this is probably a good thing.

Imagine a dystopia in which people are as accountable for their prosody as they are for their words. One consequence would be a loss of ambiguities useful in daily communication. If your boss asks you to do something ill advised, but you are unable to say *no*, you can instead say *okay* in a way that conveys that you have concerns, while saving her from losing face. While she could in theory come back with *don't talk to me in that tone of voice*, no reasonable person would do so: prosody is today not something that people can pin down, so you're not accountable for it in the same way you are for your words. This is a good thing. The uncertainties of prosodic meanings help people rub along with less friction. However, as we improve our understanding of prosody, we may come to live in a world in which the ambiguities have vanished. Imagine your mentor telling you that *your references to the Supreme Leader over the past two weeks have been statistically low on Dimension 6...* or a prosecutor closing his arguments with *Ladies and Gentlemen of the jury, the recording shows that his pitch peak on the critical syllable was delayed over 90 milliseconds. Surely, as a society, we cannot tolerate such behavior.* If we come to understand prosody too well, that knowledge could be misused to control or shut down communication. My hope is that, instead, sincere attempts to communicate will always be respected, including speakers' rights to use prosody flexibly, without fear.

Apart from such hypothetical, futuristic concerns, there are risks today. Consider an example from a dialog collected in a test of the recording setup:

1) L: *What's the last movie you saw?*
   N: *I haven't seen anything since Lincoln.*
   L: *Lincoln, okay, I haven't seen that one.*
   N: <sil:-0.8> *That was really good though. No, it was good.*
   L: *It was good?*

Here N's second turn starts early, gratuitously overlapping L's continued speech. When listening, it sounds like a dominance display. The shock here is that N was me. When I first listened to this recording fragment I was disappointed in how far my turn-taking behavior diverged from my ideals. After all, it is self-evident that all men are created equal, and I believe I treat everyone with respect. Shouldn't my turn-taking live up to this?

And yet, maybe my behavior was not really out of line. Over decades of interacting with students my turn-taking behaviors have evolved into something that works well with them. I remember that as a new professor, I consistently failed to take control in conversations with students, resulting in mushy, inefficient, confusing-for-everyone interactions. And I see other teachers frequently displaying their status in their turn-taking. So perhaps my behavior is not really that appalling. Certainly it was not fatal in our little conversation about movies: the dominance-tinted turn-taking didn't seem to bother Luis nor impede the communication of important information.[2]

However, it's easy to imagine a dystopia in which people self-limit or adjust their prosody to match their political ideals, regardless of whether doing so might make anyone happier or more effective. I think we should be cautious about judging each other's dialog behaviors based on ideology. There are too many realms of language – while hiking, in the kitchen, while shopping, at work, out with friends, and so on – too many languages in contact, too many subcultures with their own minor constructions and flavors of general constructions, too many personalities, and too many goals to expect a priori norms to always make sense. Rather, I think we should generally respect people, including ourselves, for doing whatever works for them and the people they interact with.

15.3   Dialog Prosody for Fun and Profit

While this is not a self-help book, I hope that knowledge of these constructions and patterns will be helpful, and perhaps even a source of power: the power to improve your life and the lives of those around you.

Perhaps you will apply this knowledge of prosody to workplace problems. In the early 1980s, John Gumperz, while consulting, met a group of English native speakers who felt mistreated because the cafeteria servers were always rude to them.[3] Among various cross-cultural issues, Gumperz found a solid specific complaint: the servers, all immigrants from South Asia, tended to offer side dishes using a falling pitch, perhaps

2) $gravy$

rather than the more typical rising pitch for offers:

3) $gravy$

For the native English speakers, the falling pitch was clearly rude, conveying a cold "take it or leave it" attitude, but the servers of course had no such intention. This trivial difference in behavior caused serious bad feelings, and, until Gumperz came along, no one realized the connection to subconscious prosodic behaviors and perceptions.[4]

Maybe in the good old days such problems never arose: speakers talking to others in the same village could select prosodic patterns from the common toolbox without conscious thought, and interpret what they heard reflexively, without problems. Everyone was on the same page. But now in our globally connected lives,[5] we need more awareness and more effort as we deal with people whose prosody is not what we're used to. If you do notice a prosody-based

miscommunication, perhaps you can figure out how to help, either by helping learners of English become more effective communicators; or by helping
those who deal with learners to see past the unfamiliar or awkward prosodic
behaviors to appreciate the actual intentions [6]

Or perhaps you could examine situations in your own life. A first step to
better communication can be debugging specific issues. Deborah Tannen, for
example, noticed interesting differences between her husband's conversational
practices and expectations and her own. She figured out some of the causes
of misunderstandings, tracing them back to cultural patterns, and distilled her
findings into a series of insightful books.[7]

You have to be careful, though. Professor Tannen is also famous for
cautioning her graduate students, in the first week of class, not to pay
attention to dialog phenomena when they are talking with someone they
care about. In important dialogs, the priority is to devote full attention to
working to communicate, despite any differences in communication styles.
Don't be an observer in situations where you need to be a fully engaged
participant.

Or perhaps you could use this knowledge just for fun. I like to observe
prosody while traveling. Hearing English in novel dialects makes it more interesting. And overhearing while traveling enables a helpful detachment: if you
overhear two strangers talking about a boss, you're not tempted to care who's
in the right; you can just pay attention to how they voice their complaints. And
traveling provides lots of time to ruminate, replaying what you've heard over
again in your mind, while walking to the next sight or riding the shuttle. Wher-
ever you do it, you may spot many things of beauty: stunningly appropriate
uses of standard constructions, hot new minor constructions, and fresh creative
construction combinations.

While language is a garden, to admire and study, it is also a source of power.
One special kind of language tool is the magic spell. Across cultures, spells
are sources of power, enabling individuals with special knowledge to harness
or unleash greater forces. Consider, for example, *abracadabra*, or *lumos*, or *O
great all-creating God, nourish, protect, and bless these seeds*, or my favorite:
*by the authority invested in me by the Regents of the University of Texas, I
hereby confer upon you the degree of Bachelor of Science.* As suggested by
their other names, "incantations" and "enchantments," spells should be ritually
chanted, or at least declaimed with special prosody, different from the prosody
of either speech or song. Spells are absolutely fixed in form and, on all literary
evidence, single-purpose. Having learned the spell to, say, change someone
into a newt, if you decide you'd rather change them into a frog, you can't just
modify or inflect the spell, you have to go back to the Hogwarts library for a
new one. Spells are invariably ancient – with archaic syntax or even in a dead
language – and eternally unchanging.

Prosodic constructions similarly may have ancient roots, but they are a living part of language. Mastering a prosodic construction is not just memorizing a form once and thereafter performing it unchanged forever; rather it involves sensitivity to specific situations, contexts, and aims. Prosodic constructions need to be fresh every time: selected, trimmed, and tailored to work in concert with other constructions and specific words and gestures. Unlike timelessly eternal spells, they are fundamentally part of the here-and-now of human interaction. Unlike magic spells, the larger forces you engage with prosody are not supernatural forces, but the goodwill and energies of your fellow humans. Enjoy your power, and use it for good!

Notes

Chapter 2 Bookended Narrow Pitch Regions

1. Kurumada et al. (2012); Kurumada and Clark (2017)
2. Redrawn from Kurumada et al. (2012), by permission
3. Redrawn from Kurumada et al. (2012), by permission
4. Braun et al. (2006)
5. Some discussions of this pattern focus on these alone. However, producing two pitch peaks without an interleaved region of narrow pitch is not a normal way to convey contrast. It is true that in the laboratory such examples can be obtained, for example by requiring subjects to produce contrastive intonation on short phrases such as *you like John* (Goodhue et al., 2015). However, it is not clear what this tells us about the general pattern: just as watching people in sack races may not tell us much about normal human locomotion.
6. Xu et al. (2012)
7. Calhoun (2009)
8. Ladd (1978); Laver (1994); Constant (2012); Silverman et al. (1992)
9. Liberman and Sag (1974)
10. Redrawn from Liberman and Sag (1974), by permission
11. Cutler (1977)
12. Cutler (1977)
13. Redrawn from (Hedberg et al., 2003), by permission
14. Redrawn from (Hedberg et al., 2003), by permission
15. Hedberg et al. (2003)
16. Lai (2012); see also Goodhue and Wagner (2018)
17. Lai (2012), by permission
18. Ogden (2007)
19. Ogden (2007)
20. Kay and Fillmore (1999)
21. Ogden (2007); Wright (2011)
22. Jefferson (1988); Tannen (1990); Michaud and Warner (1997); Ogden (2006); Traverso (2009)
23. Zellers and Ogden (2014)
24. Ogden (2007)
25. 't Hart et al. (2006)
26. Sometimes this construction is part of a larger pattern, a two-part structure where the contrast is made explicit, as in *you might want a drink, but you won't want any food* (Barth-Weingarten, 2009).

27. Although for another view, see Constant (2012)
28. Fillmore (1975)
29. Lakoff (1987)
30. Kochanski (2006)
31. Braun et al. (2006)
32. Pittam (1994); Cole (2015)
33. Yip (2002), although prosody in Mandarin still plays important roles in many pragmatic functions (Ward et al., 2016a).
34. Whorf (2012); Hoffman et al. (1986); Slobin (1987); Boroditsky (2001)
35. Condon (1985)
36. Gladwell (2008)
37. Ogden (2007, 2012); Petrone and Niebuhr (2013); Niebuhr (2014); Hedberg et al. (2017); Ward (2014)

Chapter 3 Downstep Constructions

1. Pike (1945); Ladd (1978); Huttenlauch et al. (2018)
2. Ladd (2008)
3. Coren (2011)
4. Ladd describes these as "stereotypical" situations, and Jeong as contexts in which there exists "a salient goal" (Ladd, 1978; Jeong and Condoravdi, 2017).
5. Ward and Abu (2016)
6. Ladd (1978)
7. Jeong and Condoravdi (2017)
8. Brown and Levinson (1987); Wichmann (2004); Kendrick and Drew (2016)
9. The initial greeting can of course do much more: it may indicate approval, register how much time has passed since the previous meeting, set the tone for the rest of the conversation, and so on (Pillet-Shore, 2012).
10. Day-O'Connell (2013)
11. Ladd (1978); Niebuhr (2015)
12. Bolinger (1986)
13. Day-O'Connell (2013)
14. Niebuhr (2015)
15. Godfrey et al. (1992)
16. The need for silence after this construction was also noted by Ladd, as reported by Gussenhoven (2004, p. 314).
17. This diagram is inspired by gestural scores as developed in articulatory phonology (Browman and Goldstein, 1992; Byrd and Saltzman, 1998).
18. Lakoff (1987); Arvaniti (2011); Walsh et al. (2010); Kapatsinski et al. (2017)
19. Gick et al. (2013); Xu (2017)
20. Grabe (1998); van Santen et al. (2006); Torreira and Grice (2018)
21. O'Connor and Arnold (1973); Selkirk (1996); Gussenhoven (2004); Arvaniti (2011); Krivokapic (2014); Windmann et al. (2015)
22. Although this alignment is often not exact (Niebuhr, 2015)
23. Niebuhr (2014)
24. Ladd (1978)
25. Ladd (1978)

26. Greenberg et al. (2009)
27. Something similar is seen for syntactic constructions (Pederson, 1991; Taylor, 2004).
28. MedlinePlus (2014); Fernald and O'Neill (1993)
29. Prosody is also important in other ways to the earliest stages of language learning (Echols, 1993; Fernald, 1989; Snow and Balog, 2002; Goffman and Westover, 2013; Balog, 2012).
30. Redrawn from Fernald and O'Neill (1993), by permission
31. Heritage and Raymond (2016)
32. Pinker (2007)
33. This construction is also common with attention-getting uses of *sumimasen*, for calling (*yobikake*), and for other social cueing functions.
34. This is *inai-inai-ba* (Fernald, 1989). Incidentally, there is a good reason why Japanese uses something other than the downstep for social cueing: in Japanese, downsteps are not available for pragmatic purposes since they are fully employed in marking word identity. Just as Mandarin has tones that distinguish phonetically identical syllables, Japanese has pitch accents (rather like downsteps), whose locations distinguish phonetically identical words. Although such downsteps play a minor role in the language in general, they are emphasized in broadcast news and babytalk, as in *mama* for *Mommy*. So this chunk of prosodic bandwidth is not available for peek-a-boo or other social cueing, except in rare cases such as occasional playful calling (Abe, 1998) and in toddlers' productions of *bai-bai*, a borrowing from English *bye-bye*.
35. Fernald and O'Neill (1993)
36. Hirst and Di Cristo (1998); Gabriel Skantze (personal communication)
37. Ladd (2008)
38. Niebuhr (2014)
39. Benedict (1967); Sakamoto and Shiyo (2004)

Chapter 4 Creaky Voice and Its Functions

1. Campbell and Mokhtari (2003)
2. Laver (1994); Titze (2008); Ogden (2017)
3. Madill et al. (2017)
4. Ward (2000, 2006); Crystal (2015)
5. I will also here overlook the other ways that the auditory perception of pitch diverges from the frequency we can measure (De Cheveigne, 2005; Moore, 2003)
6. Gick et al. (2013)
7. Gussenhoven (2004)
8. This is an oversimplification: creaky voice is not just about periodicity, and it can take various forms, which may not be entirely equivalent in function (Esling, 2013; Drugman et al., 2014; Keating et al., 2015; Madill et al., 2017).
9. Ladefoged and Johnson (2014)
10. Xu and Sun (2002)
11. Better methods for detecting creaky voice are known (Kane et al., 2013; Keating et al., 2015).
12. From the Social Speech corpus (Ward and Werner, 2013)

13. Yuasa (2010)
14. Anderson et al. (2014)
15. Mendoza-Denton (2011); Podesva and Callier (2015)
16. Laver (1994)
17. de Saussure (1915; 1959)
18. In other languages, for example in some African languages, the creaky/non-creaky distinction is phonemic (Gordon and Ladefoged, 2001).
19. Schuller et al. (2013)
20. Scherer (1986, 2003)
21. Banziger and Scherer (2005)
22. Ackermann et al. (2014)
23. Bolinger (1946); Hinton et al. (1994); Bergen (2004); Schroder (2003); Ward (2006); Dingemanse et al. (2013)
24. Gussenhoven (2004); Ladd (2008)
25. Ohala (1984)
26. Ohala (1984); see also Xu et al.'s (2013) and Puts' (2005) studies of how pitch range and other factors affect the attractiveness of different voices.
27. There are of course many other ways in which this can be done (Kennard, 2006).
28. Li and Mok (2016); Ben-Aderet et al. (2017)
29. Gussenhoven (2004)
30. Murry (1971)
31. Gussenhoven (2004)
32. This is the *ii na* construction, which in addition to creaky voice involves lengthening, high pitch, and nasalization.
33. Brown and Levinson (1987)
34. Hinton et al. (1994); Pillet-Shore (2012)
35. Hinton et al. (1994); Shintel et al. (2006); Nygaard et al. (2009)
36. Pentland (2008); Gussenhoven (2002); Vaissiere (2008); Gussenhoven (2016)
37. Bolinger (1946)
38. Oertel et al. (2011); Turnbull (2017)
39. Jeong (2016)
40. Gussenhoven (2004)
41. Gussenhoven (2004)
42. Gussenhoven (2004)
43. Freese and Maynard (1998); Jeong (2016)
44. Gussenhoven (2004); Freese and Maynard (1998); Gries and Miglio (2014)
45. Gussenhoven (2016)
46. Gussenhoven (2016)
47. Ward (2006)
48. Bolinger (1963)
49. Hinton et al. (1994)
50. Niebuhr (2010)
51. Dehe and Stathi (2016)
52. It is an open question whether we should consider such things to be words or non-lexical utterances (Ward, 2006; Dingemanse et al., 2013).
53. Cruttenden (1997)
54. Szczepek Reed (2006)

55. Hendrickson (2013)
56. Bolinger (1963)
57. Bolinger (1978)
58. Jeong (2016)

Chapter 5 Perspectives on Prosody

1. Hart (1569), as discussed by Crystal (1969)
2. Grabe and Post (2002)
3. Crystal (2015)
4. Cruttenden (1981); Geluykens (1988); Hedberg et al. (2010); Hedberg et al. (2017); Couper-Kuhlen (2012); Sicoli et al. (2015); Heritage (2012); Mok et al. (2016)
5. Heritage (2012)
6. Examples 2.9, 2.33, 3.8, and 3.30
7. Saindon et al. (2017)
8. Petrone and Niebuhr (2013)
9. Who knows?
10. Pike (1945); Crystal (1969); Laver (1994); Fox (2000)
11. Cutler and Ladd (1983); Couper-Kuhlen (1986); Ladd (2008); Wells (2006); Szczepek Reed (2006); van Santen et al. (2008); Arvaniti (2011); Xu (2011, 2015); Prieto (2015); Cole (2015)
12. Pullum (2009)
13. Pinker (1994)
14. Fraccaro et al. (2013)
15. Ingram (1992), but see also Bull and Mayer (1988)
16. Sell et al. (2010); Fraccaro et al. (2013); Pisanski et al. (2014)
17. Wells (2006); Geluykens (1988); Hedberg et al. (2010, 2017); Heritage (2012); Couper-Kuhlen (2012); Petrone and Niebuhr (2013); Sicoli et al. (2015)
18. Shriberg et al. (1998); Syrdal et al. (2010); Hellbernd and Sammler (2016)
19. Wells (2006)
20. Murray and Arnott (1993); Scherer (2003); Lee and Narayanan (2005); Schuller et al. (2013); El Ayadi et al. (2011)
21. Goodwin et al. (2012)
22. Szczepek Reed (2010); Persson (2018)
23. Lakoff and Johnson (1980); Lakoff (1987)
24. Arvaniti (2016)
25. Clark (1996)
26. Tench (1996)
27. Szczepek Reed (2010)
28. Fischer (2015)
29. Szczepek Reed (2010); Ogden (2010)
30. Walker (2017)
31. Shriberg et al. (2000)
32. Cotter (1993); Warhurst et al. (2013); Ward et al. (2018)
33. In fact, constant volume may be a property of public speaking more generally, as Sueyon Im has speculated, based on her observation that in TED talks the speakers vary their intensity little (they always speak loudly).

34. Pike (1945); Tench (1996)
35. Couper-Kuhlen (1986)
36. Ladd (2014)
37. Couper-Kuhlen (1986); Campbell and Mokhtari (2003); Ni Chasaide and Gobl (2004); Walker (2017); Couper-Kuhlen and Selting (2018)
38. Wagner et al. (2015)
39. Niebuhr and Ward (2018)
40. Brazil (1997); Halliday's strategy was similar (Halliday, 1967)
41. van Santen et al. (2006)
42. Niebuhr (2015)
43. Beckman and Hirschberg (1994)
44. Selkirk (1995); Kreidler (1989)
45. Ladd (2008); Arvaniti (2016)
46. Kurumada et al. (2012)
47. Liberman and Whalen (2000)
48. Liberman and Whalen (2000); Xu (2017)
49. Niebuhr and Ward (2018)
50. Niebuhr and Ward (2018)
51. Shriberg and Stolcke (2004)
52. But not necessarily a huge amount of computational power; for example, none of the analyses done for this book took more than 10 minutes on a thousand-dollar computer (32GB, 4.2GHz).
53. Zen et al. (2013)
54. Zimmerer et al. (2014); Mennen (2015)
55. Diepenbroek and Derwing (2013); Busa (2012)
56. Gumperz (1982)
57. Deterding (2012)
58. Dickerson (2014)
59. Barraja-Rohan (2011)
60. Szczepek Reed (2012); Romero-Trillo (2012); Ward et al. (2007); Trouvain and Gut (2007); Mennen (2015)
61. Some construction-based resources for teaching prosody to second-language learners are available at www.cs.utep.edu/nigel/patterns/

Chapter 6 Late Pitch Peak and Its Functions

1. Discovered by Gosta Bruce (Ladd, 2008)
2. Kohler (1987); Pierrehumbert and Steele (1989)
3. Barnes et al. (2012)
4. The accurate alignment of articulatory gestures – by the tongue, lips, velum, and so on – in the vowels and consonants of everyday speech is a marvel of motor control (Xu, 2017).
5. Kendon (1980); Loehr (2012)
6. Parrell et al. (2014); Krivokapic (2017)
7. Ladd (1983)
8. Xu (1999); Pierrehumbert and Steele (1989); Prieto et al. (1995); Wichmann et al. (1997); Arvaniti (2011); Dilley and Heffner (2013); Niebuhr (2007)

9. On the variety of types of suggestions and advice, see DeCapua and Huber (1995).
10. Offers come in many types, with many diverse phonetic characteristics (Ogden and Walker, 2013).
11. Torreira and Grice (2018)
12. Late peaks are of course not the only prosodic characteristic of polite requests (Wichmann, 2004).
13. Wilensky et al. (1984); Levinson (2016)
14. Traum (1999)
15. Clayman and Heritage (2014); Levinson (2016)
16. Brown and Levinson (1987)
17. Clark (1996)
18. In formal genres also, late peak has been observed to have a role in the introduction of new topics and the introduction of new information within a topic (Wichmann et al., 1997; Zellers et al., 2009; Ward et al., 2018).
19. Armstrong et al. (2015); Wilhelm (2016)
20. This has been found for American English but not for Antipodean Englishes (Ritchart and Arvaniti, 2014; Warren and Fletcher, 2016).
21. Crystal (2015)
22. Niebuhr et al. (2011); Pierrehumbert and Steele (1989); Barnes et al. (2012)
23. Blu et al. (2006); Cohen et al. (2004)
24. Brown and Levinson (1987)
25. *If I Had $1000000*, by the Bare Naked Ladies
26. Trouvain and Truong (2017)
27. Bryant and Fox Tree (2005); Rakov and Rosenberg (2013); Rao (2013)
28. Such incongruities serve, more generally, to indicate that the speaker is conveying a non-literal meaning (Landgraf, 2014; Matsui et al., 2016).
29. Oliver Niebuhr, personal communication
30. Potts (2005)
31. Pierrehumbert and Steele (1989); Hasegawa and Hata (1995); Xu (1999); van Santen et al. (2006); Niebuhr et al. (2011)
32. Bruggeman et al. (2017)
33. Hyman (2012)
34. Terken (1993)
35. Tilsen (2016)
36. Ward (2018)
37. Niebuhr and Pfitzinger (2010)
38. Xu (2001); Kochanski (2010); Niebuhr and Pfitzinger (2010)
39. Ward (2018)
40. Pierrehumbert and Steele (1989); Arvaniti and Garding (2007); Wichmann et al. (1997); Ward et al. (2018)
41. Wittgenstein (1963); Lakoff (1987); Regier (1998)
42. Wagner et al. (2014)
43. Bangerter and Clark (2003)
44. Wichmann (2000)
45. Hasegawa and Hata (1995)
46. Hasegawa and Hata (1995)
47. House (2003)

48. David House has suggested another possible account: in a culture where consensus is important, making corrections without using expanded pitch range can be a way to get them done and out of the way with minimal fuss.
49. Petrone and Niebuhr (2013); Niebuhr and Pfitzinger (2010); Petra Wagner, personal communication
50. Zarate-Sandez (2016)

Chapter 7 Expressing Positive Assessments

1. Freeman and colleagues have also observed a sharper final intensity drop in positive-polarity instances of the word *yeah* (Freeman et al., 2015).
2. This may relate to the clipped ends and to a general stiffness of the articulators (Edwards et al., 1991).
3. Ward and Escalante-Ruiz (2009)
4. Murray and Arnott (1993); Freese and Maynard (1998)
5. Diskin (2017)
6. Grice (1975)
7. For example, in the social signal processing and computational paralinguistics traditions.

Chapter 8 Superposition

1. Incidentally, the prosody of list intonation is not universal. In Jewish English, influenced by Yiddish, list intonation may have a rise-fall contour on each item (Burdin, 2014). Since a list therefore has a sequence of lows between highs, the result can sound like a litany of complaints. Rachel Steindel Burdin (personal communication) has observed that this pattern is often used to good effect in Jewish-Grandmother jokes.
2. Ogden (2017)
3. Most of the recordings were done without providing a list of topics, but after two participants reported difficulty finding things to talk about for 10 minutes, a few subsequent pairs were provided with lists of suggestions.
4. Xu (2015)
5. Ladd (2008)
6. Ward et al. (2005)
7. Black et al. (2012); Govind and Prasanna (2013)
8. Fujisaki (2004); Kochanski and Shih (2003); Chen et al. (2004); Xu (2005); van Santen et al. (2004); Hirose et al. (2016)
9. Actually, Xu and Prom-on's model was not simply additive; it attained higher accuracy by including equations to represent the dynamics of target approximation (Xu and Prom-on, 2014).
10. Portes and Beyssade (2015)
11. Xu (2015); Torreira and Grice (2018)

Chapter 9 A Big-Data Approach

1. While the factor is mathematically determined, its direction is not, and you are therefore free to attach a label that represents either direction, "fatness" or "thinness," as you please. The choice here is arbitrary: it is useful to choose a name that helps you communicate the results to fellow Cetians, but this does not contribute any explanatory value to the model. If a later researcher were to reverse your choice, that would add a minus sign to every correlation with an observable, but nothing else would change.
2. PCA is of course not the only method that supports this approach (Kakouros and Rasanen, 2016).
3. Of course, as a purely linear model, PCA will not be able to find the connection between this factor and age.
4. Similar statistical methods have also enabled human scientists to discover unexpected connections from large data sets. For example, correlations between the digit ratio (the ratio of the lengths of the index and ring fingers) and ethnicity, personality, verbal fluency, and many other things.
5. For details, see any linear algebra textbook.
6. PCA has also been applied to prosody for other purposes (Itahashi and Tanaka, 1993; Chen et al., 2005).
7. Ward and Werner (2013)
8. www.cambridge.org/Ward
9. We have occasionally also found it helpful to look at which words are statistically common at points that are strongly positive or negative on a dimension (Ward and Vega, 2012b).
10. Some of these limitations may not apply to other similar methods, such as Independent Components Analysis and Non-Negative Matrix Factorization. Other related methods have already been applied to prosody, including Functional Data Analysis and TAL (Gubian et al., 2010; Janssoone et al., 2016).
11. Fillmore et al. (1988); Goldberg (2013); Fried and Ostman (2005); Fischer (2015)
12. Of course, this is not the only way to use PCA in prosody research, and PCA is not the only big-data approach to prosody; related methods are surveyed in Ward and Gallardo (2017).
13. Technically this is the log energy. Perceptions of loudness are complex, and intensity, being a simple acoustic measurement, only approximates it (Moore, 2003; Albert et al., 2018).
14. Oxenham (2018)
15. Hermes (1998); Ladefoged (2003); Gussenhoven (2004); Chapman (2007)
16. More specifically, the proxy for lengthening is low cepstral flux, intended to reflect the perceptual degree of similarity between two sound samples (Skantze, 2017).
17. Shockey (2013)
18. Niebuhr (2017); Cheng and Xu (2013)
19. Specifically, enunciation over some window is measured by the distance between the average cepstrum, across that window, from the global-average, neutral cepstrum. This is a good indicator of reduction, but not the only one that could be used (Ernestus and Warner, 2011).
20. Coates et al. (2011)

21. There are two reasons for not using narrow windows everywhere. The first is the trade-off between the number of features we can use and the number of data points we can process, given limited computer memory. The second is that evenly spaced features can give factors that resemble the sine wave basis functions of Fourier Analysis, and are thus completely generic and uninformative, as I found in a preliminary analysis using intensity features alone. By adding a "foveal region" of closely spaced windows, we bias the PCA to find factors that highlight periods of rapid change and are centered at such points.

22. The specific windows here were chosen based on experience tuning the offsets and durations to obtain the most information possible, as judged by success in language modeling and information retrieval applications (Vega, 2012; Ward et al., 2018).

23. Other features for future work to add include nasal voice, breathiness, and harmonicity, which have clear percepts but are a little more difficult to compute directly from the signal. Other good features to explore include spectral tilt and voicing fraction; conversely, these are easy to compute but are not perceived consistently. There are also thousands of derivative features that could be included (Eyben et al., 2010).

24. Day-O'Connell (2013); Niebuhr (2015); Ward (2015)

25. Many sets of prosodic features exist, each with its own advantages, and generally tuned to one task or another, such as speech recognition (Nöth et al., 2000; Ward et al., 2011), speaker identification and speaker verification (Sonmez et al., 1998; Chen et al., 2005; Ferrer et al., 2007, 2010; Kinnunen and Li, 2010), assessing non-native speech (Chen et al., 2018), recognizing Mandarin tones (Slaney et al., 2013), recognizing laughter (Oh et al., 2013), identifying languages and dialects, and recognizing speakers' "states and traits" (Schuller, 2011), including emotion, sleepiness, intoxication, deceptiveness, likability, charisma, flirtatiousness, social roles, and various medical conditions (Fernandez and Picard, 2005; Yang et al., 2013; Tanaka et al., 2014; Ranganath et al., 2013; Eyben et al., 2016).

26. Indeed, for much prosody research, identifying units is a central concern. However, for purposes of elucidating dialog prosody, this is probably better avoided.

27. This contrasts with Batliner's application of PCA in that, among other differences, he applied PCA to a carefully selected set of timepoints, namely those at utterance ends (Batliner et al., 2001).

28. Chafe (2002)

29. Albert et al. (2018)

30. Shriberg and Stolcke (2004)

31. Lehiste and Peterson (1961); Moore (2003)

32. Gussenhoven (2004)

33. Lehiste and Peterson (1961); Whalen and Levitt (1995); van Santen et al. (2006)

34. Lehiste and Peterson (1961)

35. The fact that intensity appears to drop in steps is just an artifact of the use of non-infinitesimal windows. Other techniques can produce smoother plots, such as Functional Data Analysis (Gubian et al., 2011; Parrell et al., 2013; Jokisch et al., 2014).

36. Comprehensive basic introductions to the phonetics of prosody – acoustic, articulatory, and perceptual – include Chapter 4 of Ladefoged (2003) and Chapter 4 of Ogden (2017). A higher-level view is given by Couper-Kuhlen (1986), a brief

computational overview by Jurafsky and Martin (2009), and more on algorithms and technical aspects by Owens (1993).

37. Ward (2015)

38. The human brain clearly performs some kind of speaker normalization for pitch (Tang et al., 2017).

39. Shriberg et al. (2000)

40. Tillmann (2014)

41. Laskowski (2015); van Santen et al. (2006); Ward and Abu (2016)

42. Ward and Werner (2013); Ward and Gallardo (2015)

43. There is some evidence that friends understand each other better, and use nonverbal cues and signaling that is less explicit, so this may not have been the best choice (Cassell et al., 2007).

44. With more data the PCA computation would never have ended, given the limited memory of the machine I was using.

45. Specifically, these are dialogs 1, 4, 5, 7, 8, and 21 from the Social Speech corpus (Ward and Werner, 2013), processed using the pbook.fss feature set (Ward, 2015).

46. Ward and Abu (2016)

47. Ward and Gallardo (2015, 2017)

48. Switchboard (Godfrey et al., 1992; Ward and Vega, 2012a)

49. Maptask (Anderson et al., 1991; Ward, 2014)

50. Over the years I've used a variety of feature sets, as I've added feature types and made feature computations more robust. In addition, I've varied the window sizes and numbers depending on the data and purpose. I see this as analogous to adjusting a microscope's focus. For example, for a study of the prosody of Mandarin, where rapid pitch movements are important in conveying tones, it was helpful to use a feature set where the pitch windows were more numerous and finer grained (Ward et al., 2016a).

Chapter 10 From Patterns to Meanings

1. These correlations arise because when someone is silent there will be no evidence for pitch of any kind, meaning, conversely, that there will be a correlation between my measure of loudness and every pitch feature. Ultimately, this is because of the decision to represent silence as just a very quiet form of speaking. As a result, many dimensions will show positive loadings on all pitch features whenever there are positive loadings on loudness, although these may not really mean anything. By focusing on the difference lines we overcome this problem. I thank Stefan Benus for alerting me to this issue.

2. Lakoff (1987)

3. Thus PCA provides a new approach to the difficult problem of identifying exemplars or prototypes of linguistic constructions (Gries, 2003).

4. Wootton (1989)

5. Bavelas et al. (1995)

6. Gunthner (1999); Cervone et al. (2015)

7. The bug was using int() instead of floor(). While it may seem odd that we failed to immediately notice the absence of the expected prosodic patterns at those

timepoints, that day we were examining lower-ranked dimensions, where the superimposed contributions of higher dimensions can obscure them.

8. This may reflect the fact that the narrow pitch is the core of this construction, or that this construction is often superimposed with others which contribute more to the prosody of the bookends, or both. Another factor is that the 212-item feature set may lack the right features for the bookmarks to show up clearly. With an earlier feature set, whose pitch features covered a wider span (Ward, 2014), there was a dimension that corresponded more closely to the Bookended Narrow Pitch Construction, with the bookends visible as positive loadings in the pitch and intensity features.

9. For example, Dimension 10, when negative, usually represents the B speaker producing a late peak and, at these times the A speaker's only "action" was to remain silent. Conversely, at the positive extremes, usually the A speaker is producing a late peak while the B speaker is silent. (It's actually a little more complicated: there is also a flip-side pattern in Dimension 10, as we will see.)

10. This tendency to symmetry is stronger here than usual for PCA. This is because the features computed for the two sides are identical, and because the two sides are slightly correlated, due to a small amount of cross-track bleeding. Symmetry, if felt to be a problem, can be avoided by using various methods, including non-negative matrix factorization or clustering (Reichel, 2014).

11. Ward (2014)

12. Day-O'Connell (2013); Ladd (1978)

13. Ward and Abu (2016)

14. Ward (2014)

15. In this figure, the scale is greater than that in the others, to make the pitch tendency visible despite its modest loadings.

16. Fuchs et al. (2015); Holt and Rangarathnam (2018)

17. Pierrehumbert (1979)

18. Reichel and Mady (2014)

Chapter 11 Turn-Taking Constructions

1. Heldner and Edlund (2010); Levinson and Torreira (2015); Levinson (2016); Heeman and Lunsford (2017); Enfield (2017)

2. Levinson (2016); Bögels and Levinson (2017)

3. Local and Walker (2012); Bögels and Torreira (2015)

4. This differs slightly from earlier descriptions of this construction (Ward and Gallardo, 2017), mostly because we are now using a more robust feature set.

5. Reed (2004); Niebuhr et al. (2013); Walker (2017)

6. As argued by Levinson (2016). However, turn-final prosody might still be decisive if the speaker has a response pre-prepared and only needs to decide whether to deploy it or not (Corps et al., 2018).

7. De Ruiter et al. (2006)

8. Kendon (1967); Oertel et al. (2012); Ward et al. (2016b)

9. Levelt (1989)

10. Novick et al. (1996); Andrist et al. (2013)

11. Gravano and Hirschberg (2011); Hjalmarsson (2009)
12. Sebanz et al. (2006); Scott et al. (2009); Aziz-Zadeh et al. (2010); Menenti et al. (2012)
13. Emberson et al. (2010)
14. Johnstone et al. (1995); Turkle (2016)
15. Trouvain (2014)
16. Schoenenberg et al. (2014)
17. Johnstone et al. (1995)
18. Boltz (2005); Roberts et al. (2006); Szczepek Reed (2010); Roberts and Francis (2013)
19. Roberts (2013)
20. ten Bosch et al. (2005); Local and Walker (2012); Strombergsson et al. (2013); Witt (2015); Zellers (2016); Heeman and Lunsford (2017)
21. Sidnell (2011)
22. Sidnell (2011); Sacks et al. (1974)
23. Searle (1992); Schegloff (1992)
24. Ward and Abu (2016)
25. Clark (1996); Ward and DeVault (2016)
26. Clark (2002); Schober and Brennan (2003)
27. Among the various computational models for predicting who speaks when, the best do so without a notion of turn at all (Ward et al., 2010; Skantze, 2017).
28. Selfridge and Heeman (2010); Johansson and Skantze (2015)
29. O'Connell et al. (1990); Cowley (1998)
30. From Pixabay under a Creative Commons License
31. Ford et al. (1996); Barth-Weingarten (2013)
32. Observation by David Novick
33. Bergen (2008)
34. Johansson and Skantze (2015)
35. Kendon (1967); Mixdorff et al. (2015); Zellers et al. (2016); Torreira et al. (2015); Wlodarczak and Heldner (2016); Drummond and Hopper (1993); Homke et al. (2017)
36. Duncan Jr. and Fiske (1985); Ferrer et al. (2003); Gravano and Hirschberg (2011); Raux and Eskenazi (2012)
37. Skantze (2017); Maier et al. (2017); Shannon et al. (2017)
38. Lerner (2002)
39. Cowley (1998)
40. Trouvain and Truong (2014)
41. Kori (1987); Mowrer et al. (1987); Lasarcyk and Trouvain (2008); Oh et al. (2013); Trouvain (2014)
42. Gervais and Wilson (2005); Bryant and Aktipis (2014)
43. Wells and Macfarlane (1998); Yang and Heeman (2010); Szczepek Reed (2010); Kurtic et al. (2013)
44. Jaffe (1978)
45. Bohus and Horvitz (2014)
46. While sometimes interchangeable, different filler tokens tend to gravitate to different roles, such as turn-initial fillers or utterance-internal disfluency markers (Benus, 2009b).

47. Erard (2008); O'Connell and Kowal (2004)
48. Chafe (1980a,b)
49. Brennan and Williams (1995); Fox Tree (2001); Ward (2006)
50. Finlayson and Corley (2012); Nicholson et al. (2003)
51. Bolinger (1989)
52. Ward (2004)
53. Ferreira (2007)
54. Cowley (1998)
55. Barth-Weingarten (2013)
56. Ogden and Hawkins (2015); Benus (2009a)
57. Allwood et al. (1992)
58. Bavelas et al. (2000)
59. Ward and Tsukahara (2000)
60. Ward et al. (2012)
61. Duncan Jr. and Fiske (1985); Ward and Tsukahara (2000); Gravano and Hirschberg (2009)
62. Homke et al. (2017)
63. Ward and Tsukahara (2000)
64. Ward (2004)
65. Gratch et al. (2007b,a); DeVault et al. (2014)
66. Fujie et al. (2005)
67. Yngve (1970); Ward and Tsukahara (1999); Ward and DeVault (2016)
68. Novick and Gris (2014); Phillips-Silver et al. (2010); Filippi (2016); Wacewicz et al. (2017)
69. Cummins (2009)
70. Smelser (1993)
71. Heritage (2017)
72. Dabbs and Ruback (1987); Bohus and Horvitz (2011); Kawahara et al. (2012)
73. Stivers et al. (2009)
74. Ward and Gallardo (2017); Ward et al. (2016a)
75. Cecil (2010); Martinez (2018)
76. Cecil (2010)
77. Tannen (1989); Wieland (1991)
78. Ward and Gallardo (2017)
79. Condon (1985)
80. Ward and Tsukahara (2000); Cutrone (2005); Cecil (2010)
81. Ward and Al Bayyari (2007)
82. Ward and Al Bayyari (2010)
83. Ward et al. (2007)
84. Sacks et al. (1974)
85. Benus et al. (2011); ter Maat and Heylen (2009)

Chapter 12 Topic Management Constructions

1. Wright (2011)
2. Curl et al. (2006); Schegloff and Sacks (1973); Drew and Holt (1998); Holt (2010)

3. Couper-Kuhlen (2004); Riou (2017)
4. Yang et al. (2011)
5. Shriberg et al. (2000); Swerts (1997)
6. Schegloff and Sacks (1973); Couper-Kuhlen (2004)
7. Swerts (1997)
8. Laver (1994)
9. Laver (1994); Ishi et al. (2010)
10. Although creaky voice and breathy voice have different glottal mechanisms, both show up in the pitch plot as a scattering of values.
11. Searle (1992)
12. Ishi et al. (2010)

Chapter 13 Stance-Related Constructions

1. Biber et al. (1999); Freeman (2014); Freeman et al. (2015); Ward et al. (2018)
2. Pomerantz (1984); Ogden (2012)
3. Zaki (2014)
4. Intriguingly, Okamoto and I found experimentally that nasalization in Japanese may similarly indicate lack of surprise or novelty, at least in short responses (Ward, 2002; Ward and Okamoto, 2003).
5. Ward and Gallardo (2017)
6. Condon (1985)

Chapter 14 The Rest of English Prosody

1. Hirschberg and Litman (1993); Calhoun and Schweitzer (2012)
2. Niebuhr (2010)
3. Bolinger (1986); Selkirk (1995); Bell et al. (2009)
4. Tao et al. (2018)
5. Couper-Kuhlen (1996); Benus et al. (2011); Szczepek Reed (2010); Giles et al. (1987); Acosta and Ward (2011); Pickering et al. (2012)
6. Marsh et al. (2009)
7. Rosenberg and Hirschberg (2009); Niebuhr et al. (2016); Fernandez Gallardo and Weiss (2017)
8. The issue of individual variation, as Levinson has observed, has been neglected by most recent work in language and cognitive science, but is a critical topic for future work (Levinson, 2012).
9. Grice et al. (2017)
10. Aziz-Zadeh et al. (2010)
11. Roberts (2013)
12. Dediu and Ladd (2007); Wong et al. (2008)
13. The prosody of *whatever* can be even richer: there is more than one dimension of variation, especially when used with a touch of anger (Benus et al., 2007).
14. McCann and Peppe (2003); Irvine et al. (2016); Sorocco et al. (2009)
15. Kurumada and Clark (2017)

Chapter 15 Envoi

1. A step in this direction is my study of dialog prosody in Mandarin (Ward et al., 2016a).
2. Gladwell (2008)
3. Gumperz (1982)
4. Using inappropriate prosody for the function is only one way in which the prosody of non-native speakers can differ from that of natives (Mennen, 2015; Ward and Gallardo, 2017).
5. Piller (2011)
6. Roberts (2013)
7. Tannen (1989, 1990)

Bibliography

Abe, Isamu. 1998. Intonation in Japanese. Pages 360–375 of: Hirst, Daniel, and Di Cristo, Albert (eds.), *Intonation Systems: A Survey of Twenty Languages*. Cambridge University Press.

Ackermann, Hermann, Hage, Steffen R, and Ziegler, Wolfram. 2014. Brain mechanisms of acoustic communication in humans and nonhuman primates: An evolutionary perspective. *Behavioral and Brain Sciences*, **37**, 529–546.

Acosta, Jaime C., and Ward, Nigel G. 2011. Achieving rapport with turn-by-turn, user-responsive emotional coloring. *Speech Communication*, **53**, 1137–1148.

Albert, Aviad, Cangemi, Francesco, and Grice, Martine. 2018. Using periodic energy to enrich acoustic representations of pitch in speech: A demonstration. Pages 804–808 of: *Speech Prosody*.

Allwood, Jens, Nivre, Joakim, and Ahlsén, Elisabeth. 1992. On the semantics and pragmatics of linguistic feedback. *Journal of Semantics*, **9**(1), 1–26.

Anderson, Anne H., Bader, Miles, Bard, Ellen Gurman, Boyle, Elizabeth, Doherty, Gwyneth, Garrod, Simon, Isard, Stephen, Kowtko, Jacqueline, McAllister, Jan, Miller, Jim, et al. 1991. The HCRC map task corpus. *Language and Speech*, **34**, 351–366.

Anderson, Rindy C., Klofstad, Casey A., Mayew, William J., and Venkatachalam, Mohan. 2014. Vocal fry may undermine the success of young women in the labor market. *PloS One*, **9**, e97506.

Andrist, Sean, Mutlu, Bilge, and Gleicher, Michael. 2013. Conversational gaze aversion for virtual agents. In: *Proceedings of Intelligent Virtual Agents (IVA)*.

Armstrong, Meghan E., Piccinini, Page, and Ritchart, Amanda. 2015. The phonetics and distribution of non-question rises in two varieties of American English. In: *The 18th International Congress of Phonetic Sciences (ICPhS)*.

Arvaniti, Amalia. 2011. The representation of intonation. Pages 757–780 of: van Oostendorp, Marc, Ewen, Colin J., Hume, Elizabeth V., and Rice, Keren (eds.), *The Blackwell Companion to Phonology*. Wiley.

Arvaniti, Amalia. 2016. Analytical decisions in intonation research and the role of representations: Lessons from Romani. *Laboratory Phonology*, **7**(1), 1–43.

Arvaniti, Amalia, and Garding, Gina. 2007. Dialectal variation in the rising accents of American English. Pages 547–576 of: *Papers in Laboratory Phonology 9*. Mouton de Gruyter.

Aziz-Zadeh, Lisa, Sheng, Tong, and Gheytanchi, Anahita. 2010. Common premotor regions for the perception and production of prosody and correlations with empathy and prosodic ability. *PloS One*, **5**, e8759.

Balog, Heather L. 2012. Early prosodic production. Pages 133–146 of: Romero-Trillo, Jesus (ed.), *Pragmatics and Prosody in English Language Teaching*. Springer.

Bangerter, Adrian, and Clark, Herbert H. 2003. Navigating joint projects with dialog. *Cognitive Science*, **27**, 195–225.

Banziger, Tanja, and Scherer, Klaus R. 2005. The role of intonation in emotional expressions. *Speech Communication*, **46**, 252–267.

Barnes, Jonathan, Veilleux, Nanette, Brugos, Alejna, and Shattuck-Hufnagel, Stefanie. 2012. Tonal center of gravity: A global approach to tonal implementation in a level-based intonational phonology. *Laboratory Phonology*, **3**, 337–382.

Barraja-Rohan, Anne-Marie. 2011. Using conversation analysis in the second language classroom to teach interactional competence. *Language Teaching Research*, **15**, 479–507.

Barth-Weingarten, Dagmar. 2009. Contrasting and turn transition: Prosodic projection with parallel-opposition constructions. *Journal of Pragmatics*, **41**, 2271–2294.

Barth-Weingarten, Dagmar. 2013. From "intonation units" to cesuring: An alternative approach to the prosodic-phonetic structuring of talk-in-interaction. Pages 91–124 of: Reed, Beatrice Szczepek, and Raymond, Geoffrey (eds.), *Units of Talk: Units of Action*. John Benjamins.

Batliner, Anton, Buckow, Jan, Huber, Richard, Warnke, Volker, Nöth, Elmar, and Niemann, Heinrich. 2001. Boiling down prosody for the classification of boundaries and accents in German and English. Pages 2781–2784 of: *Eurospeech*.

Bavelas, Janet Beavin, Chovil, Nichile, Coates, Linda, and Roe, Lori. 1995. Gestures specialized for dialogue. *Personality and Social Psychology Bulletin*, **21**, 394–405.

Bavelas, Janet, Coates, Linda, and Johnson, Trudy. 2000. Listeners as co-narrators. *Journal of Personality and Social Psychology*, **79**, 941–952.

Beckman, Mary E., and Hirschberg, Julia. 1994. *The ToBI Annotation Conventions*. Ohio State University.

Bell, Alan, Brenier, Jason M., Gregory, Michelle, Girand, Cynthia, and Jurafsky, Dan. 2009. Predictability effects on durations of content and function words in conversational English. *Journal of Memory and Language*, **60**, 92–111.

Ben-Aderet, Tobey, Gallego-Abenza, Mario, Reby, David, and Mathevon, Nicolas. 2017. Dog-directed speech: Why do we use it and do dogs pay attention to it? Pages 2016.2429 of: *Proceedings of the Royal Society B*, vol. 284.

Benedict, Ruth. 1967. *The Chrysanthemum and the Sword: Patterns of Japanese Culture*. Houghton Mifflin Harcourt.

Benus, Stefan. 2009a. Are we "in sync"? Turn-taking in collaborative dialogues. Pages 2167–2170 of: *Interspeech*.

Benus, Stefan. 2009b. Variability and stability in collaborative dialogues: Turn-taking and filled pauses. Pages 796–799 of: *Tenth Interspeech Conference*.

Benus, Stefan, Gravano, Agustin, and Hirschberg, Julia. 2007. Prosody, emotions, and..."whatever". Pages 2629–2632 of: *Interspeech*.

Benus, Stefan, Gravano, Agustin, and Hirschberg, Julia. 2011. Pragmatic aspects of temporal accommodation in turn-taking. *Journal of Pragmatics*, **43**, 3001–3027.

Bergen, Benjamin K. 2004. The psychological reality of phonaesthemes. *Language*, **80**, 290–311.

Bergen, D. 2008. Humor. Pages 189–198 of: Benson, Janette B., and Haith, Marshall M. (eds.), *Social and Emotional Development in Infancy and Early Childhood*. Elsevier.

Biber, Douglas, Johansson, Stig, Leech, Geoffrey, Conrad, Susan, and Finegan, Edward. 1999. The grammatical marking of stance. Pages 965–986 of: Biber, Douglas, Johansson, Stig, Leech, Geoffrey, Conrad, Susan, and Finegan, Edward (eds.), *Longman Grammar of Spoken and Written English*. Pearson Education.

Black, Alan W., Bunnell, H. Timothy, et al. 2012. Articulatory features for expressive speech synthesis. Pages 4005–4008 of: *International Conf. on Acoustics, Speech and Signal Processing, IEEE*.

Blu, Susan, Mullin, Molly Ann, and Songe, Cynthia. 2006. *Word of Mouth: A Guide to Commercial and Animation Voice-over Excellence*. Silman-James Press.

Bögels, Sara, and Levinson, Stephen C. 2017. The brain behind the response: Insights into turn-taking in conversation from neuroimaging. *Research on Language and Social Interaction*, **50**, 71–89.

Bögels, Sara, and Torreira, Francisco. 2015. Listeners use intonational phrase boundaries to project turn ends in spoken interaction. *Journal of Phonetics*, **52**, 46–57.

Bohus, Dan, and Horvitz, Eric. 2011. Multiparty turn taking in situated dialog: Study, lessons, and directions. Pages 98–109 of: *SIGdial*.

Bohus, Dan, and Horvitz, Eric. 2014. Managing human-robot engagement with forecasts and... um... hesitations. Pages 2–9 of: *Proceedings of the 16th International Conference on Multimodal Interaction*. ACM.

Bolinger, Dwight. 1946. Thoughts on "Yep" and "Nope". *American Speech*, **21**, 90–95.

Bolinger, Dwight. 1963. The uniqueness of the word. *Lingua*, **12**, 113–136.

Bolinger, Dwight. 1978. Intonation across languages. Pages 471–524 of: Greenberg, J. (ed.), *Universals of Human Language, II*. Stanford University Press.

Bolinger, Dwight. 1986. *Intonation and Its Parts*. Stanford University Press.

Bolinger, Dwight. 1989. *Intonation and Its Uses*. Stanford University Press.

Boltz, Marilyn. 2005. Temporal dimensions of conversational interaction: The role of response latencies and pauses in social impression formation. *Journal of Language and Social Psychology*, **24**, 103–138.

Boroditsky, Lera. 2001. Does language shape thought? Mandarin and English speakers' conceptions of time. *Cognitive Psychology*, **43**, 1–22.

Braun, Bettina, Kochanski, Greg, Grabe, Esther, and Rosner, Burton S. 2006. Evidence for attractors in English intonation. *The Journal of the Acoustical Society of America*, **119**, 4006–4015.

Brazil, David. 1997. *The Communicative Value of Intonation in English*. Cambridge University Press.

Brennan, Susan E., and Williams, Maurice. 1995. The feeling of another's knowing: Prosody and filled pauses as cues to listeners about the metacognitive states of speakers. *Journal of Memory and Language*, **34**, 383–398.

Browman, Catherine P., and Goldstein, Louis. 1992. Articulatory phonology: An overview. *Phonetica*, **49**, 155–180.

Brown, Penelope, and Levinson, Stephen C. 1987. *Politeness: Some Universals in Language Usage*. Cambridge University Press.

Bruggeman, Anna, Cangemi, Francesco, Wehrle, Simon, El Zarka, Dina, and Grice, Martine. 2017. Unifying speaker variability with the Tonal Centre of Gravity. Pages 21–24 of: Belz, Malte, and Mooshammer, Christine (eds.), *Phonetics and Phonology in German-Speaking Countries*.

Bryant, Gregory A., and Aktipis, C. Athena. 2014. The animal nature of spontaneous human laughter. *Evolution and Human Behavior*, **35**, 327–335.

Bryant, Gregory A., and Fox Tree, Jean E. 2005. Is there an ironic tone of voice? *Language and Speech*, **48**, 257–277.

Bull, Peter, and Mayer, Kate. 1988. Interruptions in political interviews: A study of Margaret Thatcher and Neil Kinnock. *Journal of Language and Social Psychology*, **7**, 35–46.

Burdin, Rachel Steindel. 2014. Variation in list intonation in American Jewish English. In: *Speech Prosody*.

Busa, Maria Grazia. 2012. The role of prosody in pronunciation teaching: A growing appreciation. Pages 101–105 of: Busa, Maria Grazia, and Stella, Antonio (eds.), *Methodological Perspectives on Second Language Prosody*, Papers from ML2P 2012, CLEUP.

Byrd, Dani, and Saltzman, Elliot. 1998. Intragestural dynamics of multiple prosodic boundaries. *Journal of Phonetics*, **26**, 173–199.

Calhoun, Sasha. 2009. What makes a word contrastive? Prosodic, semantic and pragmatic perspectives. Pages 53–78 of: Barth-Weingarten, D., Dehe, N., and Wichmann, A. (eds.), *Where Prosody Meets Pragmatics: Research at the Interface*. Emerald.

Calhoun, Sasha, and Schweitzer, Antje. 2012. Can intonation contours be lexicalised? Implications for discourse meanings. Pages 271–327 of: Elordieta, Gorka, and Prieto, Pilar (eds.), *Prosody and Meaning*. De Gruyter Mouton.

Campbell, Nick, and Mokhtari, Parham. 2003. Voice quality: The 4th prosodic dimension. Pages 2417–2420 of: *15th International Congress of the Phonetic Sciences*.

Cassell, Justine, Gill, Alastair J., and Tepper, Paul A. 2007. Coordination in conversation and rapport. Pages 41–50 of: *Proceedings of the Workshop on Embodied Language Processing*. Association for Computational Linguistics.

Cecil, Matthew J. 2010. *Cross-Linguistic Variation in Turn Taking Practices: A Computational Study of the Callhome Corpus*. M.Phil. thesis, University of Colorado at Boulder.

Cervone, Alessandra, Lai, Catherine, Pareti, Silvia, and Bell, Peter. 2015. Towards automatic detection of reported speech in dialogue using prosodic cues. Pages 3061–3065 of: *Interspeech*.

Chafe, Wallace L. 1980a. The deployment of consciousness in the production of a narrative. Pages 9–49 of: Chafe, Wallace L. (ed.), *The Pear Stories*. Ablex.

Chafe, Wallace L. 1980b. Some reasons for hesitating. Pages 169–180 of: Dechert, Hans W., and Raupach, Manfred (eds.), *Temporal Variables in Speech*. Mouton.

Chafe, Wallace. 2002. Searching for meaning in language: A memoir. *Historographica Linguistica*, **29**, 245–261.

Chapman, Mark. 2007. Theory and practice of teaching discourse intonation. *ELT Journal*, **61**, 3–11.

Chen, Gao-Peng, Bailly, Gerard, Liu, Qing-Feng, and Wang, Ren-Hua. 2004. A superposed prosodic model for Chinese text-to-speech synthesis. Pages 177–180 of: *International Symposium on Chinese Spoken Language Processing*. IEEE.

Chen, Lei, Zechner, Klaus, Yoon, Su-Youn, Evanini, Keelan, Wang, Xinhao, Loukina, Anastassia, Tao, Jidong, Davis, Lawrence, Lee, Chong Min, Ma, Min, et al. 2018. *Automated Scoring of Nonnative Speech Using the SpeechRater SM v. 5.0 Engine*. Tech. rept. ETS Research Report ETS RR-18-10. Wiley Online Library.

Chen, Zi-He, Liao, Yuan-Fu, and Juang, Yau-Tarng. 2005. Prosody modeling and eigen-prosody analysis for robust speaker recognition. In: *Proceedings of ICASSP*.

Cheng, Chierh, and Xu, Yi. 2013. Articulatory limit and extreme segmental reduction in Taiwan Mandarin. *Journal of the Acoustical Society of America*, **134**(6), 4481–4495.

Clark, Herbert H. 1996. *Using Language*. Cambridge University Press.

Clark, Herbert H. 2002. Speaking in time. *Speech Communication*, **36**, 5–13.

Clayman, Steven, and Heritage, John. 2014. Benefactors and beneficiaries: Benefactive status and stance in the management of offers and requests. Pages 55–86 of: *Requesting in Social Interaction*. John Benjamins.

Coates, Adam, Lee, Honglak, and Ng, Andrew Y. 2011. An analysis of single-layer networks in unsupervised feature learning. In: *Proceedings of the 14th International Conference on Artificial Intelligence and Statistics*.

Cohen, Michael H., Giangola, James P., and Balogh, Jennifer. 2004. *Voice User Interface Design*. Addison-Wesley.

Cole, Jennifer. 2015. Prosody in context: A review. *Language, Cognition and Neuroscience*, **30**, 1–31.

Condon, John C. 1985. *Good Neighbors: Communicating with the Mexicans*. Intercultural Press.

Constant, Noah. 2012. English rise-fall-rise: A study in the semantics and pragmatics of intonation. *Linguistics and Philosophy*, **35**, 407–442.

Coren, Dan. 2011. *It's only a #%&* doorbell!* http://dancoren.weebly.com/section-3-its-only-a–doorbell.html, retrieved January 7, 2016.

Corps, Ruth E., Gambi, Chiara, and Pickering, Martin J. 2018. Coordinating utterances during turn-taking: The role of prediction, response preparation, and articulation. *Discourse Processes*, **55**, 230–240.

Cotter, Colleen. 1993. Prosodic aspects of broadcast news register. Pages 90–100 of: *19th Annual Meeting of the Berkeley Linguistics Society*.

Couper-Kuhlen, Elizabeth. 1986. *An Introduction to English Prosody*. Edward Arnold.

Couper-Kuhlen, Elizabeth. 1996. The prosody of repetition: On quoting and mimicry. Pages 366–405 of: Couper-Kuhlen, Elizabeth, and Selting, Margret (eds.), *Prosody in Conversation: Interactional Studies*. Cambridge University Press.

Couper-Kuhlen, Elizabeth. 2004. *Prosody and Sequence Organization in English Conversation: The Case of New Beginnings*. John Benjamins.

Couper-Kuhlen, Elizabeth. 2012. Some truths and untruths about final intonation in conversational questions. Pages 123–145 of: de Ruiter, Jan P. (ed.), *Questions: Formal, Functional and Interactional Perspectives*. Cambridge University Press.

Couper-Kuhlen, Elizabeth, and Selting, Margret. 2018. *Interactional Linguistics*. Cambridge University Press.

Cowley, Stephen J. 1998. Of timing, turn-taking, and conversations. *Journal of Psycholinguistic Research*, **27**, 541–571.

Cruttenden, Alan. 1981. Falls and rises: Meanings and universals. *Journal of Linguistics*, **17**, 77–91.

Cruttenden, Alan. 1997. *Intonation*, 2nd edition. Cambridge University Press.

Crystal, David. 1969. *Prosodic Systems and Intonation in English*. Cambridge University Press.

Crystal, David. 2015. *Making a Point: The Persnickety Story of English Punctuation.* St. Martin's Press.

Cummins, Fred. 2009. Rhythm as entrainment: The case of synchronous speech. *Journal of Phonetics*, **37**, 16–28.

Curl, Traci S., Local, John, and Walker, Gareth. 2006. Repetition and the prosody–pragmatics interface. *Journal of Pragmatics*, **38**, 1721–1751.

Cutler, Anne. 1977. The context-dependence of "intonational meanings." Pages 104–115 of: *Papers from the Thirteenth Regional Meeting.* Chicago Linguistic Society.

Cutler, Anne, and Ladd, D. Robert. 1983. Models and measurements in the study of prosody. Pages 1–10 of: Cutler, Anne, and Ladd, D. Robert (eds.), *Prosody: Models and Measurements.* Springer.

Cutrone, Pino. 2005. A case study examining backchannels in conversations between Japanese–British dyads. *Multilingua*, **24**, 237–274.

Dabbs, James M., and Ruback, R. Barry. 1987. Dimensions of group process: Amount and structure of vocal interaction. Pages 123–169 of: Berkowitz, Leonard (ed.), *Advances in Experimental Social Psychology, 20.* Academic Press.

Day-O'Connell, Jeremy. 2013. Speech, song, and the minor third: An acoustic study of the stylized interjection. *Music Perception*, **30**, 441–462.

De Cheveigne, Alain. 2005. Pitch perception models. Pages 169–233 of: Plack, Christopher J., Oxenham, Andres J., and Fay, Richard R. (eds.), *Pitch.* Springer.

De Ruiter, J. P., Mitterer, H., and Enfield, N. J. 2006. Projecting the end of a speaker's turn: A cognitive cornerstone of conversation. *Language*, **82**, 515–535.

de Saussure, Ferdinand. 1915; 1959. *Course in General Linguistics.* McGraw-Hill.

DeCapua, Andrea, and Huber, Lisa. 1995. "If I were you...": Advice in American English. *Multilingua*, **14**, 117–132.

Dediu, Dan, and Ladd, D. Robert. 2007. Linguistic tone is related to the population frequency of the adaptive haplogroups of two brain size genes, ASPM and Microcephalin. *Proceedings of the National Academy of Sciences*, **104**, 10944–10949.

Dehe, Nicole, and Stathi, Katerina. 2016. Grammaticalization and prosody: The case of English sort/kind/type of constructions. *Language*, **92**, 911–946.

Deterding, David. 2012. Issues in the acoustic measurement of rhythm. Pages 9–24 of: Romero-Trillo, Jesus (ed.), *Pragmatics and Prosody in English Language Teaching.* Springer.

DeVault, David, Artstein, Ron, Benn, Grace, Dey, Teresa, Fast, Ed, Gainer, Alesia, et al. 2014. SimSensei Kiosk: A virtual human interviewer for healthcare decision support. Pages 1061–1068 of: *Proceedings of AAMAS.*

Dickerson, Wayne B. 2014. A nail in the coffin of stress-timed rhythm. Pages 184–196 of: *Pronunciation in Second Language Learning and Teaching Conference.*

Diepenbroek, Lori G., and Derwing, Tracey M. 2013. To what extent do popular ESL textbooks incorporate oral fluency and pragmatic development? *TESL Canada Journal*, **30**, 1–20.

Dilley, Laura C., and Heffner, Christopher. 2013. The role of F_0 alignment in distinguishing intonation categories: Evidence from American English. *Journal of Speech Sciences*, **3**, 3–67.

Dingemanse, Mark, Torreira, Francisco, and Enfield, Nick J. 2013. Is "huh?" a universal word? Conversational infrastructure and the convergent evolution of linguistic items. *PloS One*, **8**(11), e78273.

Diskin, Chloe. 2017. The use of the discourse-pragmatic marker "like" by native and non-native speakers of English in Ireland. *Journal of Pragmatics*, **120**, 144–157.

Drew, Paul, and Holt, Elizabeth. 1998. Figures of speech: Figurative expressions and the management of topic transition in conversation. *Language in Society*, **27**, 495–522.

Drugman, Thomas, Alku, Paavo, Alwan, Abeer, and Yegnanarayana, Bayya. 2014. Glottal source processing: From analysis to applications. *Computer Speech & Language*, **28**, 1117–1138.

Drummond, Kent, and Hopper, Robert. 1993. Back channels revisited: Acknowledgment tokens and speakership incipiency. *Research on Language and Social Interaction*, **26**, 157–177.

Duncan Jr., Starkey, and Fiske, Donald W. 1985. The turn system. Pages 43–64 of: Duncan, Jr., Starkey, and Fiske, Donald W. (eds.), *Interaction Structure and Strategy*. Cambridge University Press.

Echols, Catharine H. 1993. A perceptually-based model of children's earliest productions. *Cognition*, **46**, 245–296.

Edwards, Jan, Beckman, Mary E., and Fletcher, Janet. 1991. The articulatory kinematics of final lengthening. *Journal of the Acoustical Society of America*, **89**(1), 369–382.

El Ayadi, Moataz, Kamel, Mohamed S, and Karray, Fakhri. 2011. Survey on speech emotion recognition: Features, classification schemes, and databases. *Pattern Recognition*, **44**, 572–587.

Emberson, Lauren L., Lupyan, Gary, Goldstein, Michael H., and Spivey, Michael J. 2010. Overheard cell-phone conversations. *Psychological Science*, **21**(10), 1383–1388.

Enfield, Nicholas J. 2017. *How We Talk: The Inner Workings of Conversation*. Basic Books.

Erard, Michael. 2008. *Um...: Slips, Stumbles, and Verbal Blunders, and What They Mean*. Anchor Canada.

Ernestus, Mirjam, and Warner, Natasha. 2011. An introduction to reduced pronunciation variants. *Journal of Phonetics*, **39**, 253–260.

Esling, John H. 2013. Voice quality. In: Chapelle, Carol A. (ed.), *The Encyclopedia of Applied Linguistics*. Blackwell.

Eyben, Florian, Wöllmer, Martin, and Schuller, Björn. 2010. OpenSmile: The Munich versatile and fast open-source audio feature extractor. Pages 1459–1462 of: *Proceedings of the International Conference on Multimedia*.

Eyben, Florian, Scherer, Klaus R., Schuller, Björn W., Sundberg, Johan, André, Elisabeth, Busso, Carlos, et al. 2016. The Geneva minimalistic acoustic parameter set (GeMAPS) for voice research and affective computing. *IEEE Transactions on Affective Computing*, **7**, 190–202.

Fernald, Anne. 1989. Intonation and communicative intent in mothers' speech to infants: Is the melody the message? *Child Development*, **6**, 1497–1510.

Fernald, Anne, and O'Neill, Daniela K. 1993. Peekaboo across cultures: How mothers and infants play with voices, faces, and expectations. Pages 259–285 of: MacDonald, Kevin (ed.), *Parent–Child Play: Descriptions and Implications*. State University of New York Press.

Fernandez, Raul, and Picard, Rosalind W. 2005. Classical and novel discriminant features for affect recognition from speech. Pages 473–476 of: *Interspeech*.

Fernandez Gallardo, Laura, and Weiss, Benjamin. 2017. Towards speaker characterization: Identifying and predicting dimensions of person attribution. Pages 904–908 of: Interspeech 2017.

Ferreira, Fernanda. 2007. Prosody and performance in language production. *Language and Cognitive Processes*, **22**, 1151–1177.

Ferrer, Luciana, Shriberg, Elizabeth, and Stolcke, Andreas. 2003. A prosody-based approach to end-of-utterance detection that does not require speech recognition. In: *IEEE International Conference on Acoustics, Speech and Signal Processing*.

Ferrer, Luciana, Shriberg, Elizabeth, Kajarekar, Sachin, and Sonmez, Kemal. 2007. Parameterization of prosodic feature distributions for SVM modeling in speaker recognition. Pages 233–236 of: *IEEE International Conference on Acoustics, Speech and Signal Processing*, vol. 4.

Ferrer, Luciana, Scheffer, Nicolas, and Shriberg, Elizabeth. 2010. A comparison of approaches for modeling prosodic features in speaker recognition. Pages 4414–4417 of: *IEEE International Conference on Acoustics, Speech and Signal Processing*.

Filippi, Piera. 2016. Emotional and interactional prosody across animal communication systems: A comparative approach to the emergence of language. *Frontiers in Psychology*, **7**, 1–19.

Fillmore, Charles J. 1975. An alternative to checklist theories of meaning. Pages 123–131 of: *Berkeley Linguistics Society, Proceedings of the First Annual Meeting*.

Fillmore, Charles J., Kay, Paul, and O'Connor, M. C. 1988. Regularity and idiomaticity in grammatical constructions: The case of let alone. *Language*, **64**(3), 501–538.

Finlayson, Ian R., and Corley, Martin. 2012. Disfluency in dialogue: An intentional signal from the speaker? *Psychonomic Bulletin & Review*, **19**, 921–928.

Fischer, Kerstin. 2015. Conversation, construction grammar, and cognition. *Language and Cognition*, **7**(4), 563–588.

Ford, Cecilia E., Fox, Barbara A., and Thompson, Sandra A. 1996. Practices in the construction of turns: The "TCU" revisited. *Pragmatics*, **6**, 427–454.

Fox, Anthony. 2000. *Prosodic Features and Prosodic Structure: The Phonology of Suprasegmentals*. Oxford University Press.

Fox Tree, Jean E. 2001. Listeners' uses of *um* and *uh* in speech comprehension. *Memory and Cognition*, **29**, 320–326.

Fraccaro, Paul J., O'Connor, Jillian J. M., Re, Daniel E., Jones, Benedict C., DeBruine, Lisa M., and Feinberg, David R. 2013. Faking it: Deliberately altered voice pitch and vocal attractiveness. *Animal Behaviour*, **85**, 127–136.

Freeman, Valerie. 2014. Hyperarticulation as a signal of stance. *Journal of Phonetics*, **45**, 1–11.

Freeman, Valerie, Levow, Gina-Anne, Wright, Richard, and Ostendorf, Mari. 2015. Investigating the role of "yeah" in stance-dense conversation. Pages 3076–3080 of: *Interspeech*.

Freese, Jeremy, and Maynard, Douglas W. 1998. Prosodic features of bad news and good news in conversation. *Language in Society*, **27**, 195–219.

Fried, Mirjam, and Ostman, Jan-Ola. 2005. Construction Grammar and spoken language: The case of pragmatic particles. *Journal of Pragmatics*, **37**(11), 1752–1778.

Fuchs, Susanne, Petrone, Caterina, Rochet-Capellan, Amelie, Reichel, Uwe D., and Koenig, Laura L. 2015. Assessing respiratory contributions to F0 declination in German across varying speech tasks and respiratory demands. *Journal of Phonetics*, **52**, 35–45.

Fujie, Shinya, Fukushima, Kenta, and Kobayashi, Tetsunori. 2005. Back-channel feedback generation using linguistic and nonlinguistic information and its application to spoken dialogue system. Pages 889–892 of: *Interspeech*.

Fujisaki, Hiroya. 2004. Information, prosody, and modeling – with emphasis on tonal features of speech. In: *Speech Prosody*.

Geluykens, Ronald. 1988. On the myth of rising intonation in polar questions. *Journal of Pragmatics*, **12**, 467–485.

Gervais, Matthew, and Wilson, David Sloan. 2005. The evolution and functions of laughter and humor: A synthetic approach. *The Quarterly Review of Biology*, **80**, 395–430.

Gick, Bryan, Wilson, Ian, and Derrick, Donald. 2013. *Articulatory Phonetics*. Wiley-Blackwell.

Giles, Howard, Mulac, Anthony, Bradac, James J., and Johnson, Patricia. 1987. Speech accommodation theory: The first decade and beyond. Pages 13–48 of: McLaughlin, M. L. (ed.), *Communication Yearbook 10*. Sage.

Gladwell, Malcolm. 2008. *Outliers: The Story of Success*. Little, Brown.

Godfrey, John J., Holliman, Edward C., and McDaniel, Jane. 1992. Switchboard: Telephone speech corpus for research and development. Pages 517–520 of: *Proceedings of ICASSP*.

Goffman, Lisa, and Westover, Stefanie. 2013. Interactivity in prosodic representations in children. *Journal of Child Language*, **40**, 1032–1056.

Goldberg, Adele E. 2013. Constructionist approaches. Pages 15–31 of: Hoffman, Thomas, and Trousdale, Graeme (eds.), *The Oxford Handbook of Construction Grammar*. Oxford University Press.

Goodhue, Daniel, and Wagner, Michael. 2018. Intonation, *yes* and *no*. *Glossa*, **5**(1), 5.

Goodhue, Daniel, Harrison, Lyana, Siu, Yuen Tung Clementine, and Wagner, Michael. 2015. Toward a bestiary of English intonational contours. Pages 311–320 of: *Proceedings of the 46th Conference of the North Eastern Linguistic Society*.

Goodwin, Marjorie Harness, Cekaite, Asta, and Goodwin, Charles, E. 2012. Emotion as stance. Pages 16–41 of: *Emotion in Interaction*. Oxford University Press.

Gordon, Matthew, and Ladefoged, Peter. 2001. Phonation types: A cross-linguistic overview. *Journal of Phonetics*, **29**, 383–406.

Govind, D., and Prasanna, S. R. Mahadeva. 2013. Expressive speech synthesis: A review. *International Journal of Speech Technology*, **16**(2), 237–260.

Grabe, Esther. 1998. Pitch accent realization in English and German. *Journal of Phonetics*, **26**, 129–143.

Grabe, Esther, and Post, Brechtje. 2002. Intonational variation in the British Isles. Pages 343–346 of: *Speech Prosody*.

Gratch, Jon, Wang, Ning, Okhmatovskaia, A., Lamothe, F., Morales, M., van der Werf, R. J., and Morency, L.-P. 2007a. Can virtual humans be more engaging than real ones? *Lecture Notes in Computer Science*, **4552**, 286–297.

Gratch, Jonathan, Wang, Ning, Gerten, Jillian, Fast, Edward, and Duffy, Robin. 2007b. Creating rapport with virtual agents. Pages 125–138 of: *Intelligent Virtual Agents*. Springer.

Gravano, Agustin, and Hirschberg, Julia. 2009. Backchannel-inviting cues in task-oriented dialogue. Pages 1019–1022 of: *Interspeech*.

Gravano, Agustin, and Hirschberg, Julia. 2011. Turn-taking cues in task-oriented dialogue. *Computer Speech and Language*, **25**, 601–634.

Greenberg, Yoko, Shibuya, Nagisa, Tsuzaki, Minoru, Kato, Hiroaki, and Sagisaka, Yoshinori. 2009. Analysis on paralinguistic prosody control in perceptual impression space using multiple dimensional scaling. *Speech Communication*, **51**, 585–593.

Grice, H. Paul. 1975. Logic and conversation. Pages 41–58 of: *Syntax and Semantics 3: Speech Acts*. Seminar Press.

Grice, Martine, Ritter, Simon, Niemann, Henrik, and Roettger, Timo B. 2017. Integrating the discreteness and continuity of intonational categories. *Journal of Phonetics*, **64**, 90–107.

Gries, Stefan Th. 2003. Towards a corpus-based identification of prototypical instances of constructions. *Annual Review of Cognitive Linguistics*, **1**, 1–27.

Gries, Stefan Th., and Miglio, Viola G. 2014. New information in naturalistic data is also signalled by pitch movement: An analysis from monolingual English/Spanish and Bilingual Spanish speakers. *Complutense Journal of English Studies*, **22**, 11–33.

Gubian, Michele, Cangemi, Francesco, and Boves, Lou. 2010. Automatic and data driven pitch contour manipulation with functional data analysis. In: *Speech Prosody*.

Gubian, Michele, Boves, Lou, and Cangemi, Francesco. 2011. Joint analysis of F0 and speech rate with functional data analysis. Pages 4972–4975 of: *ICASSP*.

Gumperz, John J. 1982. *Discourse Strategies*. Cambridge University Press.

Gunthner, Susanne. 1999. Polyphony and the "layering of voices" in reported dialogues: An analysis of the use of prosodic devices in everyday reported speech. *Journal of Pragmatics*, **31**, 685–708.

Gussenhoven, Carlos. 2002. Intonation and interpretation: Phonetics and phonology. Pages 47–57 of: *Speech Prosody*.

Gussenhoven, Carlos. 2004. *The Phonology of Tone and Intonation*. Cambridge University Press.

Gussenhoven, Carlos. 2016. Foundations of intonational meaning: Anatomical and physiological factors. *Topics in Cognitive Science*, **8**, 425–434.

Halliday, Michael A. K. 1967. *Intonation and Grammar in British English*. Walter de Gruyter.

Hart, John. 1569. *Orthographie*. Serres.

Hasegawa, Yoko, and Hata, Kazue. 1995. The function of F0-peak delay in Japanese. Pages 141–151 of: *21st Annual Meeting of the Berkeley Linguistics Society*.

Hedberg, Nancy, Sosa, Juan M., and Fadden, Lorna. 2003. The intonation of contradictions in American English. In: *Prosody and Pragmatics Conference*.

Hedberg, Nancy, Sosa, Juan M., Gorgulu, Emrah, and Mameni, Morgan. 2010. The prosody and meaning of wh-questions in American English. In: *Speech Prosody*.

Hedberg, Nancy, Sosa, Juan M., and Gorgulu, Emrah. 2017. The meaning of intonation in yes-no questions in American English. *Corpus Linguistics and Linguistic Theory*, **13**, 321–368.

Heeman, Peter A., and Lunsford, Rebecca. 2017. Turn-taking offsets and dialogue context. Pages 1671–1675 of: *Interspeech*.

Heldner, Mattias, and Edlund, Jens. 2010. Pauses, gaps and overlaps in conversations. *Journal of Phonetics*, **38**, 555–568.

Hellbernd, Nele, and Sammler, Daniela. 2016. Prosody conveys speaker's intentions: Acoustic cues for speech act perception. *Journal of Memory and Language*, **88**, 70–86.

Hendrickson, Robert. 2013. *God Bless America: The Origins of over 1,500 Patriotic Words and Phrases*. Skyhorse Publishing.

Heritage, John. 2012. Epistemics in action: Action formation and territories of knowledge. *Research on Language & Social Interaction*, **45**(1), 1–29.

Heritage, John. 2017. Conversation analysis and institutional talk: Analyzing distinctive turn-taking. Pages 3–17 of: *Dialoganalyse VI/2: Referate der 6. Arbeitstagung, Prag 1996*. Walter de Gruyter.

Heritage, John, and Raymond, Chase Wesley. 2016. Are explicit apologies proportional to the offenses they address? *Discourse Processes*, **53**, 5–25.

Hermes, Dik J. 1998. Auditory and visual similarity of pitch contours. *Journal of Speech, Language, and Hearing Research*, **41**, 63–72.

Hinton, Leanne, Nichols, Joanna, and Ohala, John J. (eds.). 1994. *Sound Symbolism*. Cambridge University Press.

Hirose, Keikichi, Hashimoto, Hiroya, Saito, Daisuke, and Minematsu, Nobuaki. 2016. Superpositional modeling of fundamental frequency contours for HMM-based speech synthesis. Pages 771–775 of: *Speech Prosody*.

Hirschberg, Julia, and Litman, Diane. 1993. Empirical studies on the disambiguation of cue phrases. *Computational Linguistics*, **19**, 501–530.

Hirst, Daniel, and Di Cristo, Albert. 1998. *Intonation Systems: A Survey of Twenty Languages*. Cambridge University Press.

Hjalmarsson, Anna. 2009. The additive effect of turn-taking cues in human and synthetic voice. Pages 23–35 of: *Speech Communication*, vol. 53.

Hoffman, Curt, Lau, Ivy, and Johnson, David R. 1986. The linguistic relativity of person cognition: An English–Chinese comparison. *Journal of Personality and Social Psychology*, **51**, 1097–1105.

Holt, Elizabeth. 2010. The last laugh: Shared laughter and topic termination. *Journal of Pragmatics*, **42**, 1513–1525.

Holt, Yolanda Feimster, and Rangarathnam, Balaji. 2018. F_0 declination and reset in read speech of African American and White American women. *Speech Communication*, **95**, 43–50.

Homke, Paul, Holler, Judith, and Levinson, Stephen C. 2017. Eye blinking as addressee feedback in face-to-face conversation. *Research on Language and Social Interaction*, **50**, 54–70.

House, David. 2003. Perceiving question intonation: the role of pre-focal pause and delayed focal peak. Pages 755–758 of: *International Congress of the Phonetics Sciences*.

Huttenlauch, Clara, Feldhausen, Ingo, and Braun, Bettina. 2018. The purpose shapes the vocative: Prosodic realisation of Columbian Spanish vocatives. *Journal of the International Phonetic Association*, **48**, 33–56.

Hyman, Larry M. 2012. *Do All Languages Have Word Accent?* UC Berkeley Phonology Lab Annual Report.

Ingram, Jay. 1992. *Talk Talk Talk: Decoding the Mysteries of Speech*. Anchor.

Irvine, Christina A., Eigsti, Inge-Marie, and Fein, Deborah A. 2016. Uh, um, and autism: filler disfluencies as pragmatic markers in adolescents with optimal outcomes from autism spectrum disorder. *Journal of Autism and Developmental Disorders*, **46**(3), 1061–1070.

Ishi, Carlos Toshinori, Ishiguro, Hiroshi, and Hagita, Norihiro. 2010. Analysis of the roles and the dynamics of breathy and whispery voice qualities in dialogue speech. *EURASIP Journal on Audio, Speech, and Music Processing*, **2010**, 1–12.

Itahashi, Shuichi, and Tanaka, Kimihito. 1993. A method of classification among Japanese dialects. In: *Eurospeech*.

Jaffe, Joseph. 1978. Parliamentary procedure and the brain. Pages 55–66 of: Siegman, Aron W., and Feldstein, Stanley (eds.), *Nonverbal Behavior and Communication*. Lawrence Erlbaum Associates.

Janssoone, Thomas, Clavel, Chloe, Bailly, Kevin, and Richard, Gael. 2016. Using temporal association rules for the synthesis of embodied conversational agents with a specific stance. Pages 175–189 of: *International Conference on Intelligent Virtual Agents*. Springer.

Jefferson, Gail. 1988. On the sequential organization of troubles-talk in ordinary conversation. *Social Problems*, **35**, 418–441.

Jeong, Sunwoo. 2016. Conventions in prosody for affective meanings: Non-canonical terminal contours in English polar interrogatives. Pages 907–911 of: *Speech Prosody*.

Jeong, Sunwoo, and Condoravdi, Cleo. 2017. Imperatives with the calling contour. In: *Proceedings of the 43rd Annual Meeting of the Berkeley Linguistics Society*.

Johansson, Martin, and Skantze, Gabriel. 2015. Opportunities and obligations to take turns in collaborative multi-party human-robot interaction. Pages 305–314 of: *16th Annual Meeting of the Special Interest Group on Discourse and Dialogue*.

Johnstone, Anne, Berry, Umesh, Nguyen, Tina, and Asper, Alan. 1995. There was a Long Pause: Influencing turn-taking behaviour in human-human and human-computer dialogs. *International Journal of Human-Computer Studies*, **42**, 383–411.

Jokisch, Oliver, Langenberg, Tristan, and Pinter, Gabor. 2014. Intonation-based classification of language proficiency using FDA. In: *Speech Prosody*.

Jurafsky, Dan, and Martin, James H. 2009. *Speech and Language Processing*, 2nd edition. Pearson.

Kakouros, Sofoklis, and Rasanen, Okko. 2016. Perception of sentence stress in speech correlates with the temporal unpredictability of prosodic features. *Cognitive Science*, **40**(7), 1739–1774.

Kane, John, Drugman, Thomas, and Gobl, Christer. 2013. Improved automatic detection of creak. *Computer Speech & Language*, **27**, 1028–1047.

Kapatsinski, Vsevolod, Olejarczuk, Paul, and Redford, Melissa A. 2017. Perceptual learning of intonation contour categories in adults and 9 to 11-year-old children: Adults are more narrow-minded. *Cognitive Science*, **41**, 383–415.

Kawahara, Tatsuya, Iwatate, Takuma, and Takanashi, Katsuya. 2012. Prediction of turn-taking by combining prosodic and eye-gaze information in poster conversations. In: *Interspeech*.

Kay, Paul, and Fillmore, Charles J. 1999. Grammatical constructions and linguistic generalizations: The What's X doing Y? construction. *Language*, **75**, 1–33.

Keating, Patricia, Garellek, Marc, and Kreiman, Jody. 2015. Acoustic properties of different kinds of creaky voice. In: *International Congress of the Phonetic Sciences*.

Kendon, Adam. 1967. Some functions of gaze-direction in social interaction. *Acta Psychologica*, **26**, 22–63.

Kendon, Adam. 1980. Gesticulation and speech: Two aspects of the process of utterance. Pages 207–227 of: Key, Mary R. (ed.), *The Relationship of Verbal and Nonverbal Communication*. de Gruyter.

Kendrick, Kobin H., and Drew, Paul. 2016. Recruitment: Offers, requests, and the organization of assistance in interaction. *Research on Language and Social Interaction*, **49**, 1–19.

Kennard, Catherine Hicks. 2006. *Gender and Command: A Sociophonetic Analysis of Female and Male Drill Instructors in the United States Marine Corps*. Ph.D. thesis, the University of Arizona.

Kinnunen, Tomi, and Li, Haizhou. 2010. An overview of text-independent speaker recognition: From features to supervectors. *Speech Communication*, **52**, 12–40.

Kochanski, Greg. 2006. Prosody beyond fundamental frequency. Pages 89–121 of: Sudhoff, Stefan, Lenertova, Denisa, Meyer, Roland, Pappert, Sandra, Augurky, Petra, Mleinek, Ina, Richter, Nichole, and Schliesser, Johannes (eds.), *Methods in Empirical Prosody Research*. Walter de Gruyter.

Kochanski, Greg. 2010. Prosodic peak estimation under segmental perturbations. *Journal of the Acoustical Society of America*, **127**, 862–873.

Kochanski, Greg, and Shih, Chilin. 2003. Prosody modeling with soft templates. *Speech Communication*, **39**, 311–352.

Kohler, Klaus J. 1987. The linguistic functions of F0 peaks. Pages 149–152 of: *11th Congress of the Phonetic Sciences*.

Kori, Shiro. 1987. Perceptual dimensions of laughter and their acoustic correlates. Pages 67.4.1–67.4.4 of: *XIth International Congress of the Phonetic Sciences*, vol. 4.

Kreidler, Charles W. 1989. *The Pronunciation of English: A Course Book in Phonology*. Blackwell.

Krivokapic, Jelena. 2014. Gestural coordination at prosodic boundaries and its role for prosodic structure and speech planning processes. *Philosophical Transactions of the Royal Society of London, B*, **369**, 2013.0397.

Krivokapic, Jelena. 2017. A kinematic study of prosodic structure in articulatory and manual gestures. *Laboratory Phonology*, **8**, 1–26.

Kurtic, Emina, Brown, Guy J., and Wells, Bill. 2013. Resources for turn competition in overlapping talk. *Speech Communication*, **55**, 721–743.

Kurumada, Chigusa, and Clark, Eve V. 2017. Pragmatic inferences in context: Learning to interpret contrastive prosody. *Journal of Child Language*, **44**, 850–880.

Kurumada, Chigusa, Brown, Merideth, and Tannenhaus, Michael K. 2012. Pragmatic interpretation of contrastive prosody: It looks like speech adaptation. In: *Cognitive Science Conference*.

Ladd, D. Robert. 1978. Stylized intonation. *Language*, **54**, 517–540.

Ladd, D. Robert. 1983. Phonological features of intonational peaks. *Language*, **59**, 721–759.

Ladd, D. Robert. 2008. *Intonational Phonology*, 2nd edition. Cambridge University Press.

Ladd, D. Robert. 2014. *Simultaneous Structure in Phonology*. Oxford University Press.

Ladefoged, Peter. 2003. *Phonetic Data Analysis*. Blackwell.

Ladefoged, Peter, and Johnson, Keith. 2014. *A Course in Phonetics*, 7th edition. Wadsworth.

Lai, Catherine. 2012. Response types and the prosody of declaratives. In: *Speech Prosody*.

Lakoff, George. 1987. *Women, Fire, and Dangerous Things*. University of Chicago Press.

Lakoff, George, and Johnson, Mark. 1980. *Metaphors We Live By*. University of Chicago Press.

Landgraf, Rabea. 2014. Are you serious? Irony and the perception of emphatic intensification. Pages 91–94 of: *Proc. 4th International Symposium on Tonal Aspects of Languages (TAL)*.

Lasarcyk, Eva, and Trouvain, Jürgen. 2008. Imitating conversational laughter with an articulatory speech synthesizer. Pages 43–48 of: *Interdisciplinary Workshop on the Phonetics of Laughter*.

Laskowski, Kornel. 2015. Auto-imputing radial basis functions for neural-network turn-taking models. Pages 1820–1824 of: *Interspeech*.

Laver, John. 1994. *Principles of Phonetics*. Cambridge University Press.

Lee, Chul Min, and Narayanan, Shrikanth. 2005. Toward detecting emotions in spoken dialogs. *IEEE Transactions on Speech and Audio Processing*, **13**, 293–303.

Lehiste, Ilse, and Peterson, Gordon E. 1961. Some basic considerations in the analysis of intonation. *The Journal of the Acoustical Society of America*, **33**, 419–425.

Lerner, Gene H. 2002. Turn-sharing: The choral co-production of talk in interaction. Pages 225–256 of: Ford, Cecilia E., Fox, Barbara A., and Thompson, Sandra A. (eds.), *The Language of Turn and Sequence*. Oxford University Press.

Levelt, W. J. M. 1989. *Speaking: From Intention to Articulation*. MIT Press.

Levinson, Stephen C. 2012. The original sin of cognitive science. *Topics in Cognitive Science*, **4**, 396–403.

Levinson, Stephen C. 2016. Turn-taking in human communication: Origins and implications for language processing. *Trends in Cognitive Sciences*, **20**, 6–14.

Levinson, Stephen C., and Torreira, Francisco. 2015. Timing in turn-taking and its implications for processing models of language. *Frontiers in Psychology*, **6**, 731.

Li, Yu-Fai, and Mok, Peggy. 2016. Does size matter? A preliminary investigation on the effects of physical size on pitch level in pet-directed speech. Pages 1196–1200 of: *Speech Prosody*.

Liberman, Alvin M., and Whalen, Doug H. 2000. On the relation of speech to language. *Trends in Cognitive Sciences*, **4**, 187–196.

Liberman, Mark, and Sag, Ivan. 1974. Prosodic form and discourse function. Pages 402–427 of: *Papers from Tenth Regional Meeting, Chicago Linguistic Society*.

Local, John, and Walker, Gareth. 2012. How phonetic features project more talk. *Journal of the International Phonetic Association*, **42**, 255–280.

Loehr, Daniel P. 2012. Temporal, structural, and pragmatic synchrony between intonation and gesture. *Laboratory Phonology*, **3**, 71–89.

Madill, Catherine J., Sheard, Christine, and Heard, Robert. 2017. Are instructions to manipulate specific parameters of laryngeal function associated with auditory-perceptual ratings of voice quality in nondisordered speakers? *Journal of Voice*, **31**, 540.e21–e33.

Maier, Angelika, Hough, Julian, and Schlangen, David. 2017. Towards deep end-of-turn prediction for situated spoken dialogue systems. In: *Interspeech*.

Marsh, Kerry L., Richardson, Michael J., and Schmidt, Richard C. 2009. Social connection through joint action and interpersonal coordination. *Topics in Cognitive Science*, **1**(2), 320–339.

Martinez, Claudia B. 2018. Cross-cultural analysis of turn-taking practices in English and Spanish conversations. *Vernacular: New Connections in Language, Literature, & Culture*, **3**(1), 5.

Matsui, Tomoko, Nakamura, Tagiru, Utsumi, Akira, Sasaki, Akihiro T, Koike, Takahiko, Yoshida, et al. 2016. The role of prosody and context in sarcasm comprehension: Behavioral and fMRI evidence. *Neuropsychologia*, **87**, 74–84.

McCann, Joanne, and Peppe, Sue. 2003. Prosody in autism spectrum disorders: A critical review. *International Journal of Language & Communication Disorders*, **38**, 325–350.

MedlinePlus. 2014. *Developmental Milestones Record: 9 Months*. www.nlm.nih.gov/medlineplus/ency/article/002009.htm.

Mendoza-Denton, Norma. 2011. The semiotic hitchhiker's guide to creaky voice: Circulation and gendered hardcore in a Chicana/o gang persona. *Journal of Linguistic Anthropology*, **21**, 261–280.

Menenti, Laura, Pickering, Martin J, and Garrod, Simon C. 2012. Towards a neural basis of interactive alignment in conversation. *Frontiers in Human Neuroscience*, **6**, 1–9.

Mennen, Ineke. 2015. Beyond segments: Towards a L2 intonation learning theory. Pages 171–188 of: Delais-Roussairie, Elisabeth, Avanzi, Mathieu, and Herment, Sophie (eds.), *Prosody and Language in Contact*. Springer.

Michaud, Shari L., and Warner, Rebecca M. 1997. Gender differences in self-reported response to troubles talk. *Sex Roles*, **37**, 527–540.

Mixdorff, Hansjorg, Honemann, Angelika, Kim, Jeesun, and Davis, Chris. 2015. Anticipation of turn-switching in auditory-visual dialogs. Pages 1676–1680 of: *1st Joint Conference on Facial Analysis, Animation and Auditory-Visual Speech Processing*.

Mok, Peggy P. K., Yin, Yanjun, Setter, Jane, and Nayan, Noor Mat. 2016. Assessing knowledge of English intonation patterns by L2 speakers. In: *Speech Prosody*.

Moore, Brian C. J. 2003. *An Introduction to the Psychology of Hearing*, 5th edition. Academic Press.

Mowrer, Donald E., LaPointe, Leonard L., and Case, James. 1987. Analysis of five acoustic correlates of laughter. *Journal of Nonverbal Behavior*, **11**, 191–199.

Murray, Iain R., and Arnott, John L. 1993. Toward the simulation of emotion in synthetic speech: A review of the literature on human vocal emotion. *Journal of the Acoustic Society of America*, **93**, 1097–1108.

Murry, Thomas. 1971. Subglottal pressure and airflow measures during vocal fry phonation. *Journal of Speech, Language, and Hearing Research*, **14**, 544–551.

Ni Chasaide, Ailbhe, and Gobl, Christer. 2004. Voice quality and F0 in prosody: Towards a holistic account. In: *Speech Prosody*.

Nicholson, Hannele, Bard, Ellen Gurman, Lickley, Rohin, Anderson, Anne H., Mullin, Jim, Kenicer, David, and Smallwood, Lucy. 2003. The intentionality of disfluency: Findings from feedback and timing. Pages 17–20 of: Eklund, Robert (ed.), *ISCA Tutorial and Research Workshop on Disfluency in Spontaneous Speech*.

Niebuhr, Oliver. 2007. Categorical perception in intonation: A matter of signal dynamics? Pages 642–645 of: *Interspeech*.

Niebuhr, Oliver. 2010. On the phonetics of intensifying emphasis in German. *Phonetica*, **67**, 170–198.

Niebuhr, Oliver. 2014. Resistance is futile: The intonation between continuation rise and calling contour in German. Pages 132–136 of: *Interspeech*.

Niebuhr, Oliver. 2015. Stepped intonation contours: A new field of complexity. Pages 39–74 of: Skarnitzl, R., and Niebuhr, O. (eds.), *Tackling the Complexity of Speech*. Charles University Press.

Niebuhr, Oliver. 2017. Clear speech — mere speech? How segmental and prosodic speech reduction shape the impression that speakers create on listeners. Pages 894–898 of: *Interspeech*, vol. 18.

Niebuhr, Oliver, and Pfitzinger, Hartmut. 2010. On pitch-accent identification: The role of syllable duration and intensity. In: *Speech Prosody*.

Niebuhr, Oliver, and Ward, Nigel G. 2018. Challenges in the modeling of pragmatics-related prosody. *Journal of the International Phonetics Association*, **48**, 1–8.

Niebuhr, Oliver, D'Imperio, Mariapaola, Fivela, Barbara G., and Cangemi, Francesco. 2011. Are there shapers and aligners? Individual differences in signalling pitch accent category. Pages 120–123 of: *International Congress of Phonetic Sciences*.

Niebuhr, Oliver, Gors, Karin, and Graupe, Evelin. 2013. Speech reduction, intensity, and F0 shape are cues to turn-taking. Pages 261–269 of: *Sigdial*.

Niebuhr, Oliver, Vosse, Jana, and Brem, Alexander. 2016. What makes a charismatic speaker? A computer-based acoustic-prosodic analysis of Steve Jobs' tone of voice. *Computers in Human Behavior*, **64**, 366–382.

Nöth, Elmar, Batliner, Anton, Kießling, Andreas, Kompe, Ralf, and Niemann, Heinrich. 2000. Verbmobil: The use of prosody in the linguistic components of a speech understanding system. *IEEE Transactions on Speech and Audio Processing*, **8**, 519–532.

Novick, David, and Gris, Ivan. 2014. Building rapport between human and ECA: A pilot study. Pages 472–480 of: *Human-Computer Interaction. Advanced Interaction Modalities and Techniques*. Springer.

Novick, David G, Hansen, Brian, and Ward, Karen. 1996. Coordinating turn-taking with gaze. Pages 1888–1891 of: *International Conference on Spoken Language Processing*, vol. 3.

Nygaard, Lynne C., Herold, Debora S., and Namy, Laura L. 2009. The semantics of prosody: Acoustic and perceptual evidence of prosodic correlates to word meaning. *Cognitive Science*, **33**, 127–146.

O'Connell, Daniel C., and Kowal, Sabine. 2004. The history of research on the filled pause as evidence of the written language bias in Linguistics (Linell, 1982). *Journal of Psycholinguistic Research*, **33**, 459–474.

O'Connell, Daniel C., Kowal, Sabine, and Kaltenbacher, Erika. 1990. Turn-taking: A critical analysis of the research tradition. *Journal of Psycholinguistic Research*, **19**, 345–373.

O'Connor, J. D., and Arnold, G. F. 1973. *Intonation of Colloquial English: A Practical Handbook*, 2nd edition. Longman.

Oertel, Catharine, Scherer, Stefan, and Campbell, Nick. 2011. On the use of multimodal cues for the prediction of degree of involvement in spontaneous conversation. In: *Interspeech*.

Oertel, Catharine, Wlodarczak, Marcin, Edlund, Jens, Wagner, Petra, and Gustafson, Joakim. 2012. Gaze patterns in turn-taking. In: *Thirteenth Interspeech Conference*.

Ogden, Richard. 2006. Phonetics and social action in agreements and disagreements. *Journal of Pragmatics*, **38**, 1752–1775.

Ogden, Richard 2007. Linguistic resources for complaints in conversation. Pages 1321–1324 of: *International Congress of the Phonetic Sciences*.

Ogden, Richard. 2010. Prosodic constructions in making complaints. Pages 81–103 of: Barth-Weingarten, Dagmar, Reber, Elisabeth, and Selting, Margret (eds.), *Prosody in Interaction*. Benjamins.

Ogden, Richard. 2012. Prosodies in conversation. Pages 201–217 of: Niebuhr, Oliver (ed.), *Understanding Prosody: The Role of Context, Function, and Communication*. De Gruyter.

Ogden, Richard. 2017. *An Introduction to English Phonetics*, 2nd edition. Edinburgh University Press.

Ogden, Richard, and Hawkins, Sarah. 2015. Entrainment as a basis for co-ordinated actions in speech. In: *International Congress of the Phonetic Sciences*.

Ogden, Richard, and Walker, Traci. 2013. Phonetic resources in the construction of social actions. Pages 277–312 of: Szczepek Reed, Beatrice, and Raymond, Geoffrey (eds.), *Units of Talk: Units of Action*. John Benjamins.

Oh, Jieun, Cho, Eunjoon, and Slaney, Malcolm. 2013. Characteristic contours of syllable-level units in laughter. In: *Interspeech*.

Ohala, John J. 1984. An ethological perspective on common cross-language utilization of F_0. *Phonetica*, **41**, 1–16.

Owens, F. J. 1993. *Signal Processing of Speech*. McGraw Hill.

Oxenham, Andrew J. 2018. How we hear: The perception and neural coding of sound. *Annual Review of Psychology*, **69**, 27–50.

Parrell, Benjamin, Lee, Sungbok, and Byrd, Dani. 2013. Evaluation of prosodic juncture strength using functional data analysis. *Journal of Phonetics*, **41**(6), 442–452.

Parrell, Benjamin, Goldstein, Louis, Lee, Sungbok, and Byrd, Dani. 2014. Spatiotemporal coupling between speech and manual motor actions. *Journal of Phonetics*, **42**, 1–11.

Patience, Matthew, Marasco, Olivia, Colanton, Laura, Klassen, Gabrielle, Radu, Malina, and Tararova, Olga. 2018. Initial pitch cues in English sentence types. Pages 463–467 of: *Speech Prosody*.

Pederson, Eric. 1991. The ecology of a semantic space. Pages 457–468 of: *Berkeley Linguistics Society, Proceedings of the Seventeenth Annual Meeting.*

Pentland, Alex. 2008. *Honest Signals.* MIT Press.

Persson, Rasmus. 2018. On some functions of salient initial accents in French talk-in-interaction: Intonational meaning and the interplay of prosodic, verbal and sequential properties of talk. *Journal of the International Phonetics Association,* **48**, 77–102.

Petrone, Caterina, and Niebuhr, Oliver. 2013. On the intonation of German intonation questions: The role of the prenuclear region. *Language and Speech,* **57**, 108–146.

Phillips-Silver, Jessica, Aktipis, C. Athena, and Bryant, Gregory A. 2010. The ecology of entrainment: Foundations of coordinated rhythmic movement. *Music Perception: An Interdisciplinary Journal,* **28**, 3–14.

Pickering, Lucy, Hu, Guiling Gloria, and Baker, Amanda. 2012. The pragmatic function of intonation: Cueing agreement and disagreement in spoken English discourse and implications for ELT. Pages 199–218 of: Romero-Trillo, Jesus (ed.), *Pragmatics and Prosody in English Language Teaching.* Springer.

Pierrehumbert, Janet. 1979. The perception of fundamental frequency declination. *The Journal of the Acoustical Society of America,* **66**, 363–369.

Pierrehumbert, Janet B., and Steele, Shirley A. 1989. Categories of tonal alignment in English. *Phonetica,* **46**(4), 181–196.

Pike, Kenneth L. 1945. *The Intonation of American English.* University of Michigan Press.

Piller, Ingrid. 2011. *Intercultural Communication: A Critical Introduction.* Edinburgh University Press.

Pillet-Shore, Danielle. 2012. Greeting: Displaying stance through prosodic recipient design. *Research on Language & Social Interaction,* **45**, 375–398.

Pinker, Steven. 1994. *The language mavens. Chapter 12 of: The Language Instinct.* Harper Collins.

Pinker, Steven. 2007. *The Stuff of Thought: Language as a Window into Human Nature.* Penguin.

Pisanski, Katarzyna, Fraccaro, Paul J., Tigue, Cara C., O'Connor, Jillian J. M., Röder, Susanne, Andrews, Paul W., et al. 2014. Vocal indicators of body size in men and women: a meta-analysis. *Animal Behaviour,* **95**, 89–99.

Pittam, Jeffery. 1994. *Voice in Social Interaction.* Sage.

Podesva, Robert J., and Callier, Patrick. 2015. Voice quality and identity. Pages 173–194 of: *Annual Review of Applied Linguistics, 35.* Cambridge University Press.

Pomerantz, Anita. 1984. Agreeing and disagreeing with assessments: Some features of preferred/dispreferred turn shapes. Pages 57–101 of: Atkinson, J. Maxwell, and Heritage, John (eds.), *Structures of Social Action: Studies in Conversation Analysis.* Cambridge University Press.

Portes, Cristel, and Beyssade, Claire. 2015. Is intonational meaning compositional? *Verbum,* **37**, 207–233.

Potts, Christopher. 2005. Lexicalized intonational meaning. Pages 129–146 of: Kawahara, Shigeto (ed.), *University of Massachusetts, Occasional Papers in Linguistics (UMOP) 30: Papers on Prosody.* Amherst, MA: GLSA.

Prieto, Pilar. 2015. Intonational meaning. *Wiley Interdisciplinary Reviews: Cognitive Science,* **6**, 371–381.

Prieto, Pilar, Van Santen, Jan, and Hirschberg, Julia. 1995. Tonal alignment patterns in Spanish. *Journal of Phonetics*, **23**, 429–451.

Pullum, Geoffrey K. 2009. 50 years of stupid grammar advice. *The Chronicle of Higher Education*, **55**(32), B15.

Puts, David Andrew. 2005. Mating context and menstrual phase affect women's preferences for male voice pitch. *Evolution and Human Behavior*, **26**, 388–397.

Rakov, Rachel, and Rosenberg, Andrew. 2013. Sure, I did the right thing: A system for sarcasm detection in speech. Pages 842–846 of: *Interspeech*.

Ranganath, Rajesh, Jurafsky, Dan, and McFarland, Dan. 2013. Detecting friendly, flirtatious, awkward, and assertive speech in speed-dates. *Computer Speech and Language*, **27**, 89–115.

Rao, Rajiv. 2013. Prosodic consequences of sarcasm versus sincerity in Mexican Spanish. *Concentric: Studies in Linguistics*, **39**(2), 33–59.

Raux, Antoine, and Eskenazi, Maxine. 2012. Optimizing the turn-taking behavior of task-oriented spoken dialog systems. *ACM Transactions on Speech and Language Processing*, **9**, 1–23.

Reed, Beatrice Szczepek. 2004. Turn-final intonation in English. Pages 97–117 of: Couper-Kuhlen, Elizabeth, and Ford, Cecilia E. (eds.), *Sound Patterns in Interaction: Cross-Linguistics Studies from Conversation*. John Benjamins.

Regier, Terry. 1998. Reduplication and the arbitrariness of the sign. In: *Proceedings of the 20th Annual Conference of the Cognitive Science Society*.

Reichel, Uwe D. 2014. Linking bottom-up intonation stylization to discourse structure. *Computer Speech and Language*, **28**, 1340–1365.

Reichel, Uwe D., and Mady, Katalin. 2014. Comparing parameterizations of pitch register and its discontinuities at prosodic boundaries for Hungarian. In: *Interspeech*.

Riou, Marine. 2017. The prosody of topic transition in interaction: Pitch register variations. *Language and Speech*, **60**, 658–678.

Ritchart, Amanda, and Arvaniti, Amalia. 2014. The form and use of uptalk in Southern Californian English. Pages 20–23 of: *Proceedings of Speech Prosody*.

Roberts, Celia. 2013. The gatekeeping of Babel: Job interviews and the linguistic penalty. Pages 81–94 of: *Language, Migration and Social Inequalities*. Multilingual Matters.

Roberts, Felicia, and Francis, Alexander L. 2013. Identifying a temporal threshold of tolerance for silent gaps after requests. *Journal of the Acoustical Society of America*, **133**, 471–477.

Roberts, Felicia, Francis, Alexander L., and Morgan, M. 2006. The interaction of inter-turn silence with prosodic cues in listener perceptions of "trouble" in conversation. *Speech Communication*, **48**, 1079–1093.

Romero-Trillo, Jesus. 2012. *Pragmatics and Prosody in English Language Teaching*. Springer.

Rosenberg, Andrew, and Hirschberg, Julia. 2009. Charisma perception from text and speech. *Speech Communication*, **51**(7), 640–655.

Sacks, Harvey, Schegloff, Emanuel A., and Jefferson, Gail. 1974. A simplest systematics for the organization of turn-taking for conversation. *Language*, **50**, 696–735.

Saindon, Mathieu R., Trehub, Sandra E., Schellenberg, E. Glenn, and van Lieshout, Pascal H. H. M. 2017. When is a question a question for children and adults? *Language Learning and Development*, **13**(3), 274–285.

Sakamoto, Nancy, and Shiyo, Sakamoto. 2004. *Polite Fictions in Collision: Why Japanese and Americans Seem Rude to Each Other*. Kinseido.

Schegloff, Emanuel A. 1992. To Searle on conversation: A note in return. Pages 113–128 of: Parret, Herman, and Verschueren, Jef (eds.), *(On) Searle on Conversation*. John Benjamins.

Schegloff, Emanuel A., and Sacks, Harvey. 1973. Opening up closings. *Semiotica*, **8**, 289–327.

Scherer, Klaus R. 1986. Vocal affect expression: A review and a model for future research. *Psychological Bulletin*, **99**, 143.

Scherer, Klaus R. 2003. Vocal communication of emotion: A review of research paradigms. *Speech Communication*, **40**, 227–256.

Schober, Michael, and Brennan, Susan. 2003. Processes of interactive spoken discourse: The role of the partner. Pages 123–164 of: Graesser, A. C., Gernsbacher, M. A., and Goldman, S. R. (eds.), *Handbook of Discourse Processes*. Lawrence Erlbaum.

Schoenenberg, Katrin, Raake, Alexander, and Koeppe, Judith. 2014. Why are you so slow? Misattribution of transmission delay to attributes of the conversation partner at the far-end. *International Journal of Human-Computer Studies*, **72**, 477–487.

Schroder, Marc. 2003. Experimental study of affect bursts. *Speech Communication*, **40**, 99–116.

Schuller, Bjorn. 2011. Voice and speech analysis in search of states and traits. Pages 227–253 of: Salah, Albert Ali, and Gevers, Theo (eds.), *Computer Analysis of Human Behavior*. Springer.

Schuller, Björn, Steidl, Stefan, Batliner, Anton, Burkhardt, Felix, Devillers, Laurence, Müller, Christian, and Narayanan, Shrikanth. 2013. Paralinguistics in speech and language: State-of-the-art and the challenge. *Computer Speech & Language*, **27**, 4–39.

Scott, Sophie K., McGettigan, Carolyn, and Eisner, Frank. 2009. A little more conversation, a little less action—candidate roles for the motor cortex in speech perception. *Nature Reviews Neuroscience*, **10**, 295–302.

Searle, John R. 1992. Conversation. Pages 8–29 of: Parret, Herman, and Verschueren, Jef (eds.), *(On) Searle on Conversation*. John Benjamins.

Sebanz, Natalie, Bekkering, Harold, and Knoblich, Gunther. 2006. Joint action: Bodies and minds moving together. *Trends in Cognitive Sciences*, **10**, 70–76.

Selfridge, Ethan O., and Heeman, Peter A. 2010. Importance-driven turn-bidding for spoken dialogue systems. Pages 177–185 of: *Proceedings of the 48th Annual Meeting of the Association for Computational Linguistics*.

Selkirk, Elisabeth. 1995. Sentence prosody: Intonation, stress, and phrasing. Pages 550–569 of: Goldsmith, John A. (ed.), *The Handbook of Phonological Theory*. Blackwell.

Selkirk, Elisabeth. 1996. *The Prosodic Structure of Function Words*. Erlbaum.

Sell, Aaron, Bryant, Gregory A., Cosmides, Leda, Tooby, John, Sznycer, Daniel, Von Rueden, Christopher, et al. 2010. Adaptations in humans for assessing physical strength from the voice. *Proceedings of the Royal Society of London B: Biological Sciences*, **277**, 3509–3518.

Shannon, Matt, Simko, Gabor, Chang, Shuo-Yiin, and Parada, Carolina. 2017. Improved end-of-query detection for streaming speech recognition. Pages 1909–1913 of: *Interspeech*.

Shintel, Hadas, Nusbaum, Howard C., and Okrent, Arika. 2006. Analog acoustic expression in speech communication. *Journal of Memory and Language*, **55**, 167–177.

Shockey, Linda. 2013. *Sound Patterns of Spoken English*. Wiley.

Shriberg, Elizabeth, and Stolcke, Andreas. 2004. Direct modeling of prosody: An overview of applications in automatic speech processing. Pages 575–582 of: *Speech Prosody*.

Shriberg, Elizabeth, Bates, R., Stolcke, A., Taylor, P., Jurafsky, D., Ries, K., et al. 1998. Can prosody aid the automatic classification of dialog acts in conversational speech? *Language and Speech*, **41**, 439–487.

Shriberg, Elizabeth, Stolcke, Andreas, Hakkani-Tur, Dilek, and Tur, Gokhan. 2000. Prosody-based automatic segmentation of speech into sentences and topics. *Speech Communication*, **32**, 127–154.

Sicoli, Mark A., Stivers, Tanya, Enfield, Nick J., and Levinson, Stephen C. 2015. Marked initial pitch in questions signals marked communicative function. *Language and Speech*, **58**, 204–223.

Sidnell, Jack. 2011. *Conversation Analysis: An Introduction*. John Wiley & Sons.

Silverman, Kim, Beckman, Mary, Pitrelli, John, Ostendorf, Mori, Wightman, Colin, Price, Patti, et al. 1992. ToBI: A standard for labeling English prosody. Pages 867–870 of: *Second International Conference on Spoken Language Processing*.

Skantze, Gabriel. 2017. Towards a general, continuous model of turn-taking in spoken dialogue using LSTM recurrent neural networks. In: *Sigdial*.

Slaney, Malcolm, Shriberg, Elizabeth, and Huang, Jui-Ting. 2013. Pitch-gesture modeling using subband autocorrelation change detection. Pages 1911–1915 of: *Interspeech*.

Slobin, Dan I. 1987. Thinking for speaking. Pages 435–445 of: *Berkeley Linguistics Society, Proceedings of the Thirteenth Annual Meeting*.

Smelser, Neil J. 1993. *Effective Committee Service*. Sage.

Snow, David, and Balog, Heather L. 2002. Do children produce the melody before the words? A review of developmental intonation research. *Lingua*, **112**, 1025–1058.

Sonmez, M. Kemal, Shriberg, E. E., Heck, L., and Weintraub, M. 1998. Modeling dynamic prosodic variation for speaker verification. Pages 3189–3192 of: *ICSLP*.

Sorocco, Kristen H., Monnot, Marilee, Vincent, Andrea S., Ross, Elliott D., and Lovallo, William R. 2009. Deficits in affective prosody comprehension: Family history of alcoholism versus alcohol exposure. *Alcohol & Alcoholism*, **45**, 25–29.

Stivers, Tanya, Enfield, Nicholas J., Brown, Penelope, Englert, Christina, Hayashi, Makoto, Heinemann, Trine, et al. 2009. Universals and cultural variation in turn-taking in conversation. *Proceedings of the National Academy of Sciences*, **106**(26), 10587–10592.

Strombergsson, Sofia, Hjalmarsson, Anna, Edlund, Jens, and House, David. 2013. Timing responses to questions in dialogue. Pages 2584–2588 of: *Interspeech*.

Swerts, Marc. 1997. Prosodic features at discourse boundaries of different strength. *The Journal of the Acoustical Society of America*, **101**, 514–521.

Syrdal, Ann K., Conkie, Alistair, Kim, Yeon-Jun, and Beutnagel, Mark C. 2010. Speech acts and dialog TTS. Pages 179–183 of: *Speech Synthesis Workshop*.

Szczepek Reed, Beatrice. 2006. *Prosodic Orientation in English Conversation*. Palgrave.

Szczepek Reed, Beatrice. 2010. *Analysing Conversation: An Introduction to Prosody.* Palgrave Macmillan.

Szczepek Reed, Beatrice. 2012. Prosody in conversation: Implications for teaching English pronunciation. Pages 147–168 of: Romero-Trillo, Jesus (ed.), *Pragmatics and Prosody in English Language Teaching.* Springer.

't Hart, Johan, Collier, Rene, and Cohen, Antonie. 2006. *A Perceptual Study of Intonation: An Experimental-Phonetic Approach to Speech Melody.* Cambridge University Press.

Tanaka, Hiroki, Sakti, Sakriani, Neubig, Graham, Toda, Tomoki, and Nakamura, Satoshi. 2014. Linguistic and acoustic features for automatic identification of autism spectrum disorders in children's narrative. Page 88 of: *ACL 2014.*

Tang, C., Hamilton, L. S., and Chang, E. F. 2017. Intonational speech prosody encoding in the human auditory cortex. *Science*, **357**, 797–801.

Tannen, Deborah. 1989. *That's Not What I Meant! How Conversational Style Makes or Breaks Relationships.* Ballantine.

Tannen, Deborah. 1990. *You Just Don't Understand: Men and Women in Conversation.* William Morrow.

Tao, Jiaer, Torreira, Francisco, and Clayards, Meghan. 2018. Durational cues to word boundaries in spontaneous speech. Pages 240–244 of: *Speech Prosody Conference.*

Taylor, John R. 2004. The ecology of constructions. Pages 49–73 of: Radden, Gunter, and Panther, Klaus-Uwe (eds.), *Studies in Linguistic Motivation.* Mouton De Gruyter.

ten Bosch, Louis, Oostdijk, Nelleke, and Boves, Lou. 2005. On temporal aspects of turn taking in conversational dialogues. *Speech Communication*, **47**, 80–86.

Tench, Paul. 1996. *The Intonation Systems of English.* Cassell.

ter Maat, Mark, and Heylen, Dirk. 2009. Turn management or impression management. Pages 467–473 of: *Intelligent Virtual Agents 2009; LNAI 5773.*

Terken, Jacques. 1993. Issues in the perception of prosody. Pages 228–233 of: *ESCA Workshop on Prosody.*

Tillmann, Barbara. 2014. Pitch processing in music and speech. *Acoustics Australia*, **42**, 124–130.

Tilsen, Sam. 2016. Selection and coordination: The articulatory basis for the emergence of phonological structure. *Journal of Phonetics*, **55**, 53–77.

Titze, Ingo R. 2008. The human instrument. *Scientific American*, **298**, 94–101.

Torreira, Francisco, and Grice, Martine. 2018. Melodic constructions in Spanish: Metrical structure determines the association properties of intonational tones. *Journal of the International Phonetics Association*, **48**, 9–32.

Torreira, Francisco, Bogels, Sara, and Levinson, Stephen C. 2015. Breathing for answering: The time course of response planning in conversation. *Frontiers in Psychology*, **6**, 284–294.

Traum, David R. 1999. Speech acts for dialogue agents. Pages 169–201 of: Rao, Anand S., and Wooldridge, Michael (eds.), *Foundations of Rational Agency.* Springer.

Traverso, Veronique. 2009. The dilemmas of third-party complaints in conversation between friends. *Journal of Pragmatics*, **41**, 2385–2399.

Trouvain, Juergen. 2014. Laughing, breathing, clicking: The prosody of nonverbal vocalisations. Pages 598–602 of: *Speech Prosody.*

Trouvain, Jürgen, and Gut, Ulrike. 2007. *Non-Native Prosody: Phonetic Description and Teaching Practice*. Walter de Gruyter.

Trouvain, Jürgen, and Truong, Khiet P. 2014. *Towards Unravelling Prosodic Characteristics of Speaker-Overlapping Laughing in Conversational Speech Corpora*. Verlag fur Gesparchforschung.

Trouvain, Jurgen, and Truong, Khiet P. 2017. Laughter. Pages 340–355 of: Attardo, Salvatore (ed.), *The Routledge Handbook of Language and Humor*. Routledge.

Turkle, Sherry. 2016. *Reclaiming Conversation: The Power of Talk in a Digital Age*. Penguin.

Turnbull, Rory. 2017. The role of predictability in intonational variability. *Language and Speech*, **60**, 123–153.

Vaissiere, Jacqueline. 2008. Perception of intonation. Pages 236–263 of: Pisoni, David, and Remez, Robert (eds.), *The Handbook of Speech Perception*. John Wiley & Sons.

van Santen, Jan, Mishra, Taniya, and Klabbers, Esther. 2008. Prosodic processing. Pages 471–488 of: *Springer Handbook of Speech Processing*. Springer.

van Santen, Jan P. H., Klabbers, Esther, and Mishra, Taniya. 2006. Toward measurement of pitch alignment. *Italian Journal of Linguistics*, **18**, 161–187.

van Santen, Jan P. H., Mishra, Taniya, and Klabbers, Esther. 2004. Estimating phrase curves in the general superpositional intonation model. Pages 61–66 of: *Fifth ISCA Workshop on Speech Synthesis*.

Vega, Alejandro. 2012. *On the Selection of Prosodic Features for Language Modeling*. Master's thesis, University of Texas at El Paso, Computer Science Department.

Wacewicz, Slawomir, Zywiczynski, Przemyslaw, and Chiera, Alessandra. 2017. An evolutionary approach to low-level conversational cooperation. *Language Sciences*, **63**, 91–104.

Wagner, Petra, Malisz, Zofia, and Kopp, Stefan. 2014. Gesture and speech in interaction: An overview. *Speech Communication*, **57**, 209–232.

Wagner, Petra, Origlia, Antonio, Avesani, Cinzia, Christodoulides, Georges, Cutugno, Francesco, D'Imperio, Mariapaola, et al. 2015. Different parts of the same elephant: A roadmap to disentangle and connect different perspectives on prosodic prominence. In: *Proceedings of the 18th International Congress of Phonetic Sciences*.

Walker, Gareth. 2017. Pitch and the projection of more talk. *Research on Language and Social Interaction*, **50**, 206–225.

Walsh, Michael, Mobius, Bernd, Wade, Travis, and Schutze, Hinrich. 2010. Multilevel exemplar theory. *Cognitive Science*, **34**, 537–582.

Ward, Nigel. 2000. Issues in the transcription of English conversational grunts. Pages 29–35 of: *First (ACL) SIGdial Workshop on Discourse and Dialogue*.

Ward, Nigel. 2002. Ndakko. *Nihongogaku*, April, 4–5.

Ward, Nigel. 2004. Pragmatic functions of prosodic features in non-lexical utterances. Pages 325–328 of: *Speech Prosody 04*.

Ward, Nigel. 2006. Non-lexical conversational sounds in American English. *Pragmatics and Cognition*, **14**, 113–184.

Ward, Nigel G. 2014. Automatic Discovery of simply-composable prosodic elements. Pages 915–919 of: *Speech Prosody*.

Ward, Nigel G. 2015. *MidLevel Prosodic Features Toolkit*. https://github.com/ nigelgward/midlevel.

Ward, Nigel G. 2018. A corpus-based exploration of the functions of disaligned pitch peaks in American English dialog. Pages 349–353 of: *Speech Prosody*.

Ward, Nigel G., and Abu, Saiful. 2016. Action-coordinating prosody. In: *Speech Prosody*.

Ward, Nigel, and Al Bayyari, Yaffa. 2007. A prosodic feature that invites back-channels in Egyptian Arabic. Pages 186–206 of: Mughazy, Mustafa (ed.), *Perspectives on Arabic Linguistics XX*. John Benjamins.

Ward, Nigel G., and Al Bayyari, Yaffa. 2010. American and Arab perceptions of an Arabic turn-taking cue. *Journal of Cross-Cultural Psychology*, **41**, 270–275.

Ward, Nigel G., and DeVault, David. 2016. Challenges in building highly-interactive dialog systems. *AI Magazine*, **37**(4), 7–18.

Ward, Nigel G., and Escalante-Ruiz, Rafael. 2009. Using subtle prosodic variation to acknowledge the user's current state. Pages 2431–2434 of: *Interspeech*.

Ward, Nigel G., and Gallardo, Paola. 2015. *A Corpus for Investigating English-Language Learners' Dialog Behaviors*. Tech. rept. UTEP-CS-15-33. University of Texas at El Paso, Department of Computer Science.

Ward, Nigel G., and Gallardo, Paola. 2017. Non-native differences in prosodic construction use. *Dialogue and Discourse*, **8**, 1–31.

Ward, Nigel, and Okamoto, Masafumi. 2003. Nasalization in Japanese back-channels bears meaning. Pages 635–638 of: *International Congress of the Phonetic Sciences*.

Ward, Nigel, and Tsukahara, Wataru. 1999. A responsive dialog system. Pages 169–174 of: Wilks, Yorick (ed.), *Machine Conversations*. Kluwer.

Ward, Nigel G., and Tsukahara, Wataru. 2000. Prosodic features which cue back-channel responses in English and Japanese. *Journal of Pragmatics*, **32**, 1177–1207.

Ward, Nigel G., and Vega, Alejandro. 2012a. A bottom-up exploration of the dimensions of dialog state in spoken interaction. In: *13th Annual SIGdial Meeting on Discourse and Dialogue*.

Ward, Nigel G., and Vega, Alejandro. 2012b. Towards empirical dialog-state modeling and its use in language modeling. In: *Interspeech*.

Ward, Nigel G., and Werner, Steven D. 2013. *Data Collection for the Similar Segments in Social Speech Task*. Tech. rept. UTEP-CS-13-58. University of Texas at El Paso.

Ward, Nigel G., Rivera, Anais G., Ward, Karen, and Novick, David G. 2005. Root causes of lost time and user stress in a simple dialog system. In: *Interspeech*.

Ward, Nigel G., Escalante, Rafael, Al Bayyari, Yaffa, and Solorio, Thamar. 2007. Learning to show you're listening. *Computer Assisted Language Learning*, **20**, 385–407.

Ward, Nigel G., Fuentes, Olac, and Vega, Alejandro. 2010. Dialog prediction for a general model of turn-taking. In: *Interspeech*.

Ward, Nigel G., Vega, Alejandro, and Baumann, Timo. 2011. Prosodic and temporal features for language modeling for dialog. *Speech Communication*, **54**, 161–174.

Ward, Nigel G., Novick, David G., and Vega, Alejandro. 2012. Where in dialog space does uh-huh occur? In: *Interdisciplinary Workshop on Feedback Behaviors in Dialog, at Interspeech 2012*.

Ward, Nigel G., Li, Yuanchao, Zhao, Tianyu, and Kawahara, Tatsuya. 2016a. Interactional and pragmatics-related prosodic patterns in Mandarin dialog. In: *Speech Prosody*.

Ward, Nigel G., Jurado, Chelsey N., Garcia, Ricardo A., and Ramos, Florencia A. 2016b. On the possibility of predicting gaze aversion to improve video-chat efficiency. In: *ACM Symposium on Eye Tracking Research and Applications.*

Ward, Nigel G., Carlson, Jason C., and Fuentes, Olac. 2018. Inferring stance in news broadcasts from prosodic-feature configurations. *Computer Speech and Language,* **50**, 85–104.

Warhurst, Samantha, McCabe, Patricia, and Madill, Catherine. 2013. What makes a good voice for radio: Perceptions of radio employers and educators. *Journal of Voice,* **27**, 217–224.

Warren, Paul, and Fletcher, Janet. 2016. Phonetic differences between uptalk and question rises in two Antipodean English varieties. Pages 148–152 of: *Speech Prosody.*

Wells, Bill, and Macfarlane, Sarah. 1998. Prosody as an interactional resource: Turn-projection and overlap. *Language and Speech,* **41**, 265–294.

Wells, J. C. 2006. *English Intonation: An Introduction.* Cambridge University Press.

Whalen, Douglas H., and Levitt, Andrea G. 1995. The universality of intrinsic F_0 of vowels. *Journal of Phonetics,* **23**, 349–366.

Whorf, Benjamin Lee. 2012. *Language, Thought, and Reality: Selected Writings of Benjamin Lee Whorf,* 2nd edition. MIT Press. Edited by John B. Carroll, Stephen C. Levinson, and Penny Lee.

Wichmann, Anne. 2000. *Intonation in Text and Discourse: Beginnings, Middles and Ends.* Longman.

Wichmann, Anne. 2004. The intonation of please-requests: A corpus-based study. *Journal of Pragmatics,* **36**, 1521–1549.

Wichmann, Anne, House, Jill, and Rietveld, Toni. 1997. Peak displacement and topic structure. Pages 329–332 of: *Intonation: Theory, Models, and Applications.* ISCA.

Wieland, Molly. 1991. Turn-taking structure as a source of misunderstanding in French-American cross-cultural conversation. *Pragmatics and Language Learning,* **2**, 101–118.

Wilensky, Robert, Arens, Yigal, and Chin, David. 1984. Talking to UNIX in English: An overview of UC. *Communications of the ACM,* **27**, 574–593.

Wilhelm, Stephan. 2016. Towards a typological classification and description of HRTs in a multidialectal corpus of contemporary English. Pages 138–142 of: *Speech Prosody.*

Windmann, Andreas, Simko, Juraj, and Wagner, Petra. 2015. Optimization-based modeling of speech timing. *Speech Communication,* **74**, 76–92.

Witt, Silke. 2015. Modeling user response timings in spoken dialog systems. *International Journal of Speech Technology,* **18**, 231–243.

Wittgenstein, Ludwig. 1963. *Philosophical Investigations.* Oxford: Basil Blackwell. Originally 1945.

Wlodarczak, Marcin, and Heldner, Mattias. 2016. Respiratory belts and whistles: A preliminary study of breathing acoustics for turn-taking. In: *Interspeech.*

Wong, Patrick C. M., Warrier, Catherine M., Penhune, Virginia B., Roy, Anil K., Sadehh, Abdulmalek, Parrish, Todd B., and Zatorre, Robert J. 2008. Volume of left Heschl's gyrus and linguistic pitch learning. *Cerebral Cortex,* **18**, 828–836.

Wootton, A. J. 1989. Remarks on the methodology of conversation analysis. Pages 238–258 of: Derek, Roger, and Bull, Peter (eds.), *Conversation: An Interdisciplinary Perspective.* Multilingual Matters.

Wright, Melissa. 2011. On clicks in English talk-in-interaction. *Journal of the International Phonetic Association*, **41**, 207–229.

Xu, Yi. 1999. F_0 peak delay: When, where, and why it occurs. Pages 1881–1884 of: *International Congress of the Phonetic Sciences*.

Xu, Yi. 2001. Fundamental frequency peak delay in Mandarin. *Phonetica*, **58**, 26–52.

Xu, Yi. 2005. Speech melody as articulatorily implemented communicative functions. *Speech Communication*, **46**, 220–251.

Xu, Yi. 2011. Speech prosody: A methodological review. *Journal of Speech Sciences*, **1**, 85–115.

Xu, Yi. 2015. Speech prosody: Theories, models and analysis. Pages 142–177 of: Meireles, A. R. (ed.), *Courses on Speech Prosody*. Cambridge Scholars Publishing.

Xu, Yi. 2017. Syllable as a synchronization mechanism. Pages 15–18 of: Botinis, Antonis (ed.), *Proceedings of the 8th Tutorial and Research Workshop on Experimental Linguistics*. ISCA.

Xu, Yi, and Prom-on, Santitham. 2014. Toward invariant functional representations of variable surface fundamental frequency contours: Synthesizing speech melody via model-based stochastic learning. *Speech Communication*, **57**, 181–208.

Xu, Yi, and Sun, Xuejing. 2002. Maximum speed of pitch change and how it may relate to speech. *The Journal of the Acoustical Society of America*, **111**, 1399–1413.

Xu, Yi, Chen, Szu-Wei, and Wang, Bei. 2012. Prosodic focus with and without post-focus compression (PFC): A typological divide within the same language family? *Linguistic Review*, **29**, 131–147.

Xu, Yi, Lee, Albert, Wu, Wing-Li, Liu, Xuan, and Birkholz, Peter. 2013. Human vocal attractiveness as signaled by body size projection. *PloS One*, **8**, e62397:1–9.

Yang, Fan, and Heeman, Peter. 2010. Initiative conflicts in task-oriented dialogue. *Computer Speech and Language*, **24**, 175–189.

Yang, Fan, Heeman, Peter A, and Kun, Andrew L. 2011. An investigation of interruptions and resumptions in multi-tasking dialogues. *Computational Linguistics*, **37**, 75–104.

Yang, Ying, Fairbairn, Catherine, and Cohn, Jeffrey F. 2013. Detecting depression severity from vocal prosody. *IEEE Transactions on Affective Computing*, **4**, 142–150.

Yip, Moira. 2002. *Tone*. Cambridge University Press.

Yngve, Victor. 1970. On getting a word in edgewise. Pages 567–577 of: *Papers from the Sixth Regional Meeting of the Chicago Linguistic Society*.

Yuasa, Ikuko Patricia. 2010. Creaky voice: A new feminine voice quality for young urban-oriented upwardly mobile American women? *American Speech*, **85**, 315–337.

Zaki, Jamil. 2014. Empathy: A motivated account. *Psychological Bulletin*, **140**, 1608–1647.

Zarate-Sandez, German. 2016. Categorical perception and prenuclear pitch peak alignment in Spanish. Pages 663–667 of: *Proceedings of the International Conference on Speech Prosody*.

Zellers, Margaret. 2016. Prosodic variation and segmental reduction and their roles in cuing turn transition in Swedish. *Language and Speech*, **60**, 1–25.

Zellers, Margaret, and Ogden, Richard. 2014. Exploring interactional features with prosodic patterns. *Language and Speech*, **57**, 285–309.

Zellers, Margaret, Post, Brechtje, and D'Imperio, Mariapaola. 2009. Modeling the intonation of topic structure: two approaches. Pages 2463–2466 of: *Interspeech*.

Zellers, Margaret, House, David, and Alexanderson, Simon. 2016. Prosody and hand gesture at turn boundaries in Swedish. In: *Speech Prosody*.

Zen, Heiga, Senior, Andrew, and Schuster, Mike. 2013. Statistical parametric speech synthesis using deep neural networks. Pages 7962–7966 of: *2013 IEEE International Conference on Acoustics, Speech and Signal Processing (ICASSP)*.

Zimmerer, Frank, Jugler, Jeanin, Andreeva, Bistra, Mobius, Bernd, and Trouvain, Jürgen. 2014. Too cautious to vary more? A comparison of pitch variation in native and non-native productions of French and German speakers. In: *Speech Prosody*.

Author Index

Subject Index